Foreword

It gives me great pleasure to write a forward for the book 'Living Heritage'. As the title suggests bell ringing in Wokingham has its roots in the past with a strong link to the future. Reading this book you cannot fail to be impressed by the dedication hard work and sheer fun which bell ringers have had at All Saints Tower over many centuries. While aiming for perfection bell ringers have been a very inclusive group drawing from all ages and groups in the community. The bell ringers in the All Saints band give talks to visitors during heritage day and provide tours for many community groups who are interested in finding out about the art of bell ringing.

In the past bell ringers have been drawn from many walks of life. While some of the leading lights have come from the clergy there have also been working people who were drawn to this task. Bell ringing demands skill and precision; a good ear and dedication. Learning this craft from scratch involves persistence and the ability to work as a member of a team. All the skills associated with bell ringing are invaluable for many aspects of every day work and life.

The importance of passing down the heritage of bell ringing is strongly emphasised today through training young people to become bell ringers and encouraging people to appreciate the long tradition of bell ringing through talks and demonstrations. This book brings together many facts which otherwise might be forgotten. It is informative for those who are not bell ringers themselves. Above all it reflects the enjoyment of bell ringing both for those practising their skills and for the rest of us who listen.

Tina Marinos
Chairman, The Wokingham Society
September 2009

W0013727

The production of this book was supported by a generous grant from the Wokingham Society's J H Elliston Clifton Fund.

Preface

The bell restoration at All Saints in 2004 came exactly 300 years after the original ring of six bells was installed in 1704. The restoration was a historic landmark that reminded the ringers of their history. They were already responding to the Church's initiative to move closer to the community by organising visits up the tower, and by giving talks about bells and bellringing to local community groups. While preparing material for these talks, especially those to local history societies, I found myself digging deeper into the records of our past.

Several people suggested that I should write an article about the history of ringing in Wokingham, so I kept looking for more information to fill the gaps in what I already knew. Historians will know (but I didn't at first) that the more you dig, the more you find, and also that as you answer questions, there are yet more questions that you want to answer. As the story emerged, it became more compelling and I wanted to find out more. It was too big a story to fit in 'an article', which led to the idea of a book, so I began research in earnest.

At first I just wanted to make a contribution to the historical record. Wokingham is a historic town, and here was an unexplored part of its history that I could help to make accessible to others.

I particularly wanted to show non-ringers the richness of ringing history and culture. In my talks to community groups I have always been struck by how fascinated people are when they realise just how much there is to ringing – the skill, the science, the art and the tradition. Of course the book is also for ringers, since it explores far more things than the contemporary aspects of ringing.

The last 30 years were familiar ground for me, and we have good records. I entered the story near the end of Chapter 7, so the latter part of the book draws on my personal recollections.

It was much harder unearthing the evidence for earlier periods, where the records were more sparse, but the more I dug, the more I found. Some parts of the story are very hazy, pieced together from scant surviving documents, while other parts are more rounded, especially where I was fortunate to be able to talk to people with memories of what happened at the time. Gradually I got to know more about our predecessors, and they began to feel familiar, almost like old friends.

I hope that you find the story interesting. If you are a not a ringer, I hope that through the history of this small corner of the ringing world, I may give you a view of the richness of the contemporary world of ringing and ringers.

John Harrison, September 2009

Contents

1 Introduction

The story of a group of people spanning three centuries inevitably contains many contrasts, but they are joined by a common thread. The story of bellringing in Wokingham is about generations of people linked not by blood ties, but by their service to the unique tradition of English style bellringing – an art that evolved about a hundred years before our story begins, and that thrives and continues to develop.

Through all those years, each generation of ringers learned the skills, practised the art, and passed on the love of ringing to those who came after them. The progress of ringing in Wokingham wasn't smooth and steady. At times it was was helping to make history while at other times it was in a backwater. During those three hundred years, the daily lives of ringers were influenced by the changing fortunes of the nation at large, and by war and social change.

Ringing itself was influenced by huge transformations. The Church in whose buildings most bells hang went through crisis and renewal. Its relationship with ringers went through cycles of acceptance, alienation, and active encouragement. Wokingham played a leading local role in the 'Belfry Reform' movement, which swept the land, and led to the foundation of many of our modern ringing societies.

Our story shows how the band of ringers at All Saints has waxed and waned over the years, in size, in vigour, and in achievement. It has fostered ringers who made their mark in the wider world, and it has benefitted from imported talent. We meet the characters who led the band in successive eras, and follow their achievements.

Inseparable from the ringers' story is the story of the bells that they rang, and the tower in which the bells hang. Over the years, these too have seen many changes, with periods of both decline and restoration.

Bells had been used in English churches for hundreds of years before our story begins. And as churches acquired more bells, the scene was set for the evolution of the peculiarly English art of change ringing – sounding the bells in systematically ordered sequences. This emerged sometime around 1600, along with the special way of hanging bells that makes it possible, like chicken and egg. As it spread across the country, it created a huge demand for bells[1] and the bell founders to make them[2].

Our story begins at the height of this boom, just after 1700. Wokingham's own bell foundry had closed some 80 years earlier in 1622, after 370 years in business, so it fell to the Reading founder Samuel Knight to install a ring of six bells at All Saints in 1704. Knight later moved to London, and became a rival to the Whitechapel foundry, which is now England's oldest company still doing business from the same premises.

The main part of the book is divided chronologically into six periods. This is preceded by a brief introductory chapter for non ringers, and followed by an overview of the whole history, with four annexes and an index.

---

[1] Around 1350 new rings of bells were cast during the 18th century (compared with only 350 in the 16th) and around 2000 parishes added more bells to existing rings.

[2] Around 1700, there were nearly sixty UK bell foundries, compared to half a dozen in 1300 (and only two in the present day).

2 For non ringers

(Ringers who know all this may skip to Chapter 3, on page 11)

This story is about people involved in a special activity. It will come to life more vividly for you if you understand some of the basic concepts and terminology of ringing, which can seem baffling to an outsider. But with a little explanation it all starts to fit into place, so read on ...[1]

2.1 How bells work

English style bell ringing, also called 'full circle ringing', is made possible because the bells are hung in a special way. The bell and wheel are both mounted on the headstock, which is free to rotate. Figure 1 (L) shows the bell mouth-down, at rest, but when ringing it swings through 360 degrees in alternate directions, from mouth-up to mouth-up and back again.

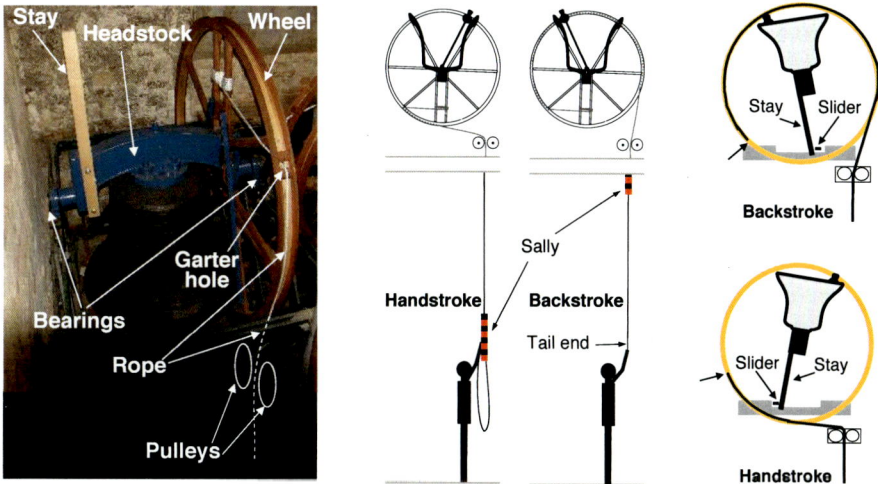

Figure 1: A bell hung for full circle ringing

The rope is attached to the wheel, and passes round it, then down through a pulley block to the ringing room many feet below. The rope is all that connects the ringer with the bell above. As the bell swings, the rope wraps alternately each way round the wheel, so that it is in tension as the bell comes to rest at the end of each swing, see Figure 1 (centre). This means that at one end of the swing (called the handstroke) the ringer has surplus rope and therefore holds the 'sally', the fluffy coloured part that is some way from the rope end. At the other end of the swing (the backstroke) the ringer holds the end of the rope, and the sally may disappear through the ceiling.

The bell can be rested when mouth up, with the stay resting against the slider bar underneath the bell taking its weight, see Figure 1 (R). The slider moves to let the bell go just beyond the balance point in each direction, so it can rest at either stroke.

---

[1] This section is based on 'About Bellringing' on All Saints tower website: http://AllSaintsWokinghamBells.org.uk/

The clapper strikes on opposite sides of the bell at each stroke. As the bell comes to rest the clapper keeps going, so it strikes the leading edge each time. The ringer controls the bell by exerting more or less force as required on each swing.

Figure 2: All Saints bells (L) 'down' for safety and (R) 'up' ready for ringing

2.2 Ringing in sequence

Ringing many bells in sequence is the essence of the English style (in contrast to the random sounds that are traditional in many parts of the world) but to achieve this, and keep the bells in the correct sequence, it is essential to be able to control the period of swing accurately. To change accurately from one sequence to another, which is the essence of change ringing (see below), requires even more control over the swing period. Swinging the bell near to the balance point makes this precision control possible, by varying the height to which it swings on each stroke. Swing a little higher and it rings more slowly, swing a little less high and it rings more quickly. There is a physical limit to how much the timing can be varied between successive swings of a bell, so the bells still can't play 'tunes' in the normal sense.

2.3 Bell music

Almost all rings of bells have notes in a diatonic scale. The key varies with the weight of the bells (heavier bells have a deeper tone) but ringers don't refer to the actual notes when ringing. They number the bells from the highest note (number 1) also called the Treble, down the scale to the lowest note, also called the Tenor. The most basic sequence is 'rounds', where the bells ring after each other running down the scale. All ringing normally starts and ends with rounds. Figure 3 shows three popular sequences, in musical notation and also as numbers. The diagrams show a ring of 8 bells with Tenor in C, but they could be in any key, and the numbers would still be the same.

1 2 3 4 5 6 7 8   1 3 5 7 2 4 6 8   1 5 2 6 3 7 4 8

Figure 3: Rounds, Queens and Tittums, in musical notation and as numbers

2.4 Change ringing

The sequence can be changed by successively swapping adjacent pairs of bells. In 'call changes' this is done periodically, one change at a time. In 'method ringing' the sequence changes continually, with most bells changing place most of the time.

Figure 4 shows four successive sequences at the start of one simple method. The red lines show the changes between the sequences – the crosses show a pair of bells swapping place, and the vertical lines show a bell staying in the same place.

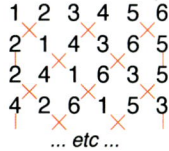

$$
\begin{array}{cccccc}
1 & 2 & 3 & 4 & 5 & 6 \\
2 & 1 & 4 & 3 & 6 & 5 \\
2 & 4 & 1 & 6 & 3 & 5 \\
4 & 2 & 6 & 1 & 5 & 3 \\
\end{array}
$$
... etc ...

Figure 4: Progressive changes, as used in method ringing

To achieve the changes, individual bells must swing more quickly (to move earlier in the sequence) or more slowly (to move later in the sequence). Each ringer is continually altering the timing of his or her bell by making it swing a little higher or less high, to fit accurately into the overall rhythmic pattern.

2.5 Method names

All change ringing methods have a name.   Like botanical names for plants, most method names have three parts, eg 'Plain Bob Doubles', 'Norwich Surprise Minor', 'Kent Treble-bob Maximus''.

- The first part is the specific name (often named after a place, but can be named after many other things).

- The second part is the type (to do with the way the method is constructed).

- The third part refers to the number of bells, see Table 1.

Bells	Name	Bells	Name
3	Singles	4	Minimus
5	Doubles	6	Minor
7	Triples	8	Major
9	Caters	10	Royal
11	Cinques[2]	12	Maximus
13	Sextuples	14	14-in
15	Septuples	16	16-in

Table 1: Family names for change ringing methods

2.6 Learning & ringing methods

Methods run for scores or hundreds of sequences, but ringers don't even attempt to remember all of the numbers. Instead, they think of the paths of each bell. For example, imagine joining up all the lines in Figure 4 that connect the '2's (and

---

[2] Pronounced 'sinks', but from the French 'cinque' (and 'caters' is from 'quatre').

continuing a lot longer). Figure 5 does this, and shows the path of bell number 2 in Plain Bob Major. It is much easier to remember the pattern than to remember 112 sequences of 8 numbers. The pattern is cyclic (the bottom joins to the top) and has the added bonus that the other bells follow the same pattern, but start at different points on the line. More complex methods have more complicated lines, which most ringers learn in terms of clusters of sub-patterns within an overall pattern.

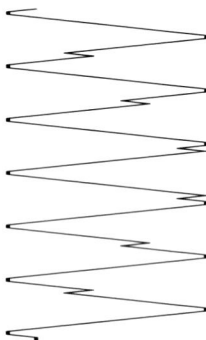

Figure 5: The pattern of Plain Bob Major

2.7 Performances: courses, touches, quarter peals and peals

The simplest performance is a 'plain course' of a method, at the end of which the sequence returns to rounds. The ringing can be varied to make it longer (or sometimes shorter) by calling a 'touch'. At key points, a 'conductor' makes a call ('Bob' or 'Single'), which alters the sequence, like switching onto a different track.

For most ringing (services and practices) there are more ringers present than bells, and different people ring each touch, with touches normally lasting 5 - 10 minutes.

Longer performances have pre-arranged bands with one person per bell. The commonest performance is a 'quarter peal' , which typically takes between 40 and 50 minutes. Less common is a peal, which takes between 2½ and 4½ hours, depending on the weight of the bells. About 5000 peals and 13,000 quarters are rung per year.

2.8 Bands of ringers

An active tower has a band of ringers responsible for ringing (and often also for maintaining) the bells. The band recruits, trains and develops new ringers to replenish those who move on or give up.

Training is a lengthy process, first learning to handle a bell safely (like learning to stay on a bike), then learning to control the bell's speed (like learning to cycle in a straight line and turn corners), then learning to synchronise the bell with others (like cycling in formation) and finally, learning how to ring methods.

As a rule of thumb, a healthy band needs at least twice as many ringers as bells.

2.9 Ringing jargon

For a list of ringing terms used in this book, see the glossary on page 145.

3 Early years: Up to the mid 19th century

In the beginning – Some time between 1189 and 1193, Bishop Hubert of Salisbury dedicated the 'Chapel of Wokingham' to All Saints, and it became the Parish Church. The outer bases of the west porch, and the archway of the door at the bottom of the stairs date from around 1370. The tower was erected in the 15th century, probably around 1450 when the church was rebuilt. It was already common for the larger parish churches to have three or more bells, and although we don't know how many bells Wokingham had when the tower was built, a century later in 1553, it had four bells. (There was also a sanctuary bell, not hung in the tower.)

Ringing the Curfew – The first mention of ringing in Wokingham is in Richard Palmer's charity of 1664. He gave lands, the profits from which were to be paid:

> 'to the Sexton of the Parish Church of Wokingham, or to such other persons as the Trustees think meet, to ring the greatest bell belonging to the said Parish Church that shall be fit to be rung, half an hour every evening at eight o'clock and every morning at 4 o'clock, or as near those hours as may be, from the 10th of September to the 11th of March in each year for ever.'

His stated object was to promote:

> 'a timely going to rest in the evening, and early risings (things ordinarily attended and rewarded with thrift and proficiency), and that strangers who should happen to lose their way in winter might be informed of the time of night, and receive some guidance; and also that all those whose care of being mindful of their latter end should incline them thereunto, might at the ringing of the evening bell think of their own passing and day of death, and at the ringing of the said morning bell might think of the resurrection and call to their last judgement.'

Palmer's belief that the sound of a bell would act universally as an alarm clock, a navigation beacon, and a religious observance, perhaps mirrors the complementary roles of ringing and bell towers in modern society. Ringing is intimately coupled with church worship, but ringing also has an affectionate place in the heart of the vast number of people who never worship in church. And as anyone who has ever used an Ordnance Survey map knows, church towers are supremely useful landmarks.

Palmer specified the greatest bell because it would also be the loudest, and as we saw above, there were four bells at All Saints long before the 1660s.

Secular ringing – In mediaeval times, bells had many secular as well as religious functions, being used to signal events to the local community. Ringing was the principle means of making a loud noise on occasions of public rejoicing. It had developed into a secular sport, something that might have existed alongside ringing for religious purposes as it does today, were it not for the strictures of the reformation, which pushed ringing even further from the Church. At a time when many injunctions banned ringing in connection with church services, particularly ringing several bells together 'in peal', it was the secular function that kept ringing alive. Fortunately, although the reformers swept away many 'superstitious' accoutrements of our parish churches, they removed few bells, perhaps because their use was too deeply embedded in the civic life of the community. For example, we know about the four bells in 1553 when '152 ozs. of plate at Wokingham were seized for the King's use', leaving just 'one chalice of 13 ozs', and the bells. [21]

Wokingham's ringers would have been paid to ring for public events, as they were elsewhere, but they must also have practised, and no doubt rang for pleasure as well. The custom in most places was to pay the Sexton of the church to open up the tower when they wished to ring. Ringers in places like London had a choice of many towers, but Wokingham ringers had just the one.

This pattern of ringing would have been established long before 1704, the real start to our story, with the installation of a new ring of six bells, which would undoubtedly have provided a major boost to ringing in the town.

3.1 Wokingham in the 18th century

To contemplate what ringing was like in the 1700s we first need to remember how different the world was. When Samuel Knight installed the six bells at All Saints, Queen Anne was on the throne. Europe was still in the 'Little Ice Age', with Frost Fairs held on the frozen Thames in London. Johnson's dictionary, Handel's Messiah and the adoption of the Gregorian calendar (which led the peasants to demand 'Give us back our 11 days') were all decades away. America was still a colony, and the slave trade was flourishing. England's population was a seventh of what it is today.

Wokingham was a long established market town, but it was tiny by modern standards and to our eyes would have seemed more like a large village[1].

The social context – The pace of life was slower, and work was physically harder for most people. There were no modern conveniences, and everyday life was more cruel and violent. For example, Wokingham has the dubious distinction of being the last town in England where bull baiting took place. This was a major civic event, not just for the townsfolk, but for the gentry, aldermen and burgesses, who turned out in state to see it. George Staverton, whose family name is preserved in local house and street names, left property in 1661 to provide a bull for baiting in the Market Place each St Thomas day (21st December).

Parliament's first attempt to outlaw this gory sport in 1802 failed, with claims that it was a 'conspiracy of Jacobins and Methodists' and a 'preliminary step to the overthrow of the government'. Even after it was eventually outlawed in 1821, the bull was still paraded through Wokingham before being killed, and in 1835 the mob seized the bull and baited it. Barbarity to the bull was matched by fighting among the crowds. The 1700s were plagued by a group known locally as 'the fighters', who went round the crowds provoking and picking fights with anyone they fancied.

The 18th century was also the era of 'The Wokingham Blacks' – not a rugby team, but a dangerous gang of criminals who operated in and around the town, with their faces blacked to avoid recognition[2]. They started as a society to poach deer from Windsor Forest, and then graduated to other forms of crime, with widespread

---

[1] In 1801 the population was only 2281, and growing rapidly, so it was probably well under 2000 during most of the 18th century, compared with well over 30,000 now.

[2] The "Black Act" of 1723 made it a criminal offence to blacken the face.

housebreaking, blackmail and murder. At one time, William Shorter's house in Wokingham commanded nearly all criminal activity in Eastern Berkshire. The authorities of the day were powerless against them, and only when voluntary groups of citizens banded together to hunt them down were they eventually brought to justice. Dozens of them were either hanged or deported at every assizes.

Things seem to have changed by the middle of the 19th century, when Wokingham had become a much more law abiding place. An 1850 report said:

> 'The sessions are held in the Town Hall every April and October, but so exemplary is the general conduct of the inhabitants that few cases of delinquency are ever brought before them'.

Maybe Victorian values were having their effect on the previously troublesome parts of Wokingham society.

Public entertainment – For most people in the 18th century, there was very little of the entertainment that we take for granted today. Even the upright piano, that pillar of Victorian domestic music making, wasn't due to make its appearance until the latter decades, and wouldn't become widely available until the following century. So such entertainment as there was was public. Theatre going was popular in the latter part of the century. For example, in 1768, the *Reading Mercury* records:

> Mr Linnet's Company of Comedians is now at Wokingham and there is a very genteel Theatre fitted up for them in Rose Street.

No theatre building is known, and 'fitted up' suggests that it might have been temporary. But it must have been reasonably substantial, since seats were advertised as: 'Boxes 3/-, Pit 2/-, Gallery 1/-[3]. Advertisements a couple of years later simply referred to: 'Oakingham Theatre' or 'the theatre in Wokingham'.

The plays 'met with universal applause' and the titles advertised in successive weeks in November 1768 give us a glimpse of the contemporary repertoire:

> 'Monday a Tragedy entitled Romeo and Juliet, Wednesday The Miser, Friday King Richard the Third, with entertainments that will be expressed in the bills'

> 'Monday (by particular desire of several ladies) a Comedy entitled The Miser, to which will be added a Farce called High Life Below Stairs. Wednesday The Fair Penitent, Friday King Henry IV, with the humours of Sir John Falstaff'

> 'Monday (by particular desire) a Comedy Busy Body ... Wednesday The Revenge ... Friday The Provoked Husband or A Journey to London with Devil to Pay or Wives Metamorphosed'

But the 'genteel theatre' being advertised so elegantly amidst tinctures and elixirs to cure all manner of ills was no doubt for the genteel privileged few, while for ordinary folk communal entertainment seems to have centred on the inns and ale houses, with which Wokingham was well supplied[4].

There were in fact few public gathering places in Wokingham apart from the church and the inns. The Town Hall was in a decrepit state, and in 1763 when the

---

[3] Equivalent to £17-50, £13-00 and £6-50 in modern currency.
[4] See The Inns and Public Houses of Wokingham [11].

Corporation couldn't afford to repair it, they leased it to William Wheatley of the Bush Inn. The terms of the lease allowed them to use of it for their meetings, but for some fifteen years, even they met in one of the inns or up-market ale houses. The church too seems to have been dependent on the inn keepers – The Bush and The Rose supplied most of the sacramental wine to All Saints (some three dozen bottles a year) and it was not uncommon for an inn keeper to be a churchwarden. So it is easy to see how the inn keepers could have controlled the provision of Wokingham's entertainment, much of which seems to have been competitive spectator sport. The inn keepers sponsored pigeon shooting, cudgelling, quarter-stick matches, cock fighting, and one of the most popular – bellringing contests.

3.2 Prize ringing

With ringing being seen as a sport in the 17th and 18th centuries, it is no surprise that it developed into a competitive one. Bands from different towns and villages vied with each other for supremacy, and prize ringing took place in many parts of the country, from at least the early 1700s. For some reason ringing competitions became particularly prevalent around Reading and Wokingham later in the century.

In Cyril Wratten's articles in the subject [17] he observed that 'There was scarcely a town or village within a 15 mile radius of Reading that did not have at least one match during the period, while in a number of places they were almost an annual event'.

Wokingham was very much a part of this. At least four of the inns in the town sponsored ringing contests at All Saints between the 1760s and 1780s: The Ship, The Bush, The Six Bells (in Cross Street from 1777 to 1793) and the Half Moon (on the site of the modern Post Office from 1770 to 1786).

The inn keepers provided the prizes, and they covered their costs with the profit from what competitors and spectators ate and drank during the day. As a condition of entry, the inn keepers required the members of each competing team (called a 'sett' or 'company') to eat and pay for 'the ordinary', which was a set meal provided by the inn, usually at a cost of one shilling. Some innkeepers added extra rules forbidding the consumption of food or drink at any other establishment. We don't know whether that happened in Wokingham but with something approaching twenty inns and ale houses in the town centre[5], there would have been plenty of opportunities for participants to stray to other premises.

The first prize was normally a set of hats, often embroidered with gold or silver lace or tassels – one for each ringer and one for their 'umpire'. Larger contests might have had a second prize, a set of gloves or a set of handbells, and very occasionally a third prize of ribbons. The ringers competed for the honour of winning rather than monetary gain. These were not just one-off affairs. Jacob Peacock of the Half Moon organised a contest at All Saints in July 1781, and in Spring 1782 after moving to the Six Bells, he organised another one, offering three guineas to the winning team if they didn't approve of the hats. Six weeks later he organised yet another contest, so they must have been good for business.

[5] See [11].

During a contest, each team had to raise the bells, ring a period of rounds and then lower the bells again. This differs from most modern ringing competitions, where the bells are already 'up'[6] before the competition. A requirement for 15 minutes of rounds was typical, but sometimes it was 10 and sometimes 20. In once case (at Padworth in October 1777) each band had to ring rounds for an hour!

The local band was barred from entering the contest (but presumably was still encouraged to take part in the eating and drinking). Obviously ringers familiar with the quirks of their own bells have an advantage, but such a rule is rarely applied in modern ringing contests. Bellhanging in the 1700s wasn't what it is today – many bells would be considered 'difficult' by modern standards, so maybe knowing the bells was a bigger success factor than it would be with a modern ring of bells.

The judging arrangements in the area round Wokingham were different from most parts of the country (though they later spread elsewhere). Instead of the organiser providing the judge (as we do today) or choosing a judge from the ringers present, the custom around Wokingham was for each team to bring an umpire with them, and for the umpires then either to form a judging panel, or to draw lots for who should judge each test piece, working in groups of three.

Wokingham ringers would not have rung in any of the contests at All Saints, and with no mention of a Wokingham victory in contests elsewhere, we can't even be sure that they entered any contests at all. On balance though, with so much activity in the area, and with so many contests being held in their home tower, it seems very likely that they would have entered some contests in nearby villages, even if they weren't good enough to win any.

There is no evidence that prize ringing continued long here, and it probably died out. But where ringing competitions did continue, by the end of the century rivalry became less friendly, more intense, and more personal, as bands developed stronger identities. We might draw parallels with football in the modern age. In places where prize ringing persisted into the 19th century, notably in the industrial towns, things deteriorated. Competitions were often accompanied by gambling and violence – a far cry from the harmless public entertainment of the late 18th century.

3.3 The spread of change ringing

Change ringing[7] – the continual, systematic variation of the order of the bells that is a characteristic of English ringing – evolved in the early 1600s. At first it developed in centres like London, Cambridge and Norwich, but it soon spread to other cities, and progressively to towns and villages. Change ringing was established in towns near Wokingham by at least the early 1700s. We know this, because peals[8] are recorded from 1730 onwards in many towers within easy travelling distance (see Table 2) and it would take a band a long time to progress from having no knowledge of change ringing to being capable of ringing a peal. Even today, developing a change ringing band from scratch takes many years, and in the early days it would have taken much

---

[6] See pages 7-8 for a fuller explanation.
[7] See Chapter 2.
[8] Continuous performances of 5000 or more rows (often mis-named changes).

longer, without the supporting infrastructure of information, training and widespread experience that modern ringers enjoy. Ringing changes on bells not hung to modern standards would also have been more of a challenge, certainly for a peal[9].

Both Reading towers with bells rang peals through the mid 18th century (five at St Lawrence between 1734 & 1767 and three at St Mary's between 1740 & 1744).

Tower	Date of first peal	Miles from Wokingham
Farnham	1730	14
Reading St Lawrence	1734	7
Reading St Mary	1740	7
Windsor Curfew Tower	1748	11
High Wycombe	1751	16
Basingstoke St Michael	1754	15
Guildford St Nicholas	1762	16
Guildford Holy Trinity	1769	16
Windsor St John Baptist	1798	11

Table 2: Early peals rung around Wokingham

There are records of a few change ringing competitions (which went against the general trend here of rounds ringing). The prize was different too, being a silver cup, rather than the hats for rounds ringing competitions. At Sonning in 1783, the cup was won by the College Youths[10] competing against Oxford and Farnham. There is no indication that Sonning ringers were involved, or were capable of ringing changes at the time. There were similar competitions at Wallingford in 1776 and 1785.

Wokingham in a backwater – With change ringing established in nearby towns like Reading, why was ringing in Wokingham (and the surrounding villages) still limited to rounds? One might have expected change ringing to spread out from Reading to its neighbours. It provided far more variety and challenge than just ringing rounds, as demonstrated by the way it had already spread elsewhere, and dominates today. Travel wasn't an issue, since we know that ringers travelled further than this to compete in prize-ringing competitions. We can only assume that the two fraternities of change ringers and rounds ringers didn't mix. Perhaps they were antagonistic towards each other, as they often were in later centuries, with rounds ringers scorning 'scientific' ringers and change ringers looking down on 'stony[11]' ringers.

One suspects that the large number of rounds ringing competitions promoted by the inn keepers, helped to bind rounds ringers together. The competitive element would certainly have honed the skill and dedication needed to ring more accurately than the other competing teams. It is easy to imagine that bands who had acquired prowess as rounds ringers in the competitions might not want either the distraction, or the embarrassment, of going back to being a novice, which they would have needed to, to

---

[9] Typically around three hours ringing.
[10] Ancient Society of College Youths, then based mainly in London.
[11] A derisory term for rounds ringing, also sometimes 'Churchyard Bob' or 'Graveyard Bob'.

learn the completely new skills of change ringing. In the short term too, their striking (the ability ring with an even rhythm) would have deteriorated markedly (especially with 18th century bell hanging) before they acquired the skills to ring changes of comparable quality to their rounds ringing. Perhaps the challenge of perfect rounds ringing seemed to them an adequate alternative to the intellectual stimulus that change ringing could have offered, as indeed it does today in parts of Devon where call changes (rather than change ringing methods) are rung to a very high standard. Cyril Wratten [17] argues that the Devon tradition can trace its roots to the customs of the 18th century Berkshire competitions, of which Wokingham was a part.

So when did change ringing come to Wokingham? There is no evidence either way until quite late in the 19th century, as we shall see in Chapter 4.

3.4 Wokingham ringing in the early 19th century

The little we know about ringing life in Wokingham between the late 1700s and the mid 1800s suggests it was similar to the pattern elsewhere. The ringers must have rung in order to practice, and to train new ringers, but we don't know whether they rang for church services, or how often.

They were paid to ring, normally in beer, and they often rang on occasions of public rejoicing. For example, they were paid when they rang for the proclamation of peace in 1813. Exactly which proclamation it was, and how many times they rang for it (them) is unclear, but the payments were spread over several months. They were also paid for frequent 'ringing days', which might have been for other public celebrations or perhaps just for public entertainment.

From 1808 to 1820, the Churchwarden's accounts show payments of almost £25 for ringing, with an average of around £4[12] per year. The amount paid for ringing events was almost always 10/-[13]. Typically the expense was described as 'ringing day', 'ringing beer' or 'cash for ringers'. Half of the entries were paid to a named recipient, and in six cases the recipient so named was an inn. It seems likely that the men, women or married couples named in other payments could have been innkeepers, though it is possible that some of them were ringers.

During the same period, the churchwardens spent nearly as much money on bellropes as they did on ringers' beer, making six payments of £3-3-0[14] each. Rope wear is inevitable, especially without the benefit of modern pre-stretched polyester top ends, which reduce the worst wear in modern ropes.

Then and now – One of the earliest pictures of the church dates from this same period, and is reproduced in Figure 6. The tower is more or less as it is now[15], apart from absence of the clock and flagpole, and the presence of a large drainage spout from the tower roof. Most of the rest of the building has changed quite dramatically.

---

[12] Over £200 in modern currency.

[13] About £23 in modern currency.

[14] About £180 in modern currency, enough for two modern ropes. In an era when rope was far more widely used, in industry and sailing ships, it could have bought more.

[15] The apparent absence of the west window and doorway on the shady side of the tower must be an omission by the artist, since the window is believed to date from the 15th century.

Figure 6: All Saints in 1812 [16]

- A parapet wall has been added above the clerestory.
- The dormers over the south aisle have been removed.
- The south window has been altered.
- The porch has been rebuilt.
- There is a new chancel and Lady Chapel.
- The wooden lychgate has been replaced by one built of stone
- The wall is no longer sagging and propped up by timber struts.
- People don't sit on the pavement as the 21st century lorries roar by!

3.5 Notable ringers

Thomas (& Mary) Houlton – There are no surviving records of the ringers in this period, but there is a strong possibility that Thomas Houlton may have been a ringer. In the churchwardens' accounts, all the payments for bellropes were made to him (apart from one paid to Mary Houlton, presumably his wife). Unless he was a bellrope maker, he could have been the ringer responsible for maintaining the bells (the steeplekeeper in modern parlance). There is also a suggestive later link between the name of Houlton and ringing. From 1881 (the earliest formal records of ringers in Wokingham) right through to 1948, there were Houltons (E, T, H and W[17]) ringing in Wokingham (at St Paul's, which didn't exist in the early 1800s). Ringers often follow their parents into the tower, with ringing families spanning several generations, so it is possible that Thomas Houlton buying ropes in 1810-20 was an earlier member of the Houlton ringing dynasty, and rang at All Saints. If he was, then he is the earliest Wokingham ringer whose name we know.

---

[16] Engraving by John Harris, reproduced by courtesy of Shirley Colwill
[17] William Houlton was in the 1923 peal band pictured in Figure 33.

What about Mary? Could she also have been a ringer? For a woman to ring at that time would have been very unusual. A few women rang before the Victorian era, but they were more likely to be the daughters of the gentry ringing in estate churches along with their brothers and fathers, rather than ordinary townswomen, and there is no evidence that the Houltons were other than ordinary folk.

3.6 The bells

Wokingham bell foundry – None of All Saints known bells came from the Wokingham foundry, but a few words about it are in order. It operated from some time around 1350 to 1622, a period of nearly 300 years.

It is popularly assumed that the foundry was in Bell Foundry Lane, but this myth was laid to rest when the land behind Broad Street was being redeveloped, and the precursor archaeological excavations discovered remains of foundry slag.

So why was the eponymous lane so called? It was previously known as Bell Foundry Farm Lane, and the most likely explanation is that the founders owned a farm there.

Roger Landen, perhaps the most famous of the Wokingham founders, ran the foundry in the mid 15th century. Figure 44 shows his foundry mark, and his name appears in two local street names: Landen Close and Landen Grove. Unhelpfully for visitors, they are on opposite sides of the town. Landen Close is off Finchampstead Road, to the south of the town, and Landen Grove is off Reading Road to the northwest.

Since the foundry was only a few minutes walk from the church, it seems highly likely that it would have cast some if not all of the four bells that were here in 1553, though there are no records. After all, with a foundry on the doorstep, why go farther afield to buy bells, especially in an era of limited transport?

Quite a few Wokingham foundry bells do survive to the present day, but none of them is in Wokingham. The nearest is the Treble at Arborfield, which was cast in Wokingham around 1399.

The foundry business transferred from Wokingham to Chertsey in 1622. And when All Saints wanted six new bells installed some 80 years later, they went elsewhere.

All Saints' bells – The Reading founder Samuel Knight cast a ring of six new bells for All Saints in 1703-4 and hung them in 1704. Knight subsequently moved to London, and became a major competitor to the Whitechapel Foundry.

We can only speculate on what Knight's bells replaced. Was it still the four bells that were here in 1553, or had they since been augmented to five? It seems reasonable to assume that the old bells were of poor quality, or total replacement wouldn't have been necessary. Nor do we know whether Knight supplied a new frame, or adapted the old one to take six bells, as is often done when a few more bells are added.

Other work was probably associated with the new bells. For example, one of the main roof beams is carved '1702', see Figure 9(R), so perhaps the roof was restored just before the bells. The other beam (at right angles to it) is carved 1613, which might have marked an earlier restoration, or perhaps it came from another building.

Table 3 shows the inscriptions on Knight's bells, as far as we know them.

Bell	Inscription	Marks
Treble	*(unknown)*	*(unknown)*
2	S.K. 1704	Knight's shield
3	S.K. 1703	Oak leaves & acorns
4	*(unknown)*	*(unknown)*
5	JOHN HAWES ROBART HUNT CW 1704 S ¤ K	Knight's shield
Tenor	JOHN HAWES ROBART HUNT CW SAMUEL KNIGHT MADE THIS PELE 1703	Oak leaves & acorns

Table 3: Inscriptions on the original bells

Figure 7: Inscription detail on 5th[18] – (L) Churchwarden symbol, (R) SK shield

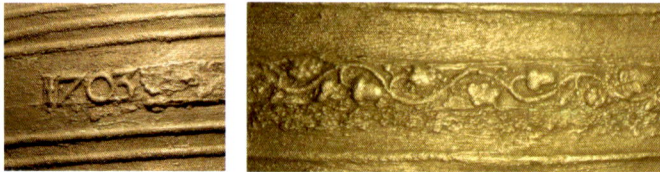

Figure 8: Inscription detail on Tenor – (L) Date (R) Oak leaves

Figure 9: Tower roof beams (L) 1613, (R) 1702

Only the heaviest two bells of Knight's installation remain, but we can deduce a lot about it.   The bells would have been cast with canons, see Figure 10 – metal loops cast on the top of the bell, through which passed forged iron straps to fix the bell to the headstock. Canons are also visible on the later bells, see Figure 11.

The headstocks were massive timber baulks, probably Elm, to which the wheel, stay and gudgeons[19] were also bolted, as shown in Figure 10.   The clappers would have been hung with baldrics[20] from iron staples cast into the inside of the bell's crown.

The frame would also have been timber, probably Oak.   Circumstantial evidence suggests that it was a few feet higher in the tower than the modern frame, whose top

---

[18] Bells 5 and 6 of the 1704 ring are now bells 7 and 8 of the modern ring.

[19] Metal shafts at each end of the headstock that fit into the bearings so the bell can rotate.

[20] Metal straps, lined with leather .

is level with the bottom of the doorway into the bell chamber. That is convenient when the frame fills the whole space, like the modern frame. But the old 6-bell frame is unlikely to have filled the space, and would have sat on top of the bell chamber floor, which would have been level with the door. This is consistent with FE Robinson's comment[21] that there was insufficient space above the old frame to hang two new bells, and that a new frame should be 3 or 4 feet lower than the old one.

The bells would have hung on plain bearings, bronze blocks with a channel in which the gudgeon pins on the ends of the headstock sit, see Figure 10 (R). Plain bearings run less freely than ball bearings (not available in 1704) and need regular lubrication. The whole installation would have needed a lot of maintenance, with the continual need to add oil or tallow to the bearings, and dozens of bolts to be kept tight as the timber expanded and shrank with the weather.

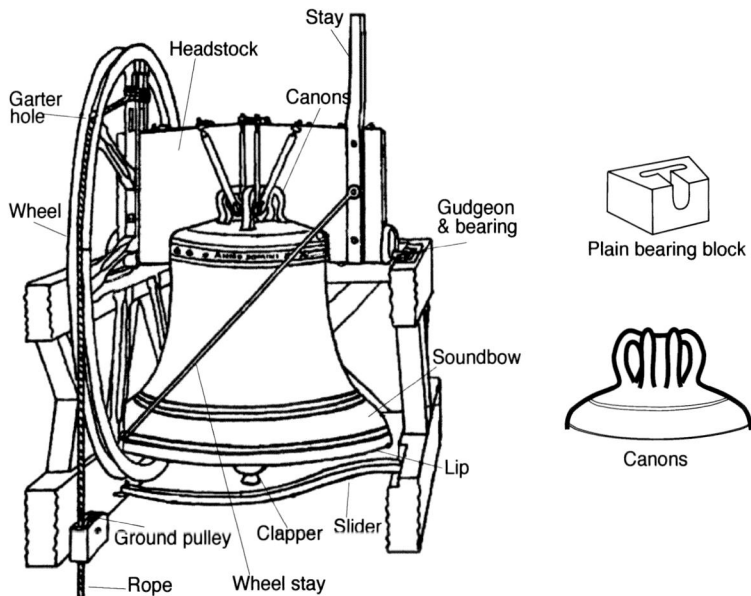

Figure 10: (L) Typical traditional bell hanging (R) Details

Misrepresentation? – The weight of the Tenor tells an interesting story. It was always listed as 19½cwt, and this was never challenged until 2004 when the bell weighed in at 16 cwt 10 lbs. Why the discrepancy? Part was due to the removal of the canons in 1903, which might have reduced 19½ cwt to 18 or perhaps 17½ cwt, but that still leaves a couple of hundredweight unaccounted for.

The weight of a bell can never be accurately known until after it has been cast, finished and tuned, because of uncertainties in the casting process. In former times, it was the custom to order bells by weight. So if you ordered a bell of a given weight, that was what you expected to receive. If a casting turned out to be on the light side,

---

[21] See page 40.

the founder would have had little incentive to inform his client that the bell weighed less than what had been paid for (or even to weigh it himself). In the case of All Saints Tenor, the crown was thinner than expected for a typical Knight bell, so it probably did emerge from casting a bit lighter than expected.

Repairs – Barely sixty years after installation, the bells needed attention, as we can see from an announcement in the *Reading Mercury and Oxford Gazette* in 1767:

> May 23 – This day was opened, at Oakingham in this county, A Peal of Six Bells, new hung by Robert Turner, Bell Hanger to Messrs. Lester and Pack.

One might expect a rehang after so short a period to have entailed little more than lifting the bells, replacing the bearing bushes and possibly replacing the gudgeon pins, a job that could be carried out by a local blacksmith. But Turner was a noted bellhanger, and to have such a person rehang the bells within a comparatively short space of time seems unusual if Knight's frame and fittings were new in 1704. Churchwardens only spent money when they had to! A major rehang suggests some serious deterioration of the installation. One possibility is that the bell frame itself needed attention. That would be more likely if Knight had re-used and adapted the existing frame, rather than installing a new one. If there were still only four bells in the tower previously, then he would have had to extend the frame, by adding extra bell pits alongside it, which might have been an unsatisfactory solution.

Another forty years on, and the bells needed yet more work. This time, two bells were replaced with new ones (Treble and 4th, see Figure 11) though we don't know exactly why. Bertram Long's notes [24] say that the new bells were cast 'when the old ones were split or otherwise injured'. The phrase suggests that he didn't really know what was wrong with them. Thomas Mears of Whitechapel provided the two new bells, both appropriately inscribed 'T Mears of London fecit 1814'. Table 4 shows expenses related to the work, which added up to a total of £126-7-11[22].

Figure 11: Thomas Mears' 1814 bells (picture taken in 2004)

---

[22] Equivalent to about £6000 in modern currency.

Cash to forward of Messrs Mears Bellfounders	£25
Wm Norton for carriage of old bells	£2
Exp for taking down, putting up bells, etc	£1-4-0
Expense to London on account of the bells	£1-0-0
By cash paid to Messrs Mears Bellfounders, London	£97-1-11
Expense with bellfounder	2/-

Table 4: Expenses for the work in 1814

3.7 The clock

What does the clock have to do with bellringers? Strictly nothing, but as it lives in the tower it is common for the ringers to look after the clock as well as the bells, which they have at All Saints for as long as anyone can now remember.

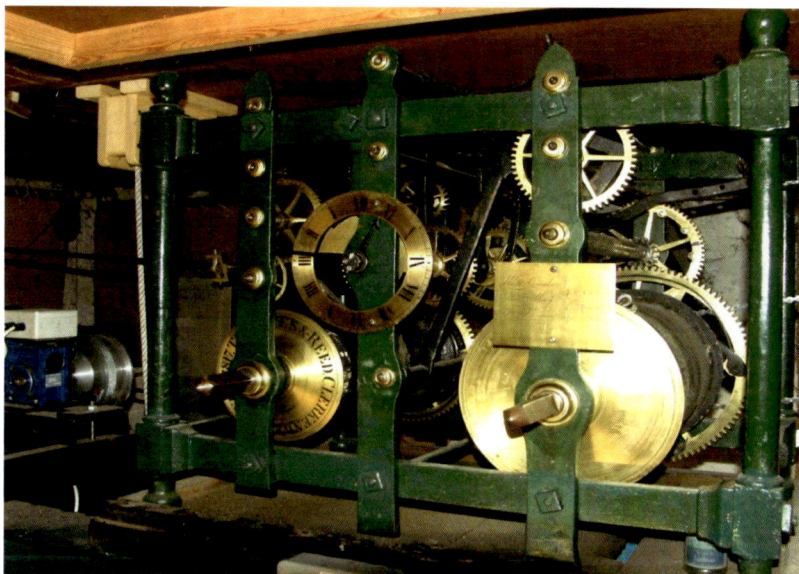

Figure 12: The clock in All Saints (taken in 2008)

The clock is a two train bedstead design, with a deadbeat escapement. It was built by Thwaites and Reed of Clerkenwell, London and installed in 1817, just thee years after Thomas Mears had replaced the two bells. The clock drives dials on the south and west faces of the tower, and the mechanism is still in action after nearly two hundred years, as shown in Figure 12.

The numbers on the adjustment dial run anticlockwise because it is on the opposite end of the shaft driving the west face. The smaller drum on the left (inscribed with the maker's name) drives the clock hands and the larger drum on the right drives the strike mechanism. The square shafts sticking out from each drum are where the handle was fitted to wind the clock, but since 2005 this chore has been taken over by auto-winder mechanisms, one of which is visible at the extreme left.

The clock now strikes the hours on an unmarked bell, mounted externally on the tower roof. It was added much later, in 1898 when the clock was repaired. Prior to that the clock probably struck on the Tenor bell, which is the more usual arrangement. The hammer would have struck the side of the bell, so the impact didn't start the bell swinging, and would have been fitted with a mechanism to hold it clear of the bell and wheel during full-circle ringing.

The south face of the clock is clearly visible in the 1832, engraving reproduced in Figure 13, whereas it wasn't there in Figure 6, which was drawn twenty years earlier. The other obvious change, is the addition of an extra dormer window in the middle of the south aisle.

Figure 13: All Saints in 1832[23] (complete with clock)

---

[23] Engraving by WA Delamotte Jnr, Sandhurst. Reproduced by permission of Wokingham Society

4 The late Victorians (1860 - 1900)

The 1860s represent a convenient point to move out of the conjectural world of Wokingham's ringing 'pre history' to get a clearer picture of what really happened. The church has a complete set of the Parish Notices (which later became the Parish Magazine) dating from 1865. In the early years they were as much about the life of the town (railway timetables, opening hours of banks, the soup kitchen, 'St Paul's Coal Club', etc) as about the life of the church (service times and church business, including the tower, bells and ringers). From the 1880s the Deanery and Diocesan ringing societies also have records, and the first ringing periodical appeared[1].

4.1 A period of change

The 19th century was a time of major change for England, and even more so for the Church. The ringing Exercise also changed dramatically, in what proved to be a transition from what had gone before, into the modern era.

The industrial revolution had drastically changed social conditions, and by the early 19th century the church had become lax in many ways, with its buildings often neglected. In 1831 a group of young High Church men struck out at the Church's complacency and launched what become the 'Oxford Movement'. It swept away old practices, and in the process triggered a wave of 'restoration' of church buildings, removing the physical signs of the old ways, including box pews, musicians' galleries, and the iconic triple-decker pulpits. The major restoration and enhancement of All Saints church building was no doubt part of this movement.

The reforms hardly touched the ringers who had operated more or less independently of the church since before the Reformation, but their ways were in similar need of improvement. Many seem to have spent much of their time in the ale house, and even in the tower there was gambling and drinking. The ringers could be as unruly as the church musicians had been. They often rang when they felt like it, with scant regard for the church. We don't know if this applied to Wokingham, but it may well have done. Our church building was sadly decayed, and we had plenty of ale houses. Whether things were as bad here as elsewhere though, we can only speculate.

With conditions improving in other areas of the church, lack of reform in the tower led to increasing tension between clergy and ringers, and sure enough after a couple of decades a group of reforming clerics inspired by the Oxford Movement turned their attention to ringers. Rev. HT Ellacombe, an engineer turned priest who was Rector of Clyst St George in Devon, improved things in his own Parish. Then with others, notably Cannon Woolmore Wigram, he stirred up other clerics to do likewise. This became known as the 'Belfry Reform' movement, and it really took hold when churches started to band together to support each other, and encouraged their ringers to form guilds and associations that would promote good practice.

Across the country the ideas took root, and in a few short decades led to the foundation of many of our modern ringing socoeties. Wokingham was at the heart of the process that gave birth to the Oxford Diocesan Guild of Church Bellringers, now

---

[1] The Bells News and Ringers' Record, from 1881

the largest in the world. It was founded in 1881, but the seeds were sown in the preceding few years, with the formation of smaller bodies that then became absorbed into it. One of these was the Sonning Deanery Society of Change Ringers.

4.2 Wokingham's role in Sonning Deanery

Wokingham was near the centre of the Deanery. In 1864, when St Paul's church was built, the town had acquired its second ring of bells, and it played a central role in the foundation of the Sonning Deanery Society of Change Ringers. On 23rd October 1879, the Chapter of the Rural Deanery of Sonning resolved:

> 'That the Bell-ringers of the Deanery be incorporated in a Society for the encouragement of Change Ringing, and that the following be appointed a Committee for carrying this resolution into effect:– Revds Dolben Paul, R. H. Hart-Davis, H. C. Sturges, J. F. Eastwood, and J. Fanklin Llewelyn, together with Mr. A. Hill, of All Saints Wokingham, and Mr. R. Blake of St. Paul's Wokingham.'

Of the priests, Paul (Bearwood), Hart-Davies (Sonning) and Sturges (Wargrave) were all ringers. Eastwood was curate at All Saints, but as far as we know not a ringer, though he was tower secretary from his arrival in 1879 till his early death three years later. The only laymen on the committee were Hill and Blake. Robert Blake, 46, was the sexton and Tower Foreman at St Paul's. He was an obvious establishment choice to be part of such a body. In contrast, Albert Hill was a young man of 24. He was clearly an able ringer, and he become Foreman at All Saints a few months later.

At the inaugural meeting of the society, the two Wokingham towers, joined by Arborfield, Hurst, Sonning & Wargrave, became founder members (shown bold in Figure 14). It is interesting to note that of the six founding towers, all but Arborfield now have eight bells, whereas of the eleven non-founding towers, only three have more than six bells – Twyford and Easthampstead with eight, and Warfield with ten.

The Society sought to encourage mutual support between the ringers throughout the Deanery. To this end it soon established the custom of holding ringing meetings at different towers, but Wokingham continued to be the focus of Deanery ringing for several generations. The Annual Meeting was held in Wokingham until 1970, since when it has rotated round different towers. In the early years, the meetings were held in The Terrace Room, but later they alternated between St Paul's Parish Rooms, and All Saints Church House (opened in 1902). The ringers' services prior to the AGM, usually had an invited clergyman to give the address.

The only elected officers were the 'administrative' roles of Chairman, Secretary and Treasurer, all held by clergymen in the early years. There was no equivalent of the Ringing Master who plays a lead role in a modern ringing society. Ringing events were organised and run by a committee of all the tower Foremen[2]. It sounds egalitarian, but in practice it was down to individuals to take a lead. As one of the committee that brought the Society into existence, Albert Hill (Foreman at All Saints) would have had influence, and he seems to have played a significant role in shaping the society's development. At the 1891 AGM, he was one of those advocating that a small group of experienced Branch ringers visit neighbouring towers to help advance

---

[2] See 'What's in a name' on page 28

their change ringing. At the 1893 AGM, he and J Ford (Foreman of Sonning) offered advice 'as to the simplest method of instructing beginners in the art of change ringing'. As we shall see later, some of Albert's successors at All Saints also made significant contributions to ringing in the Deanery and beyond.

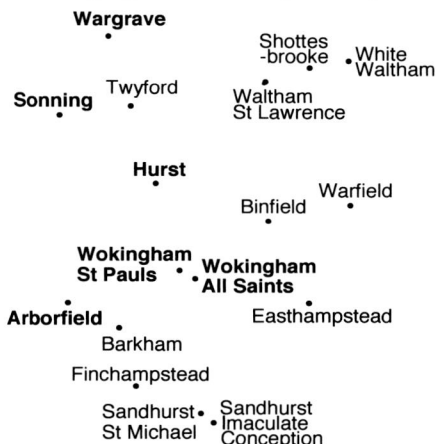

Wargrave

Shottes-brooke • White Waltham

Sonning Twyford

Waltham St Lawrence

Hurst

Warfield
Binfield

Wokingham St Pauls • **Wokingham All Saints**

Arborfield • Easthampstead

Barkham

Finchampstead

Sandhurst • Sandhurst St Michael • Imaculate Conception

*Figure 14: The modern Sonning Deanery Branch, with founding towers in **Bold**[3]*

Promoting change ringing – Change ringing was at the heart of Belfry Reform, as exemplified by the resolution to form the Sonning Deanery Society. Full membership required that 'he can take his own Bell in a Set of Bells in a Plain Course of Grandsire Doubles[4]', as stated on the membership certificate. Some ringing societies still require change ringing ability prior to election, but the Oxford Diocesan Guild of Church Bellringers does not do so (as reflected in its title), so modern ringers can become full members before they learn to ring changes.

Change ringing was not just a desirable addition to reform, it was the vehicle through which the clergy aimed to achieve the reformed behaviour of ringers. Note the order of objectives in the Sonning Deanery Society's inaugural document:

'This Society has been formed for the encouragement of Change Ringing, and the cultivation of order, moral tone, and reverence in Belfries.'

Likewise, a year later the Oxford Diocesan Guild's three 'objects' were:

(1) to recognise the true position of Ringers as Church Officers,
(2) to cultivate the art of Change Ringing, and,
(3) to promote Belfry Reform where it is needed.

It might seem odd that the reforming clergy should insist on change ringing as the means of improving ringers' behaviour and moral tone, since it had evolved outside the church's influence as a mainly secular activity, and it bore no recognisable relationship to any liturgical music. So what was the connection?

---

[3] Binfield, Easthampstead and Warfield, were in the Maidenhead Deanery of the Church until 1921. White Waltham was in East Berks & South Bucks Branch of the Guild until 1985.

[4] Grandsire Doubles was normally the first method learned, though it is now less likely to be so.

Ringing a bell is essentially a craft activity. The core skills needed are good physical co-ordination. Working men of the era used many such skills: the skill of a mower using a scythe in a corn field, or the skill of a blacksmith wielding a hammer in a smithy. Rounds ringing, especially to competition standard, requires rhythmic accuracy and a good ear. These too are skills of a type that would be familiar to men who used their hands all day long, and whose livelihood depended on the quality of their work, but who otherwise had few aspirations or pretensions.

In contrast, change ringing adds a completely different dimension. Varying the order of the bells continually while ringing requires greater co-ordination to swing the bells at different speeds, but above all it requires an intellectual input. Change ringing relies on complex rules that must be memorised and interpreted continually while ringing. The reformers must have felt that an activity requiring engagement of the mind as well as the body would bring with it the other more worthy mental habits and attitudes of the professional classes. It is perhaps noteworthy that in its early years during the 17th and 18th centuries, it was the young gentry who drove forward the the art and science of change ringing, rather than the artisans.

This close link between change ringing and moral tone is readily apparent in the early records of the Sonning Deanery Branch. At the 1882 AGM in Wokingham, the secretary reported that change ringing had been introduced to all towers in the Deanery and that 'Churchyard Bobs[5] had been buried once (and it is to be hoped) for ever'. He spoke of 'the great changes in the tone of the ringers, and the even greater change in the tone of their bells'. In the following year, after the AGM service at All Saints, he made similar remarks:

> 'No one could doubt that the Guild was doing a most useful work for the Church. The hearty service in the church, and the general goodwill expressed was of itself evidence of a higher tone among ringers, and of a greater care for a long neglected corner of our parish church.'

While he was talking generally, it is reasonable to assume that these remarks applied to the ringers at All Saints, where he was speaking.

What's in a name? – The term 'Foreman', for what is normally called a 'Tower Captain', appears amost nowhere outside Sonning Deanery. It was used at All Saints in 1873, and we know that Wokingham played a key role in founding the Sonning Deanery Society. We may speculate about a possible connection.

4.3 The band and ringing

The Parish Magazine first mentions ringing in October 1870, for the wedding of Rev. William Townsend Henman: '... various marks of respect and affection shown by the inhabitants of Wokingham ... when the Old Church bells rang out a merry peal of sympathetic gladness'. Gladness is common enough at weddings, but we might pause to wonder whether our modern understanding of 'sympathetic' was intended.

A new beginning – In 1873, six years before the decision to found the Sonning Deanery Society, there was a notice that probably marks the start of change ringing at

---

[5] One of several derisory terms for rounds ringing.

All Saints. Coincidentally also in 1873 the Vestry Meeting voted to accept the 1858 local government act in the town & parish of Wokingham – it seems strange to us that the citizens would have a choice about such things.

We saw in Chapter 3 how rounds ringing persisted in this area long after change ringing was established in nearby towns, and it seems likely that things remained much the same into the mid 1800s. But that changed in 1873, when Rev Henry George Bird came to All Saints as Assistant Priest[6], bringing with him the agenda of Belfry Reform. In September, shortly after he arrived, the Parish Magazine announced the formation of a 'Society of Honorary Change Ringers' whose rules were to be agreed at a meeting on the 13th. It announced that 'any person wishing to become a member should send his name to Mr Bird at once'.

The Rector, Rev Edward Sturges, presided at the meeting, and was elected Treasurer, Mr C Brooker was elected Secretary and Bird was elected Foreman. That suggests that he was a ringer, which is quite possible – in those days many clergy took up ringing whilst at University, although only a few of them became proficient and continued in later life. Even if he was a ringer we don't know how experienced or how good he was. If he was a non-ringing figurehead, then he would have needed to appoint some other experienced ringer to be responsible for teaching.

The new society's role was 'to help the paid ringers, and in other ways to encourage the art of bell-ringing'. In reality, it was probably a means of supplanting the old guard, using the technique neatly described some fifty years later in an SPCK leaflet[7]:

'Leave the 'old lot' as they are, telling them that they shall still ring on occasions of payment but that for other ringing, and in particular for ringing for church services, a new company is being founded, the members of which pledge themselves to learn, or do their best to learn, change ringing. This they will do for the glory of God and without any pecuniary reward. The result soon follows. The old company may or may not survive over the next Christmas season, the season of tips, Christmas boxes and the like, but before another such season comes around, bereft often of some of their own younger and more enterprising members, who have gone over to the other side, they collapse of inanation. Left out in the cold, they leave the junior and more energetic society in possession of the field.'

The ringers (presumably the Honorary Ringers) are mentioned a couple more times that year. In May there was a cricket match between choir and ringers of All Saints & St Paul's (it doesn't say whether it was joint choir v joint ringers or joint All Saints v joint St Paul's) and at All Saints tide (November) there was a social gathering for:

'63 Church Helpers, comprising Clergy, Churchwardens, Organist, Choirmen, District Visitors, Sunday and Evening School Teachers, Church Decorators, Missionary Collectors, Bellringers and other Church Officers'.

The ringers may have been last in the list, beneath decorators and collectors, but at least they were recognised as church officers, which was one of the key objectives of the Belfry Reform movement. The report goes on to say that after the meal:

---

[6] Coincidentally, in the same year, the new Rectory was built. It has since been demolished to make way for new housing at the end of the 20th century.

[7] The Bellringer (Plain Guides to Lay Work No. 8) by Rev. CDP Davies. [18]

29

'... we entered on the discussion of some of our church work. The Churchwardens, who were all with us, each spoke some encouraging words; and interesting speeches were made on the subjects of Church Decoration, Sunday Schools, Night Schools, Missionary Work, and Bellringing'.

A set of new handbells was purchased[8] for use by the honorary ringers. The bells were presumably intended to facilitate learning the basics of change ringing methods without the added complication of having to manhandle the tower bells while doing so, and without the unpleasant sounds that would emanate from the tower with a complete set of beginners all learning together, and no doubt struggling. For this purpose they probably rang one bell each[9]. This style of method learning is less common today, when most ringers learn directly on tower bells, within the context of a band that can already ring methods. Also, modern bells are better hung, and easier to handle. Many towers, including All Saints, have inherited a set of handbells from former years, though they often hang unused in the tower[10].

Progress? – The 1873 band must have made some progress, because the following summer they performed after a dinner at the Town Hall for parishioners. St Paul's ringers 'played a tune on their hand-bells', and All Saints' ringers 'gave a clever specimen of change-ringing'. There was a toast to Mr Millard 'for his service rendered in training the All Saints' Ringers'. Millard is absent from the Sonning Deanery Society records, which begin six years later. Perhaps he rang at St Paul's, which with a fairly new ring of bells may have had a more experienced band.

Bird left after two years, and without him perhaps the band lost momentum. Or perhaps their 'cleverness' with handbells didn't transfer into the tower, where the challenge of bell control would have compounded the mental task of ringing changes. We don't know what they achieved, but any success seems to have dissipated, because when records of the Oxford Diocesan Guild begin seven years later, All Saints had only one member (Albert Hill) capable of ringing changes, and three probationers, whereas St Paul's had ten change ringing members. We don't know whether Albert was in Bird's band (the only one to make the grade) or whether he learnt change ringing before he came to Wokingham, which seems quite possible. Ringing is a team activity, and it would have been difficult for him to have become a competent change ringer in a tower where no one else was.

The developing band – When Albert became Foreman in 1880, he probably had to start more or less from scratch to develop an effective change ringing band. Progress seems to have been slow if we compare Guild membership at All Saints with the ringers listed in the Parish Magazine in January 1889. Albert Hill, Sam Paice and Frank Mower were all Guild members before 1889, but the others listed only became probationers some years later: Fred Mattingley (1890), A Jones, J French (1892), H Sargeant, F Lush (1895), W Lush (1899)[11]. Note that 'probationer' didn't

---

[8] They cost between £7 and £8. This was almost certainly the set made by William Blews & Son of Birmingham, which is still in use.

[9] It is more normal to ring changes with a bell in each hand, see Figure 80 (on page 131).

[10] All Saints handbells are regularly used by an active tune ringing group, see page 114.

[11] If they were the same Lushes, see pages 33-34.

necessarily mean a novice ringer, it meant a ringer who had not yet met the Guild's requirement as a change ringer.

All Saints doesn't seem to have been the only tower in the Deanery that was slow making the transition to change ringing. At the 1885 Branch AGM, the secretary (Rev JF Llewelyn) 'made some remarks upon the general condition of the Branch':

> 'The reports which he had received from the leaders of the several Belfries did not tell of the progress in Change-Ringing which he had hoped, and looked for. He would remind all present that although great improvement had taken place in the tone of the Ringers themselves, and the condition of the Belfries, still they must not forget that one of the chief objects of the Guild was also "to cultivate the art of Change Ringing".'

Pressure of business led Albert Hill to resign as Foreman in 1896 after 16 years in post. He was a blacksmith, having been apprenticed to his father, but the 1901 census also describes him as a farmer so maybe he had taken on an extra business. Sam Paice seems to have been the obvious candidate to replace him as Foreman, and he served until his death 26 years later.

All Saints and the Guild – The Guild undoubtedly influenced the development of ringing at All Saints, especially change ringing, through its objectives and by practical assistance. The Guild appointed several qualified instructors who worked to help local towers. The Guild's first report lists eleven of them. Mr JR Haworth was engaged as 'Instructor in Change Ringing for the Towers of Sonning Deanery'. He was a member of the College Youths[12]. From Monday to Saturday, 17-22nd April 1882, he was in Wokingham, and each evening went to a different Branch tower. He gave instruction to the ringers of All Saints and St Paul's on the Saturday. When he reported about Wokingham to the Guild, he said:

> 'April 22nd 1882 "Belfry and bells in good order. Rung the course of Grandsire Doubles by memory; but for the first time rang the peal 120 changes. Understand clearly my remarks about ringing by method. Mr Hill is of great service." '

Ringers from all over the Diocese used to come together for the annual Guild Festivals, and the Parish Magazine regularly announced and reported on them. In July 1882 it said: 'ringers from Wokingham were well represented'. They travelled by train, and the previous month's notice had helpfully included train times:

> 'Ringing members to leave Wokingham at 8.59 am, and Reading at 9.50 am, and return from Oxford at 7.55pm.'

Of over 200 ringers at the 1886 Festival in Abingdon, 13 were from Wokingham (both churches). In 1895, the Festival was in Wokingham, with the service at the Parish Church, the business meeting at the Town Hall and the dinner in a large tent. It was claimed to have been 'perhaps the most successful hitherto carried out'.

The Branch provided more than practical support. When Rev John Frederick Eastwood died on 5th March 1882, at the very young age of 26, 'Muffled peals were rung on March 9th in all the churches [of the Deanery] in respect of his memory'. Like most of the clergy, he was an honorary member of the Branch, but he seems to

---

[12] The Ancient Society of College Youths, one of two premier ringing societies.

have taken a particular interest in the ringers. He was tower secretary at All Saints, a role that seems to have gone with being Assistant Priest.

Visiting ringers – While the band was building up its capabilities, there were no published performances by them, but some visiting bands did publish performances at All Saints in *The Bell News* [15]. For example:

> December 15th 1883 '... 5 St Lawrence ringers & 1 St Giles rang 720 Grandsire Minor with 34 bobs and 2 singles. Also several six-scores of Grandsire Doubles.'

> November 5th 1890 '... 8 members from Reading rang 720 Woodbine, also 720 Bob Minor and 120 Grandsire Doubles.'

On June 19th, 1897, the Saturday before Queen Victoria's Diamond Jubilee, there is another report, seemingly by a visiting band, though one of the locals was involved:

> June 19th '... midnight ringing to celebrate Queen Victoria's diamond jubilee, with several six-scores of Grandsire Doubles with F Mower one of the local ringers on 3rd. Also 360 College Single. Thanks for permission and for providing tea at such short notice. '

On the great day itself, the following Tuesday, ringing accompanied the ox roasted in the marketplace, the children's races in Langborough, and other public festivities. This was definitely by the local ringers, ten of whom were named in *Bell News:*

> 'Ringing at 6am, and at intervals throughout the day, several more six-scores'.

Rogue handbell ringers – An unusual notice appeared in December 1896 suggesting the presence of dissent within the band.

> The Hand-bell Ringers. The Ringers of the Church Tower do not go around with handbells. A party of young men practice in the Parish Room at the Rectory, by the Rector's permission twice a week during part of the winter. Three are church ringers, and the remaining two are not. They purpose going round at Christmas with the bells as they did last year. Any gifts will be handed to their Treasurer and the money divided among them after Christmas, and will they assure us be usefully spent. But it is only right that it should be known that money given to them will not go to the Church Ringers and must not be instead of the subscriptions which are kindly given to secure for the Church Ringers a small annual payment for their constant services. There are no other Handbell ringers connected with All Saints Church in any way. The young men we have referred to called themselves last year "The Rectory Handbell ringers" which was misleading, and this year propose to call themselves in future "The Christmas hand-bell ringers".'

We can only guess at the politics that lay behind this notice. What is even more surprising is to find a very similar announcement forty years later, in 1935.

> 'It is not generally known that the ringers who go round at Christmas time and call themselves "The All Saints Ringers" are not connected with the ringing at All Saints Church.'

So had the issue festered for forty years behind the scenes, with another generation taking over from the first lot? Or did lightning strike in the same place twice, and the new group was not related to the earlier one? We do not know.

4.4 Notable ringers

Albert J Hill was born in Devizes, moved to Hampshire as a child, and then came to Wokingham. It's not clear where he learnt to ring, but it could have been before he came here. He was an able ringer, and made a significant impact both at All Saints and in Sonning Deanery, having helped to set up and develop the Society/Branch. In 1894 he became the first layman (since 1881) to serve as a Branch representative on the Guild General Committee. Prior to that, each Branch had a single clerical representative. At 24 he became Tower Foreman (22 years earlier than this picture in 1902) and held the post for 16 years. The band prospered under his leadership – ten of the thirty or so ringers in his charge went on to serve for more than a decade, and some for many decades more. He was a blacksmith like his father, and later took up farming.

Samuel Paice (Sam) was a postman. Appropriately for a ringer, he lived in a house called 'Ringwell' in Goodchild Road. He was another incomer[13], having probably learnt to ring in Yateley, where he grew up, and he brought valuable skills to All Saints. He moved to Wokingham in his mid twenties, and shortly afterwards became the first member of the All Saints band to ring a peal, in June 1883 at St Paul's. He was also in the first peal rung entirely by members of Sonning Deanery, at Sandhurst on 11th March 1899, when he and five Sandhurst ringers rang a peal of 5040 Minor, in two and a half hours. It was only the second peal rung on the bells. Sam became Foreman at All Saints in 1896, and served until his death in 1920.

F & W Lush are two names in the ringing record that are likely to draw the eye of any Wokingham historian. It is well known that the brothers Frank and Walter Lush were coach builders, with customers including King Edward VII, Empress Eugenie of the French, and Prince Christian of Schleswig-Holstein. But were they also the ringing Lushes?

Wokingham had two F Lushes (both unhelpfully called Frank) and two W Lushes (Walter and William) around that time. The younger Frank was a carpenter and joiner, and William was a solicitor's clerk. They were all descended from George Lush, as shown in the selective extract from the family tree in Figure 15.

---

[13] This was a time when many people moved into Wokingham. In 1881 one in every six households had a head, or husband/wife, born outside the town.

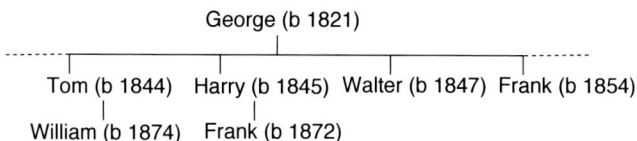

Figure 15: Selective extract from the Lush family tree

The Parish Magazine listed F & W Lush as ringers in 1889, but the Oxford Diocesan Guild records[14] for All Saints show no Lushes until 1895 (F) and 1898 (W). F Lush rang until 1946, and so must have been the younger Frank, since his coach-builder namesake died in 1907. Beyond that, we are into speculation, since in 1989, all four men were of ages when they could have rung (15, 17, 37, 42).

Figure 16: Records of Lushes as ringers

William lived with his parents in Reading from at least 1891 until after he married in late 1899, so it was probably Walter who rang here in 1898. If he was also the W Lush mentioned in 1889, and if he wasn't interested in change ringing, maybe he only joined the Guild egged on by his nephew, the young Frank, who by then was making good progress. That would be consistent with giving up after a few years as a 'probationer'. His absence from the 1902 picture (on page 41) suggests that he also gave up ringing, and there was no longer a W Lush in the band.

That still leaves the question of whether Frank the elder or Frank the younger was mentioned in 1889. It could have been Frank senior, who like Walter, never took to change ringing, but unlike him gave up ringing some time in the early 1890s, to be followed by young Frank who then made rapid progress. It seems less likely that Frank Junior would have already acquired the status of being on of the eight 'stated ringers' in 1889 at the age of 17, but then took a further six or so years to master basic change ringing.

So the likely scenario would appear to be that the coachbuilders, Walter and Frank senior, were ringing in 1889, and may well have been in Bird's 1873 band (then in their early twenties) but they never mastered change ringing. Frank probably gave up some time in the early 1890s but Walter hung on and joined the Guild for a few years after young Frank encouraged him to do so. But as a non-changeringer[15], Walter gave up in 1900, leaving young Frank to go on ringing into the 1940s.

William Loader seems not to have been notable as a ringer, but he achieved considerable fame outside the tower. He was a farrier based in Peach Street[16], and appears regularly to have distinguished himself in competitions. For example, in

---

[14] Which began in 1880.

[15] He was a 'probationer', ie a non change ringing member, for his four years in the Guild.

[16] Possibly at the Old Forge 45-47 Peach Street, now converted to offices.

1899, the Parish Magazine reported that: 'William Loader of Peach Street, one of our Bellringers, at the recent Royal Counties Show at Windsor, again took 1st prize for shoeing carriage horses'. William's grave is appropriately surrounded by an example of the blacksmith's craft, see Figure 17.

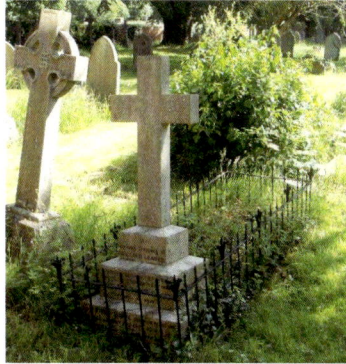

Figure 17: Wrought iron around the grave of William Loader, farrier

4.5 Restoration of the tower

The mid-late 19th century at All Saints seems to have been a time of almost continual restoration. The roof was rebuilt in 1845, with a vast programme of repair and modification in the 1860s. The scale of this work is clear from the faculty:

> 'Thoroughly repair the whole edifice of the church, enlarge the chancel by forming a new South aisle to the same, and the rebuilding of the North aisle thereof; to erect a new North wall to the North aisle of the nave, to heighten and restore the tower, to entirely remove the galleries at present existing and substitute new and open sittings for the present pews and fittings in the church, to new pave the church throughout, to lower the soil around the outside of the church [as shown in plan] to rebuild the porch & repair the cross, to restore the parapets which have been taken away...'.

This must have caused major disruption for the whole congregation, and almost certainly will have interfered with regular ringing while the work was in progress. One change in particular – opening the archway between the ringing room and the nave, thus converting it into a gallery – radically altered the perceived relationship between the ringers and the congregation. They were no longer remote and hidden, but visible to anyone in church who cared to turn and look up.

At first sight, this move was very much in the spirit of the Belfry Reform movement, but that might not have been the main motivation. As the faculty stated, more drastic work was originally planned for the tower, though lack of funds prevented it being done. The abandoned plan was ambitious – to add an extra 16 feet to the tower, with the bells higher so that the ringing room floor could be above 'the grand West window'. That suggests that integration of the ringers was not the motivation for opening up the arch, but rather it was intended to replace a blank west wall with an unfettered view of the window, a major source of light. In fact had the tower been extended, as originally envisaged, the ringers would have been out of sight again.

35

Whatever the motivation, inter-visibility between the ringers and the congregation has been a positive feature of All Saints, though it also brought some problems[17].

The large opening in the east wall of the tower, and the large window in the west wall, make it less rigid than if it had a solid base, so there is more tower movement[18] than desirable. We should be thankful that the funds did run out, because moving the bells higher in the tower would have made the movement worse – 10 to 15 feet might have doubled the force on the tower – making the bells even harder to ring.

Work on the bells – In July 1873 the bells were reported to be in a bad state, with one or two 'in a condition dangerous for ringing'. Warners[19] inspected them and offered 'to rehang them, to tune the treble bell, and to put them into thorough order' for £75-10s. The announcement concluded: 'Still the sum is a large one, what are we to do?' The prospect of more fund raising must have seemed daunting so soon after the major effort to restore the church building only eight years earlier. Daunted or not, six months later it was announced that: 'We are happy to say that the re-hanging of the Bells of the Old Church has been completed'.

What did 'rehang' mean? Warners' report noted that 'in case of the restoration of the Tower, this work will not need repetition, as the bearings of the bells can be shifted into a new chamber'. This suggests that the work was mainly confined to replacement of bearings and gudgeons[20], perhaps with some repairs to any fittings that needed it. If so, then it could all have been done without removing the bells from the tower. Was any retuning done, or was it deemed a luxury and not undertaken?[21]

Another insight into what might have been done comes from a press report[22] during the 1903 restoration, which referred to the old timber frame as having been 'renewed 30 years ago'. So there might have been a new frame in 1873. If so, it seems odd that it wasn't mentioned at the time. Maybe 'renewed' in the 1903 report referred to some sort of bracing or strengthening.

Fighting decay – In 1875, the tower was back in the headlines, with another complaint that the 'unsightly gallery for the bellringers is a most serious blemish to the beauty of the Old Church.' At the same time, and rather more seriously, a piece of stone had fallen out of the tracery of the West window, and more stone was loose. The chickens were coming home to roost from the 1860s' decision to delay work on the tower 'hoping for more time before making the extra effort to complete that part of the work'. Some work was clearly urgent, though comfortingly the surveyors reported that 'the walls were sound' and that restoration could be done 'without altering in any way the appearance of this venerable and interesting tower'.

---

[17] See pages 91 & 124

[18] Some tower movement is normal when bells are ringing, and occurs in all towers. All Saints is well short of the worst towers, but moves somewhat more than ideal.

[19] Warner and Sons, bell founders of Cripplegate, London.

[20] Stubs that protrude from the end of the headstock and rest in the bearings, so the bell can rotate.

[21] The bell Warners offered to retune was one of the bells replaced in 2004, because it could not be tuned sufficiently to bring it into a proper relationship with the other bells (using the modern understanding of bell tuning, which wasn't available in 1873).

[22] See page 42

That last comment is interesting, given that not many decades previously the appearance of the tower had been radically changed by removing the old rendering and exposing the dark puddingstone underneath [23].

The project was clearly about more than solving the safety problem. Its objectives included removal of the 'unsightly ringers' gallery', and remedying 'the draughts which now render the seats at the west end of the Church almost useless during the Winter months'. The whole cost was estimated at £1150, a large sum in those days, and fund raising began immediately. But with memories of how protracted that could be, the intention was to delay start of the work until enough money had been raised.

This policy of waiting was not to everyone's liking, and in March 1877 (two years into the fund raising) the Rector received the following apocalyptic anonymous letter.

"LET WOKINGHAM TAKE WARNING AND EXERT ITSELF"
"The tower of the parish church of Coychurch, near Brigend, fell down on Saturday evening, destroying the south aisle and a harmonium, and disturbing several monuments. The body of the church was restored a few years ago, but the tower was neglected for want of funds."

This must have inflamed the divisions within the Parish. A few months later, the report of a meeting of the Restoration Committee 'to consider what repairs were necessary to secure the free stone from further accident' said that their 'decision was not known' but it reiterated their unwillingness to start work with the 'limited funds as yet at their disposal'. Even so, they reluctantly authorised some remedial work, but regretted spending money 'for such a temporary purpose'. The stonework was examined, and some loose stone removed 'to ward off danger to people using the West door'.

The following spring (1878) they let a 'carefully revised contract' for £1000 (almost the whole of the money raised so far) for the 'outside work' to be done during the summer, and hoped for 'every exertion' to raise an extra £500 so the 'inside work' could follow on. They managed to raise £160 (including £50 from the Queen) but it was all spent by the autumn. They contracted a further £50 for the inside of the West window and plastering, and reckoned that a further £200 would be enough to complete the work. They set up a £200 guarantee fund to enable work to proceed, with £25 each from the clergy and wardens, and they made an 'earnest appeal' for further contributions.

The inside work included reconstruction of the existing screen[24] and the ringers' floor. This was another controversial decision. The gallery was clearly not liked (presumably because it partly obscured the west window). With the dream of a taller tower long gone, they had considered moving the ringers down to the ground floor, but rejected it because it 'would interfere somewhat with the use of the West door, and increase the difficulty of preventing the cold draughts'. There was no mention of the drastic effect that such a move would have had on the ability to ring the bells. This is another case where external factors happily prevented a change for the worse

---

[23] See page 129
[24] Presumably this refers to the partition between the nave and the porch, beneath the gallery.

as far as the ringers were concerned. Even with the gallery, the length of rope drop is considerable. Long ropes expand and contract with the weather, and are very springy when new[25]. There was not even a rope guide above the ringers, to constrain what can be quite unruly movement of the rope. It is unlikely that the old bells were any easier to handle in the 1870s than in the 1950s when visiting ringers, unfamiliar with the bells' quirks, had great difficulty handling them. Having even more rope to ring from the ground floor would have made things far worse.

The tower restoration was finally finished in 1880. The cost had risen to nearly £1500, but the money had not all been raised. No doubt fund raising dragged on for a while until the next round of restoration (a new organ in the late 1890s to replace the one built in 1864) and the installation of incandescent lighting shortly afterwards.

There was a further enhancement to the tower in 1885, when the stained glass of the west window was installed in memory of Commodore Elliot Morres (who had been largely instrumental in saving the nave and roof, despite a strong lobby to pull it down). The window design, by Burkson & Gryffs, represents the Te Deum.

Figure 18: (L) Ringing gallery[26], (R) Details from the west window

---

[25] Both of these problems are now eliminated by using pre-stretched polyester for the main part of the rope, but until the late 20th century all bell ropes were made entirely of natural fibres.

[26] The picture of the gallery was taken in 2009, after the rood screen was moved to the back of the nave, and new doors installed between the nave and porch.

In September 1890, only 17 years after the previous 'rehang' in 1873, the following announcement appeared out of the blue:

> 'The bells have been thoroughly looked to by Messrs Warner & Sons. The bearings and gudgeons have been renewed, and the whole of the fittings overhauled.'

Why did the bearings need renewing after so short a time? Was the original job deficient perhaps? The work cost £25, much less than the original quotation[27] for the 1873 work, but rather more than one might expect for putting right a faulty job.

Please Sir, can we have more bells? – Oliver Twist asked for more gruel after his meal, but Sam Paice asked for more bells after his. Interestingly, the report doesn't come from the Parish Magazine, but from the more distant pages of *The Bell News*, early in 1899. We can only speculate on what was being said in private. This is what was published:

> 'At All Saints Rectory, Wokingham, on Saturday last New Year's Eve, Rev Canon and Mrs Sturges, with their usual liberty gave the annual supper to the bell ringers and choir. After supper, the usual toasts were proposed, and S Paice, responding for the ringers, expressed hope that many improvements connected with the grand old church would this coming year be crowned by the addition of two new bells to the present ring of six.

> The Rector, in reply, stated that the subject of two additional bells had previously been considered, and it was thought the strength of the tower was not equal to the extra weight, but if a reliable authority could be got to report on the matter, he had no doubt that the necessary funds would be forthcoming. The ringers and others trust that now the thin end of the wedge has been inserted, the breach will continue to open until the new bells are admitted.'

It is easy to understand the desire for more bells. The daughter church of St Paul's had enjoyed a superior modern ring of eight for 35 years, while the mother church still had a 200 year old, indifferent ring of six. The first peal in the Sonning Deanery was rung on the modern bells of St Paul's, in 1864, and by the turn of the century 19 of the Deanery's 33 peals had been rung there, yet no one had ever rung a peal at All Saints. We don't know for sure, but it seems likely that no one wanted to spend three hours of hard work to ring a badly-going old six.

Whether caused by the Foreman's after dinner remark or not, the ball was now rolling, and in February 1899 the Parish Magazine referred to a 'long felt view' that adding two new Trebles might 'be a proper and acceptable gift for the Parish' that might 'add to the melody, smoothness and softness of the music from the tower'.

The Rector had said that he was open to the opinion of a 'reliable authority', and no less an authority than FE Robinson[28] was asked to inspect and advise. He said that two new bells couldn't be hung in the existing frame, and that there was insufficient space to hang them above it. The existing frame would of course have been a six bell frame, so we should interpret this to mean that the existing frame couldn't be extended sideways by adding two new pits to accommodate the extra bells.

---

[27] We don't know final cost in 1873. The scope of work may have been reduced from that quoted.
[28] Master of the Oxford Diocesan Guild of Church Bellringers, see pages 53-56.

Robinson recommended a modern iron frame to take 8 bells on one level (which is what we now have). An iron frame generally takes less space than an equivalent timber one, because timber side members need to be much thicker for the same strength (and in very old frames are often even thicker than a modern timber frame would be). A new frame can also have the whole layout optimised to fit all the bells.

Robinson also recommended mounting the frame 3 or 4 feet lower than the existing one, in order to reduce the stress on the tower, and to improve the tone for listeners outside. Tower movement varies as the cube of the height of the bells, so lowering them four feet might reduce movement by 15%. The 'tonal improvement' probably means that individual bells adjacent to the sound openings tended to 'shout', whereas when they are a below the sound openings, the sounds of the bells blend together better.

There is another practical reason for lowering the frame though. The original timber frame stood on the belfry floor, and one would have been able to walk in alongside it. The bigger eight bell frame fills the room, and had it been installed at the same height, it would have been impossible to get in without climbing through the side of the frame. With the frame lower, the door gives entrance at frame top level, which is more convenient. There is a walkway over the only narrow strip of unused space along part of the east wall[29].

As explained above, Robinson's recommendations were well founded, but they seem to have struck an alarming note in the Parish, because the article containing the report went on to say that the Rector and Churchwardens 'certainly will not allow anything of the kind to be done without the most careful consideration from every point of view and advice had from other experts'. Was this just routine administrative caution? Or did they doubt the engineering wisdom of a ringing priest, albeit such an eminent and accomplished one? Was iron considered to be a new-fangled material, compared to good, old fashioned English oak? Or were there perhaps undercurrents of opposition to the whole augmentation project within the Parish? We don't know.

Robinson estimated the cost as £152, and in August 1899 an appeal was launched to raise £150 from the whole community of the town:

'This is a matter that does not exclusively interest the congregation, and it is hoped that all in the neighbourhood round our town, lovers of the music of Church Bells will be found ready to contribute to this important improvement in the peal from our old church tower.'

As we shall see in the next chapter, things did indeed move forward in the new century, but not without some surprises along the way. And the cost of the work proved to be far more than Robinson's estimate.

---

[29] See Figure 66 (on page 120)

5 The Edwardians (1900 - 1917)

In spring 1900 the bells rang joyfully before noon to mark the relief of Ladysmith. The empire was at its height. The old Queen was still on the throne (though she would not be for much longer). No doubt 1900 brought as much euphoria and future gazing as we experienced a century later in the year 2000 (but without the widespread fear of the Millennium bug[1].)

The confident spirit of the age comes across in the oldest surviving picture of the band, taken in 1902, which still hangs in the tower, see Figure 19.

Figure 19: Ringers at the time of King Edward's coronation in 1902
(L-R) G Bacon, F Lush, 'F Moor'[2], G Cole, A Hill, F Mattingley, S Paice, J French

5.1 New bells for a new century

The last chapter closed with a fund to augment the bells from six to eight being set up in the dying months of the old century. The appeal was to the community at large, not just to church members. That was probably a wise move, given the other calls on the Church's resources around that time.   The Churchwardens' account was overdrawn in 1900 because of roof repairs. In 1901 they needed £100 to fix the heating, and April 1902 saw the opening of Church House[3], which hadn't all been paid for, and took a further couple of years to clear the debt.

---

[1] Software failures caused when the date changed from '99' to '00', ie from '1999' to '2000'.

[2] The names are written on the picture, but this one is a mystery. There is no record of any ringer called F Moor. Frank Mower rang from 1885 to 1905, and was 32 at the time. 'Moor' must be a misprint for Mower, but it is odd that no one opened up the picture to correct the name.

[3] The hall in Easthampstead Road, which was sold for private residential use in 2004, after it and the 1960s Church Annexe were both replaced by The Cornerstone community centre.

Response to the bells appeal was slow. In January 1902, the Fund had hardly moved for two years, with only £15-11-8 in hand (including £2 from Sonning Deanery ringers) and a further £13-4-0 of promises. The target of £150 must have seemed a long way off with barely £30 raised. A report gloomily concluded:

'... in the absence of any sufficient response to the appeal, the Rector and Churchwardens will probably determine to return the contributions made'

Later that year, Webb & Bennett ('the well known Church Bell-hangers'[4] according to the Parish Magazine) reported on the bells. Their conclusion corresponded closely with Robinson's opinion of three years earlier:

'...[we]... find them all sound, but much worn where the clappers now strike. They should be quarter turned[5] for the clappers to strike on a new place. The 2nd and 3rd bells are not good they should be recast ... If two new trebles are added a new frame will be required to get them on one level. We strongly advise a wrought iron frame fixed to steel girders securely built into the Tower walls. The girders would strengthen the tower, as they would be tyes to the walls. The new frame will be lower than the present one.'

The price, for two new bells, quarter turning and rehanging in a wrought iron frame resting on steel beams, was £328-17s – more than double Robinson's estimate.

The remark about strengthening the tower seems to have caused even more consternation among the parish worriers (like Robinson's original recommendation) because in the Parish Magazine, the report was accompanied by a disclaimer:

'The remark by Messrs Webb & Bennett that the new frame "would strengthen the tower" might seem to indicate that the Tower needed strengthening. The remark is not so intended. The Tower was restored in 1882, at a cost of £1500, Mr Morris being the architect and Mr Wheeler of Reading the contractor, and is strong and sound as any church tower could be.'

Notwithstanding the earlier gloom, resolve returned, and on 13 November 1902, the vestry took the decision to apply for a faculty 'to recast 2 & 3, which are out of tune; quarter turn the other four, which have all worn very thin where the clapper strikes; add two new trebles; rehang the whole on a wrought iron frame on steel girders with a new floor under the Bells'. Things then moved speedily. The faculty was granted, and in early 1903 the order placed 'with the assurance that the bells would be ready for use by Easter Day'. With only £46 raised, this must have been a bold decision.

Held up by a wing and a prayer – There was a surprise in store when the belfry was cleared out at the end of January, as revealed in a report in the Reading Mercury. As we might expect, it reported that the timber frame, 'renewed thirty years before', was in fairly good condition, but it went on ...

'It rested on a floor supported by massive oak beams, 10 or 12 inches square in the section. These were intended to support the bells and frame, weighing together 6 tons[6], not only as a dead weight, but when violently vibrating from the ringing. On

---

[4] They were based in Kidlington, and undertook quite a bit of work in local towers
[5] Mounting the bell rotated by 90°, so that the clapper strikes a fresh part of the soundbow.
[6] Probably an over statement. The bells themselves weighed just over 3 tons.

taking off the floor, which was rotten, the beams were found to be in an advanced state of decay. In some cases the wood was eaten away, leaving only 4 or 5 inches of material, and that little better than tinder. In some cases the joints of the cross pieces had quite perished, so that these beams were only held in place by the floor boards. '

The report speculated that the decayed beams had been in the tower since it was built around 1450, and that since there was evidence of re-use, they might even have been part of earlier churches, dating from 1300 or from the Norman period. The discovery seems to have caused concern:

'The New Bells Fund, opened in August 1899, for the completion of the peal of bells, was merged in Jan 1903, into a new fund for the Restoration of the Belfry, when it was found that besides adding the new bells much additional work was required to put the existing bells and belfry into a proper state of repair.'

It's rather odd. Even though they didn't know about the rotten timber at the start, installing a new frame lower than the old one, would entail complete removal of all the old floor and beams anyway. So what extra work did the new discovery entail? One might have expected an article pointing out that the planned work was timely!

Quick work – When the order was placed in January, Webb & Bennett promised that the bells would be ringing again by Easter (which was late in 1903, on 12th April). The dedication service was confidently set for Easter Eve, with the full order of service published in the April Magazine, which said that the work expected to be completed 'so far as we can judge, in a very substantial and workmanlike manner'.

The work did complete on time, and the Rector dedicated the bells[7] as planned. Residents within earshot heard them ring out for five minutes at the climax of the service, around 8-30pm on the Saturday evening. Of course they would also have rung joyfully the following morning, Easter Day. The dedication was a major event, with the full order of service printed in the Parish Magazine.

Evensong said up to the end of the 3rd Collect.

Hymn 396 pt II sung while the Clergy and Choir take their places near the Tower.

(The Rector) Let us pray.

Almighty God, who by the mouth of Thy servant Moses didst command to make two silver trumpets for the solemn assemblies, be pleased to accept our offering of these bells, and grant that through generations to come they may call together Thy faithful people in this place, to praise and worship Thy holy Name, through Jesus Christ our Lord. Amen.

Grant, O Lord, that whosoever shall be called by these bells to this Thy House, may enter it with praise and thanksgiving and finally have a portion in the new song, among the harpers harping with their harps in Thine House not made with hands, eternal in the heavens, through Jesus Christ our Lord. Amen

Grant, O Lord, that whosoever shall hear the sound of these bells and be hindered by sickness or other cause from coming to Thy House, may be helped by their voices to ascend hither in heart and mind and share in the communion of Thy Saints, through Jesus Christ our Lord. Amen

---

[7] Unlike a century later, when the Bishop performed the task.

Grant, O Lord, that they who hear these bells may be aroused thereby to harken unto Thy call to draw near unto Thee, the God of their salvation, through Jesus Christ. Amen.

O Lord God, who hast commanded every man to offer unto Thee of Thy gifts committed unto him, with a willing heart and according to his ability, accept, we beseech Thee, the offering now made by Thy servants and grant them grace evermore to offer themselves unto Thee through Jesus Christ our Lord. Amen.

The Bells will then ring for five minutes.

The Clergy and Choir returning to the Chancel, Hymn 125 will be sung, and concluding Collects for Evensong said.

The final reckoning – Only £200 had been raised when the work finished, and fund raising continued for a long while afterwards. A month later, the fund stood at £241-6-3, of which £1-18-6 was 'Mr Foreman Paice's collection'. Sam Paice, together with ten members of his family, around a dozen of his friends (all named) and 'a visitor to the belfry', had each contributed amounts ranging from 6d to 5/-. In February 1904 (when the Church House building fund was still short of its target, by £86) the final account appeared:

Receipts: Subscriptions, collections and entertainments £285-9-3, Sale of old timber £4-0-0, Interest on account £1-16-8, Grant from Rector's Fund £10, Grant from Churchwarden's Fund £39-12-1. Total £340-18-0.

Expenditure: Webb & Bennett £335, Mr Hughes (Cartage, &c) £1-18-0, Mr Goatlee (printing) £2-9-0[8], Faculty £1-1-0, Sundries (per Rector) 10s. Total £340-18-0.

The same article records the bell hanger's verdict on his own work:

'Mr Webb, of the firm of Webb & Bennett, who have done the work, rang in a peal[9] on the 9th of last month, with members of the Diocesan Guild of Bellringers, and afterwards reported to the Rector that everything was in excellent order, and that the Bells went very smoothly and would probably remain without need of any attention for many years.'

The bellframe – Webb & Bennett's work is instantly recognisable, by the characteristic 'Meccano-like' X-frame. The original design came from Whites, who soon rejected it, but Webb & Bennett kept turning them out. They were blacksmiths before they turned to bell hanging, and it must have been much more rewarding for a blacksmith to forge all those angles, and to rivet all those cross braces, than to subcontract an iron founder to cast all the frame sides that account for the majority of a conventional metal frame. The clappers at All Saints were part of an unusual batch made half of wrought iron (the traditional material) and half of steel, forge welded together – by a blacksmith of course.

There are no contemporary pictures of the 1903 frame. Figure 20 was taken while the bells were out in 2004. The blue paint and vertical grey tubes are modern. The central portion of the frame has been removed and tied alongside the nearer part, so that the bells could be lowered down through the central hatch in the floor below.

---

[8] Equivalent to over £200 in modern currency.
[9] There is no record of a peal. It was probably just a short test ring.

Figure 20: Webb & Bennett frame (photographed in 2004)

Despite their enthusiasm for iron frames, Webb & Bennett hung the bells on traditional timber headstocks. These were massive baulks of elm. The largest ones, on 7th and Tenor, see Figures 21 and 22, were about four feet long and a foot and a half deep (1200 x 450 mm), and weighed around 100 lb (45 kg).

Figure 21: 7th headstock (after removal in 2004)

The bells – Four existing bells were retained in 1903. The two largest Knight bells from 1703/4, had their canons removed (presumably they were considered too weak, or maybe they were cracked) and their crowns drilled to take bolts that fixed them to the headstock, as shown in Figure 22. Modern practice would be to cut off the canons neatly, but in 1903 they smashed them off with a sledge hammer, leaving damage on the crown, which is visible in Figure 24. The two 1814 Mears bells[10] kept their canons. The four new bells (two replacements and two extra ones) all had Doncaster heads (a shallow form of canon), as shown in Figure 23

---

[10] See Figure 11 on page 22.

Figure 22: Re-used 1703/4 bells in the 1903 installation[11] (L) 7th (R) Tenor (8th)[12]

Figure 23: New bells in the 1903 installation[13] (L) 2nd (R) 5th

---

[11] The diagonal wheel braces date from 1955 not 1903.

[12] It is bigger than the 7th, but appears smaller in this picture, which shows the whole headstock.

[13] The diagonal wheel braces, bearings and greasers date from 1955 not 1903.

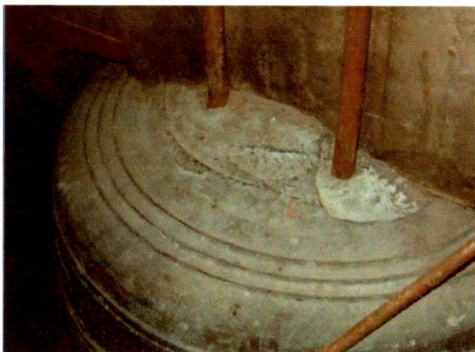

Figure 24: Scars where canons[14] were removed from the 1703 bell

5.2 Ringing

The 1903 rehanging and augmentation was a turning point for the band. The restoration project itself must have created an upsurge of interest in bells and ringing, which stimulated recruitment. The flow of new members who were trained over the ensuing years was far greater than in the 1890s when there had been hardly any.

The rehung bells helped the ringing too. They would have been easier going, and with eight bells instead of six they offered new possibilities in method ringing. For the first time in forty years, All Saints had a ring of bells that could be compared with what the daughter church at St Paul's had enjoyed for all that time.

The band became much more active, ringing both quarter peals and peals. This almost certainly reflects an enhanced standard of routine ringing as well.

Peals[15] – No doubt attracted by the newly augmented bells, a visiting band from Oxford rang the first peal ever at All Saints, exactly three weeks after the dedication, on 2nd May, see Figure 25. They were led by non other than Rev F E Robinson, who was an avid peal ringer, always keen to ring on a new set of bells. At the time, he was probably unaware that five years hence he would be living in Wokingham. The peal was of Stedman Triples, with Robinson conducting. Eight weeks later he rang another peal at All Saints, this time of Double Norwich Court Bob Major, conducted by J Hunt. Then in August the following year, he conducted another peal of Stedman Triples, and in November another visiting band rang a peal of Superlative Surprise Major, conducted by R E Hibbert.

How did the locals feel about all these peals by outsiders on their new bells? In modern times, visitor peals on new bells are often only allowed after the local ringers have rung the first one, but it wasn't so in this case. The locals took quite a while to develop themselves to peal ringing standard, which was hardly surprising from where they started. A peal is a significant undertaking, eight bell ringing was new to them, and most of them had no previous peal ringing experience.

---

[14] The canon loops would have extended a couple of inches above the top of the picture.
[15] Set piece performances of 5000+ rows (often mis-named changes), taking around 3 hours.

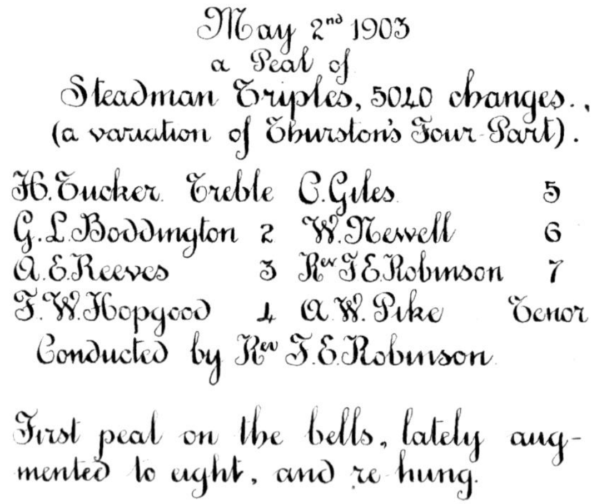

May 2nd 1903
a Peal of
Steadman Triples, 5040 changes.,
(a variation of Thurston's Four Part).

H.Tucker Treble	C.Giles	5
G.L Boddington 2	W.Newell	6
A.E Reeves 3	Rev J E Robinson	7
J.W Hopgood 4	A.W.Pike	Tenor

Conducted by Rev J.E Robinson

First peal on the bells, lately aug-
mented to eight, and re hung.

Figure 25: The first peal at All Saints

On 5th June 1906, five All Saints ringers rang in a united band at St Paul's for what was described as 'a most creditable, and at the same time disappointing, attempt' to ring a peal of Grandsire Triples:

> 'They rang with good striking until 3 hours and 6 minutes, then, when only about a minute more was required, a mistake was made. We heartily congratulate them on this most creditable performance and sincerely sympathise with them in their disappointment at not making it a very little better and thus accomplishing the first peal by local ringers at the Parish Church.'

Losing a peal in the last half hour is a real disappointment, but losing one in the last minute must have been absolutely devastating. But they tried again and nearly four years after the dedication, on 6th February 1907, they rang the first local peal at All Saints, see Figure 26 (top L). Six of the band were All Saints ringers, and the other two (including the conductor W Houlton) were from St Paul's. Three years later, on 5th February 1910 came the first peal rung entirely by All Saints ringers, see Figure 26 (top R). The peal boards recording these landmark peals hang in the tower.

In all, there were nineteen peals at All Saints in the dozen years before the First World War, and well over half of them included local ringers. This was a significant achievement for a band that until then had no previous experience of peal ringing.

Five of the peals were rung at the beginning of February, and the peal book tells us that three of them were rung in honour of the Rector's birthday. It seems fair to assume that they all were, although no dedication is given for the others.

Other notable peal dedications during this period included the Rector's induction in 1904, Rev F E Robinson's funeral in 1910, see Figure 26 (bottom), the Patronal Festival, and significant events in the lives of several ringers: Eddie Whittingham's wedding, Albert Hill's 23rd wedding anniversary, Sam Paice's 30th[16], and Bill (WJ) Paice's birthday.

---

[16] For some reason, this was not originally recorded in the All Saints peal book,

Another notable performance was on 27th April 1912, though the entry in the peal book gives no hint of its significance. On that day, a band of experienced ringers led by Alf Pulling from Guildford, including Rev C W O Jenkyn (Master of the Oxford Diocesan Guild) and other ringers from Reading, Caversham and Guildford, rang peals at both Wokingham towers. They rang Bristol Surprise Major at All Saints in the morning and then London Surprise Major at St Paul's in the afternoon. This feat was not repeated for nearly a century[17].

The two 1910 peal boards were unveiled at a ceremony on July 23rd 1910, which was Bertram Long's sixth anniversary as Rector. Ringers from Guildford, Caversham, Binfield, Sandhurst, Hurst and Wokingham attended the event, along with Rev C W O Jenkyn (the newly elected Guild Master) and Canon GF Coleridge (who eventually succeeded Jenkyn as Master). The address was on 'the meaning of pealboards, as records of work in God's church, as well as human achievement'. The ceremony included ringing touches of Stedman Triples, Superlative Surprise Major, Double Norwich Court Bob Major and Plain Bob Major, with conducting shared by Hunt, Pulling, Menday and Paice, all of whom had rung in the peals commemorated.

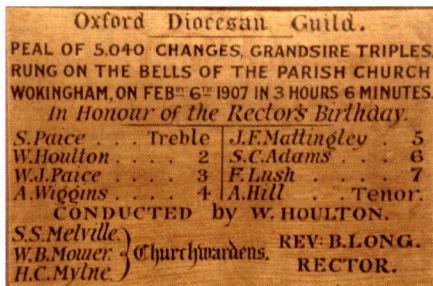

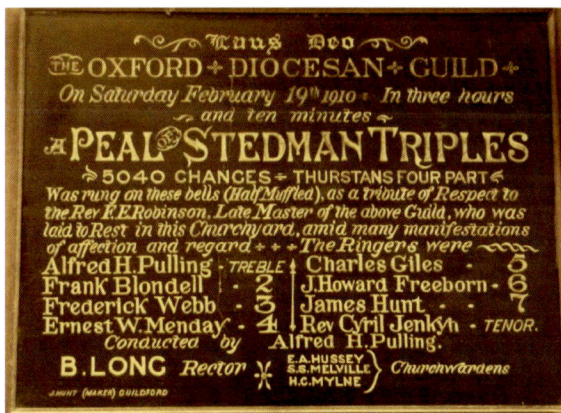

Figure 26: Early peal boards at All Saints [18]

---

[17] The next was on10th May 2008 by a local band, and shortly afterwards by a visiting band.

[18] The paint on the upper part of the 1910 peal board (upper right) has crazed, hence the poor reproduction here.

Quarter peals[19] – There are no records of quarter peals rung at All Saints before the 1903 augmentation, but a few shorter performances were published in the previous twenty years[20]. The earliest quarter peal that we know of was in March 1904, within a year of the bells being rehung.

Table 5 lists (known) quarter peals from this period, drawn from various sources[21]. They were all of Grandsire Triples, and all rung by the local band, with occasional assistance from St Paul's ringers.

Most were rung between 1904 and 1909, and it seems odd that quarter peal ringing should dry up after that, especially since the band was still strong enough, and active enough, to continue ringing one or two peals a year up to 1914.

Date	*Dedication*
26 March 1904	To commemorate 30 years of ministry by Canon Sturges
31 October 1905	To commemorate the 'Nelson Centenary' [Trafalgar] (see below)
5 November 1905	All Saints tide
14 January 1906	Welcome to HWC Erskine, organist - before evening service
10 June 1906	For evensong on Trinity Sunday & 21st birthday compliment to the conductor, WJ Paice
1 November 1906	All Saints day – dedication festival
6 February 1908	Birthday compliment to the Rector
19 April 1908	Easter morning service
4 October 1908	Harvest - morning service
15 November 1908	'The Editor's Quarter Peal[22]' to welcome Rev FE Robinson on his first Sunday in the parish
3 January 1909	Evening service
14 October 1909	Wedding of Miss Barnard of Frog Hall to Clifford Wells BA, Master of Wellington College
6 February 1916	The Rector's birthday

Table 5: Quarter peals rung between 1904 and 1919, all of Grandsire Triples

The report of the quarter peal for the Trafalgar centenary includes a note that three of the ringers then went and helped to ring 1568 changes at St Paul's. This is a non-standard length (the norm is closer to 1260) and when such performances are rung, there is normally some connection between the length of the performance and the event being commemorated. In this case though, it is hard to see a connection between 1568 and the battle of Trafalgar in 1805. Perhaps it was a peal attempt that had to be called round early because one of the band was indisposed.

The curfew – Chapter 3 told how Richard Palmer set up a charity in 1664 to pay for a curfew bell to be rung morning and evening 'for ever' in Wokingham. For ever is a long time, and many things change. In 1897, the charity trustees published a thinly veiled statement that they were turning a blind eye to a reduction of curfew ringing:

---

[19] Set piece performances of around 1260 rows, taking 45 - 50 minutes.
[20] See Chapter 4.
[21] The Bell News up to 1909, and The Ringing World from 1911, plus the Parish Magazine.
[22] Composed by the Editor of the Bell News, Harvey Reeves.

'... The charity is only £2 a year. The population round the Church has greatly increased since the charity was established in 1664. Customs have changed and men's nerves have grown more sensitive. The Trustees on these accounts are not diligent to enquire whether the evening bell is rung for the full half-hour and no one among them rises early to be able to witness whether the 4 am bell is rung every morning or any morning.'

Things came to a head just before the war in 1914. The finely balanced applecart was upset when the current owners of the land that provided the income 'declined to make any payment until such claim was substantiated'. The land had been through several hands, and it seems that the conveyancing had not been too meticulous.

The trustees declared that 'The bell has always been rung, so far as we know, in the evenings, but we have no information to show when the morning ringing was discontinued', which was hardly surprising, given their comment seventeen years earlier. The trustees discontinued the order to pay the sexton.

The Rector and Churchwardens decided to continue it on their own responsibility, since 'it would have been the greatest pity if the old custom had been dropped'. Unfortunately, between them they didn't manage to stop the story leaking out.

'The idea, however, had become current that the bell was to be stopped, and the statement was published in the Press throughout England. Such publicity, if it has produced the false impression that Wokingham is unmindful of the value of maintaining ancient customs, has at least had other good results. More than one offer was made to pay for the Bell for a year or two, and another was made, through the Editor of the Berkshire Gazette (in which, we believe, attention was first called to the matter), by a gentleman, who desired to be anonymous, to re-endow the Charity in perpetuity.'

So the problem resolved itself, and Wokingham wasn't nationally branded for vandalising ancient customs, but the people of Wokingham weren't allowed to know who had saved them from this fate.

'The donor desires that his name should not be publicly announced until after his decease : we may, however, perhaps say that he is not a resident of Wokingham, nor, so far as we know, connected with the Town.'

The War – It is hard for us to imagine the effect of the war on Wokingham as the horrors unfolded, and as more and more menfolk went to serve abroad. Over half of the ringers were engaged on active service, and at least one was killed. Parishioners, despite being remote from the battle, were reminded of it by a bell rung every weekday at noon 'as a call to all to offer up a prayer for our sailors and soldiers'.

Ringing continued in an austere atmosphere. Rev CWO Jenkyn (Guild Master) wrote that it was '... no time for peal ringing or tours ...' and he suggested 'muffled ringing limited to Good Friday[23], All Souls Day (2 Nov), New Year's Eve, the burial of an incumbent, warden or ringer, or other occasion of great public mourning'.

---

[23] This is particularly interesting. It implies that half muffled ringing on Good Friday was acceptable at that time in this Diocese. In modern times, it is often frowned on (along with any ringing in Holy Week, even for services) though not uncommon in some parts of the country.

In November 1916, the Defence of the Realm Act decreed that no bells were to be rung for services starting more than 1½ hours after sunset. The Parish decided to discontinue the 8 o'clock curfew bell, and unlike two years earlier the decision generated no complaint.

The ringers' weekly newspaper, *The Ringing World*, reflected the mood of the times, with a series of articles about ringers killed in action. In November 1916, it featured Albert Victor Loader, who learnt to ring at All Saints in 1913, at the age of fifteen:

Heroes from the Belfry 'Pte. Albert Victor Loader, Civil Service Rifles. Joined the All Saints Wokingham band three years ago and rapidly made himself proficient in Grandsire Triples, and by the time he attained the age to be able to enlist, could ring Stedman Triples. He was a regular and painstaking ringer, ever ready to assist ringing for any special service, keenly alert and anxious to do his very best in every department of life. He was in the office of the Town Clerk of Wokingham. He fell in his first action on October 7th.'

Two weeks after his death, on Oct 22nd, the Parish Magazine tells us there was 'muffled ringing in his honour and memory by his comrades'.

The curate-secretary – Many curates appear to have held the post of tower secretary at All Saints in the late 19th and early 20th century. The records only show two laymen holding the post, and one of them was in 1873 when, as we saw in Chapter 4, the curate was the Foreman. From then up to 1921, all but one known secretary was also the assistant priest of the day, so we may reasonably speculate that the two jobs went together.

At the 1907 AGM, the Rector prefaced the election by saying that the Secretary need not be a cleric, which supports the presumption that it normally was. On that occasion, a change was forced by Rev. AP Carr's departure, but there was no obvious reason why his successor, Rev EW Moberly, who was also present at the meeting, could not have been appointed in his place. Why was Carr suited to the post, and Moberley not? We know that Carr joined the Cambridge University Guild of Change Ringers in January 1893, while at Emmanuel College. As noted earlier, it was quite common for priests to take up ringing while they were at university, though many didn't continue, as Carr seems not to have done, since there is no record of him ever ringing at All Saints. Perhaps he had a special sympathy for the ringers, which Moberly lacked.

Following the Rector's hint, a layman called Dr Nash was elected as secretary. Maybe there was something that made him particularly suitable for the job, but whatever it was remains obscure. We know nothing about him, except that he had not lived in Wokingham very long[24]. He was not a church warden, nor did he ring, so the reason for his appointment remains a mystery.

---

[24] He is not recorded in the 1901 census.

5.3 Notable ringers

We know very little about most of the thirty odd people who rang at All Saints between 1900 and the first world war. Some lasted less than a year before giving up, while others went on as loyal members of the band for decades. For example, Jack French rang for 51 years (1895 to 1945), Frank Lush for 52 years (1895 to 1946) and Eddie Whittingham for 66 years (1903 to 1968). Some names stand out though.

Samuel Paice, whom we met in the previous chapter, was Foreman through the period of the augmentation, and oversaw the rise in the band's capabilities, including their first peals. He remained Foreman until he died in 1920. Like his predecessor, he played a significant role outside the tower in Sonning Deanery, and he represented the Branch on the Diocesan Guild General Committee for fourteen years.

When the 1905 Branch AGM was concerned that quarterly meetings weren't very effective in promoting change ringing, Sam was one of three people chosen to form a committee 'to arrange meetings as seemed most appropriate for this purpose'. At the 1910 AGM, it was Sam who suggested introducing monthly combined meetings at Branch towers – something that continues to this day – and he was appointed along with two others to another special committee to make it happen.

At the same meeting, Sam proposed a special Summer meeting of the Guild at Wokingham 'as an expression of thankfulness on the part of the whole Guild for the Master's wonderful restoration to health after his late severe illness'. The Master was of course Rev FE Robinson, who had recently moved to Wokingham and become Branch Chairman as well as Guild Master. He had indeed made a remarkable recovery, but when Sam's proposal was referred to the Guild committee it all came to nothing, because within the month Robinson was dead. After Sam died in 1920, the minutes record him modestly as 'a very great helper to the Branch and ringing generally'.

William J Paice (Bill) was Sam's son, and he was clearly a high flyer. He rang his first peal at St Paul's in 1905, a year after joining the Guild. The next year he composed and conducted a quarter peal of Grandsire Triples for his 21st birthday, in January 1906. The year after that he conducted his first peal (Carter's 12 part Grandsire Triples) at All Saints. He moved to Caversham where he rang at St Peter's, and then he moved to Finchampstead where he became tower captain. He was a Guild instructor[25], and served as Sonning Deanery Branch secretary from 1927-1942. He moved to London and rang at both St Mary Abbotts, Kensington and at St Paul's Cathedral. In 1947 he was elected a member of the Ancient Society of College Youths. He moved again to Surrey, and finally settled in Sandhurst. He rang a total of 104 peals. At his funeral on 12 Sept 1958, prominent members of the Guild rang handbells over his grave.

Rev. FE Robinson was without doubt Wokingham's most famous ringer. He achieved his fame before he moved here, but All Saints churchyard has the privilege of housing his grave. Francis Edward was born in Begbroke, Oxon on 6th January

---

[25] See page 31.

1833, son of Rev Francis Robinson. At Winchester he excelled in maths. He only gained 4th class honours[26] at Exeter College Oxford, but a family connection got him a job as a clerk at the Old Bank in Oxford. He became a partner, but in 1868, several years after the death of his first wife, he was called to Holy Orders. He served his curacy at Tubney, Berks, and then in 1878 was presented with the vicarage of Drayton, where he remained for thirty years. He had several serious illnesses, and was persuaded to retire to Wokingham in 1908. The rest worked wonders, and within a few months he was fit, and as active as ever. In 1910, he rang a peal on 22nd January, prior to the Sonning Deanery Branch AGM, which he chaired (having been the natural candidate for chairman as soon as he moved here). He travelled to Beech Hill that night, and took four services the following day, which was very cold. He had a seizure, but recovered by the Friday, and began to arrange a peal for Easter Monday. He had a second seizure, and at 3pm on 16th February, he died.

He was a founder of the Oxford Diocesan Guild of Church Bellringers. When in Reading on 13th November 1880 the meeting to consider the formation of a Guild came to elect a committee, Robinson rose from the floor with a prepared list of names of who should be on it. The list included 7 clergymen and 7 well known ringers, and of course it included Robinson himself who was both a ringer and a clergyman. At the inaugural meeting in Oxford on 17th January 1881, he was duly elected as the Guild's first master, and held the post until his death 29 years later.

During his last ten years he had several illnesses and tried to step down each time, but the committee persuaded him to stay on. He set the pattern of long serving clerical masters, which lasted for nearly a century, until the 1970s. Since then, masters have all been laymen, and have served shorter terms of office, with 7 masters in 30 years.

Figure 27: Rev. FE Robinson, as he appears in many towers in Oxford Diocese

[26] David Herschell attributes this to Oxford's low standing in maths at the time (Ringing World, 7 Jan 1983)

Three days after his death, a peal was rung in his memory, recorded on a peal board in the tower[27]. Rev C W O Jenkyn[28] described the ringing at his funeral thus:

'...over his grave there poured forth the muffled strains of the old Four Part of Stedman Triples which, in one or other version, will be inseparably connected with his memory'

Several hundred people came to the funeral, as can be seen from a contemporary photograph, Figure 28 (upper). The cedar tree, just to the left of his grave, now completely overshadows it, as shown in the 2006 picture, Figure 28 (lower).

Figure 28: FE Robinson's grave (above) at his funeral in 1910, (below) in 2006

Robinson is buried along with his wife Mary Caroline and his daughter Vera. The grave alongside his (whose matt stone surface bears extensive lichen, unlike the polished stone of his) has the names of three other members of the family: Grace Robinson, and her sisters Caroline and Constance Mary Spon, see Figure 29.

Robinson was above all an extremely capable and prolific ringer. He was the first person ever to ring 1000 peals, something that is now more common[29]. He rang his

---

[27] Figure 26 on page 49.

[28] Robinson's successor as Master of the Oxford Diocesan Guild of Church Bell Ringers, writing in the Guild's Annual Report.

[29] Many ringers have rung 1000 peals, and the 5000 peal record has been passed.

1000th peal at Drayton on 9th August 1905, see Figure 30. He conducted it, and the method was Stedman Triples, of which he was particularly fond. In all, FE Robinson rang about 1250 peals, in more than 450 towers. They included the first all-clerical peal and several record lengths, see Table 6.

Figure 29: Close up of FE Robinson's family graves

DRAYTON, Berks.
On 9th August, 1905, in 2 hours 47 minutes.
5040 STEDMAN TRIPLES

J. W. Washbrooke Jnr.	Treble	C. H. Fowler	5
G. A. Smith	2	H. Miles	6
F. Hopgood	3	Rev. F. E. Robinson	7
J. W. Washbrook	4	Rev. G. F. Coleridge	Tenor

Conducted by Rev. F. E. Robinson

Figure 30: FE Robinson's 1000th peal

Length	Method	Time	Place
10,080	Double Norwich Court Bob Major	5 hours 58 min	Appleton
11,328	London Surprise Major	6 hours 6 min	Drayton
12,096	Double Norwich Court Bob Major	7 hours 10 min	Boyne Hill
12,041	Stedman Caters	7 hours 26 min	Appleton
13,265	Grandsire Caters	8 hours 5 min	Appleton
15.041	Stedman Caters	9 hours 16 min	Appleton

Table 6: Long lengths in which FE Robinson rang

Robinson was a proficient wood carver. He carved the organ case, choir stalls and bench ends while at Drayton and left a chancel screen partly carved when he died.

Rev Bertram Long – Long wasn't a ringer, but from 1905-1923 he was listed along with his ringers in Oxford Diocesan Guild records, unlike all his fellow clergy who were listed separately as Honorary Members. He was very supportive of his ringers, and obviously felt great affinity with them. They clearly held him in great esteem, for example ringing many peals to mark his birthday. So it is fitting to end this chapter by mentioning him as a much loved 'honorary member'.

6 Between the wars (1918 – 1939)

The war had been a terrible experience, but the country, and ringing, survived. Life began to return to normal, and ringing at All Saints carried on and developed.

Ringers seem to have become very conscious of their role in the scheme of things. Just before the end of the war, during the Branch AGM service at All Saints, the Rural Dean, Rev. Canon GF Coleridge gave an address on the theme 'every man according to his ability'. Predictably he talked about the war and those who had been called abroad on active service, then he spoke about those left behind to keep things going at home, and in particular about bellringers:

> '... many ladies and younger lads had taken their place and kept the bells going, with an energy and zeal which would always be remembered in the ringing world!'

After the service, the minutes tell us that 'the national anthem was heartily sung'. At the following year's service, after the war had ended, Rev Joshua Anderson, Rector of Arborfield spoke about the work of church bellringers, comparing it to the bells, which 'always did their work well and were always true'. He said that ringers were privileged to have been able to announce the armistice and to call people to come and thank God. Some years later, also at All Saints, the Rector, Canon Bertram Long preached 'a very appropriate and practical sermon on ringing & churchmanship [and] by comparisons he drew many points of work and duty as Bellringer & Churchman.' For the next several years, reports refer to the addresses as 'inspiring' or 'helpful and inspiring'. No doubt the preachers chosen were good at their craft, but we might surmise that their listeners also wanted to be inspired to lift their post-war spirits.

Ringing did indeed play a full part in the rejoicing when the war ended. In July 1919 'at an early hour the bells of the churches rang out' as part of a Celebration of Peace We don't know for how long they rang out, but it must have added to the joy of the people of Wokingham, who had much else to occupy them that day. There were processions, a luncheon on Langborough recreation ground 'prepared by the wives and widows of men who served', sports, a tea, a concert in the market place, and a dance in the Drill Hall. Two years later, in July 1921, when the war memorial was dedicated, the ringers again played their part: '... before the service a half muffled peal[1] was rung on the tower bells and an open peal afterwards'.

6.1 The band

Numbers recovered quickly after the war, but Sam Paice's death a couple of years later in 1920 was a sad loss. He had led the band for over two decades, he had overseen the restoration of the bells, and he had developed a band capable of ringing both quarter peals and peals. Fred Mattingley acted as Foreman 'most efficiently ... with the hearty support of the band' between Sam's death and the next AGM, but declined an invitation to continue, because he didn't feel he could give 'all the time that he felt was required of the office'. So Bill Brooks was elected, and he held the post for over forty years. He was well liked by the rest of the band, but as we shall see, the band did not regain the momentum that Sam had built up.

---

[1] This was a layman's description. They weren't 'peals' in the true sense of 5000+ rows.

The end of the curate-secretary – In the last chapter, we observed that, with the exception of the mysterious Dr Nash in 1907, the roles of tower secretary and assistant priest seem to have gone together. The last curate secretary appears to have been Rev Frederick McDuff Christian Hare, who was curate from 1915 to 1921. He was still listed as tower secretary in March 1921 shortly before he left the Parish, but there is no further mention of any secretary at all. The AGM reports for 1924 and 1925 (the only surviving ones until 1935) both record that Bill Brooks was re-elected Foreman, but do not mention a secretary. That contrasts with previous reports, which had always named both Foreman and Secretary. Is it a coincidence that the post of Tower Secretary disappeared in the year that Brooks became Foreman?

Female ringers – During the Victorian era, ringing had been an almost exclusively male activity, though there were exceptions. For example attendance records at Kensington show that women rang in the 1850s. In Brighton in 1892 Mrs George Williams rang the Trebles[2] in a handbell peal of Grandsire Triples, conducted by her husband, and a few years later, in 1896, Miss Alice White rang in a tower bell peal at Basingstoke. Finally in 1912, the first peal rung entirely by women, was at Cubitt Town, East London, followed a few months later by the foundation of The Ladies' Guild of Change Ringers. This was when women were campaigning for suffrage.

Wokingham wasn't so progressive. The first woman to ring in a peal at All Saints[3] was a visitor, Miss M Chillingworth, but home grown women ringers only appeared when the war had drained the country of its menfolk and pushed women into many hitherto male activities. Four women became members in 1918, and so had probably learnt towards the end of the war. Misses E and M Fielder were only members for a year, but the other two, Miss M Vera Robinson and Miss Alice H Walker, both went on to serve tower and church for many years (see below on page 60).

A happy occasion – This period began with a happy event for one All Saints ringer.

Figure 31: George Cole's wedding in February 1918

---

[2] 1 and 2
[3] Plain Bob Major for All Saints dedication festival on 1st November 1913.

George Cole had been a member since 1901, and was married in February 1918. The picture in Figure 31 was taken at his home opposite the church (now demolished and replaced by Westende Flats). The preponderance of women in the picture reflects the number of men who were away. Arthur Jones (just behind the bride and groom) rang at St Paul's, and maybe influenced George to move his allegience from All Saints to St Paul's a year or so later, where he rang until 1927.

6.2 Notable ringers

William James Brooks (Bill) learnt to ring in Kent, where he was a gardener at Hever Castle. He moved to Wokingham in his twenties, and served in France in the War. He was invalided out with shrapnel wounds, which made him walk with a limp. He lived at 13 Langborough Road and was a gardener at Southlands[4] in Gypsy Lane. He was 32 when elected Foreman in 1921, at the AGM after Sam Paice's death, and he remained in post until he died in 1963, a total of 42 years divided almost equally before and after the Second World War. Bill was a quiet, genteel man, well liked by those who knew him. Over the years he served the church in many roles: as sidesman, as PCC member, as church warden, and as secretary of the Saturday Evening Entertainments Committee. He also served Sonning Deanery Branch at different times as Vice Chairman and as Branch representative to the Oxford Diocesan Guild. Bill was a competent ringer, but not a prolific peal ringer. He was nearly thirty when he rang his first peal, and only rang a handful in total – seven at All Saints, six at St Paul's, and probably not many more[5].

Rev AGG Thurlow (Gilbert) must come a close second to FE Robinson in terms of fame achieved in ringing outside Wokingham. He was born in Felixstowe in 1911, and as a student he rang with the Cambridge University Guild. He studied at Cuddesdon Theological College and served his curacy at All Saints from 1934-39. During this short time he made a positive contribution in the tower (as well as his clerical duties of course) and also gave slide lectures of his travels. So popular were these that when he returned to give a lecture shortly after leaving Wokingham, he had an audience of 300 people. During his subsequent clerical career he was Precentor at Norwich Cathedral, Vicar of Great Yarmouth, and Dean of Gloucester Cathedral, where he had a hand in the restoration of the bells. He rose to the highest ringing office, serving as President of the Central Council of Church Bell Ringers from 1963-1969. He retired to Chichester, and died in 1991, a few years after welcoming All Saints ringers when they rang there during the choir's 'cathedral week' in 1986[6].

---

[4] Now demolished.
[5] His obituary said he rang most of his peals at All Saints.
[6] See page 116

Frederick James Mattingley has the distinction of being the shortest serving Foreman at All Saints. He was a blacksmith by trade, and took up ringing while in his teens. He was almost 50, and had rung at All Saints for 31 years when Sam Paice died in the autumn of 1920. He seems to have been considered Sam's natural successor. He stepped into the Foreman's shoes until the AGM the following January, when he was asked to carry on, but declined because he didn't feel he could give the time that the office required. He only rang for four more years, and died in 1925. The picture of him here was taken much earlier, when he was 30.

Mabel Vera Robinson (Vera) was Rev FE Robinson's daughter. She learnt to ring in her thirties, becoming a member at 34. She was the first Wokingham woman to ring a peal at All Saints, on 7th February 1924. Appropriately, the method was Stedman Triples, her father's favourite, and equally appropriately, Rev CWO Jenkyn, who succeeded her father as Master of the Oxford Diocesan Guild, rang in the peal with her. She was neither as prodigious nor as proficient a ringer as her father, but she served the band diligently for many years, ringing regularly until the 1940s, after which she became a life member of the Oxford Diocesan Guild. She was active in other areas of Parish life, for example as a sidesman, as a member of the Rural Deanery Conference, and (well after she had given up ringing) as organiser of the Murdoch Road Christian Stewardship area, where one report talks about 'evening bible study formed under the inspiring leadership of Miss Robinson'. She gave couples about to be married a copy of *The People's Life of Christ*[7]. Vera left Wokingham in 1965 to look after sick relatives in Oxford, and died in 1979. She is buried with her father[8].

Alice Holdsworth Walker was 37 when she joined the band, even older than Vera who was a close friend. Alice became deeply involved in church life after coming to Wokingham with her family in 1901. She was Assistant Organist for a while, and over the years ran many church groups. She became the first Diocesan Sunday Schools Organiser. During the mid 1930s, she was known for her 'delightful illustrated lectures' with intriguing titles such as 'Rare Birds of Wokingham' or 'Birds, Butterflies and possibly a Bat'. She never became a proficient ringer, but she continued until just before the second war, when she gave up ringing but remained very active in the Parish. Throughout the 1930s, Alice (with a team of helpers) organised the meat tea for the Sonning Deanery Branch AGMs that were held in Church House. She died in 1955, aged 74, and her obituary (written by Vera, who presumably based it on reality) says that as well as learning to ring herself, Alice 'encouraged many a young lad to take up the art'.

Vera and Alice seem to have made their presence felt outside Wokingham. Quite early in their ringing careers, they were mentioned in reports of Sonning deanery

---

[7] At least she did in the 1930s, when Joan Blackman and John (AJN) Rance were married.
[8] See Figure 29 on page 56.

Branch meetings. For example, in 1924 a discussion about the possibility of instituting combined practices was reported to involve 'Misses Robinson & Walker, and Messrs Moth, Paice, Rance, and others'. Moth & Rance were both Foremen of other towers, and [WJ] Paice was the high flyer we met in Chapter 5, who later became Branch secretary. So the ladies were mixing it with the Branch heavyweights. Having come to ringing later in life, they were probably more articulate than the average youth who had a similar level of ringing experience. Had they become ringers earlier, as most men did, perhaps they too would have achieved greater prowess as ringers and progressed to positions of leadership.

6.3 The ringing

We know relatively little about the ringing in this period. There are no tower records prior to 1935, and few articles in the Parish Magazine. John Rance, who often rang with the band during the late 1920s and 1930s remembers them ringing little other than Grandsire Triples [7]. Few of the ringers had any particularly talent, and most probably never travelled beyond their own tower, despite opportunities to do so. Keener ringers in the Sonning Deanery Branch used to visit towers in the East Berks and South Bucks Branch, where they could ring more advanced methods, including Surprise methods.

There was an interesting comment in the minutes of the 1932 Sonning Deanery AGM saying that three towers (All Saints Wokingham, Twyford & Sonning) 'had made good progress with the Stedman method'. What exactly constituted good progress is unclear. It sounds somewhat short of 'success', and might simply imply that they had persevered in attempting to ring it. Stedman is not the simplest method, but it is a part of most ringers' basic repertoire, and much liked for its music and variety.

Peals – A year after the war, in December 1919, a Wokingham band rang a peal at Hurst. The Parish Magazine described it as 'an interesting achievement' and noted that 'Mr S Paice, Foreman of the tower, has taught nearly all the members to handle a bell, and given the early instruction to all in change ringing'. The band clearly thought it important too, because, rather unusually, it appears in the All Saints peal book. Without doubt it was a significant achievement, and it was the first peal for four of the band (including Bill Brooks who was soon to become Foreman).

St Nicholas, Hurst, Berks			
On 6th December 1919, in 3h 17m			
5040 Grandsire Triples			
JJ Parker's one-part. * = First peal			
EC Clark*	Treble	NC Lawrence	5
F Lush	2	H Lovelock*	6
WJ Brooks*	3	WJ Paice	7
S Paice	4	E Brant*	Tenor
Conducted by William J Paice			
Rung by members of All Saints Wokingham			

Figure 32: The first post-war peal by a Wokingham band

The first post-war peal rung at All Saints was on 5th February 1921 (just after Bill Brooks became Foreman) and was the third of the 'Rector's birthday' peals to be recorded on a peal board in the tower.

Laus Deo

Oxford Diocesan Guild.

PEAL OF GRANDSIRE TRIPLES 5,040 CHANGES RUNG ON THE BELLS OF THE PARISH CHURCH WOKINGHAM, ON FEB: 5ᵀᴴ 1921 IN 3 HRS: 21 MINS:

(In Honour of the Rector's Birthday.)

E. CLARK. - TREBLE.	W. J. BROOKS. - 5.
W. J. PAICE. - - 2.	F. LUSH. - - 6.
N. C. LAWRENCE. - 3.	H. LOVELOCK. - 7.
G. COLE. - - 4.	E. BRANT. - TENOR.

CONDUCTED BY W. J. PAICE.

E. A. Hussey. ⎫
J. C. Hammond ⎬ Churchwardens.
E. Ward. ⎭

REV: B. LONG.
RECTOR.

Figure 33: The first post-war peal rung at All Saints

It was followed by three more February peals in 1925[9], 1927 and 1932, all of which must surely have been more Rector's birthday peals, though the peal book records only one of them as such. The 1927 peal, was jointly dedicated to the Rector's and Vera Robinson's birthdays. The Parish Magazine was complimentary about the 1932 peal, which it described as 'a well struck peal of Grandsire Triples'.

Figure 34: William Houlton, Bill Paice, Frank Lush, Bill Brooks, George Cole, Samuel Adams, William Boyles, (behind the camera) John Rance

---

[9] The peal book records this as 5 February 1924 (which was a Friday), but the Felstead database, based on published reports, has it as 5 February 1925 (which was a Saturday).

The picture in Figure 34, opposite, appears with no caption at the front of the first All Saints ringers' scrap book (begun in 1978). Identifying the ringers was an interesting piece of detective work. The posed shot suggests a special occasion. Seven ringers in the picture, plus one behind the camera, suggests an eight bell performance. The style of dress points to the inter-war period, and the window behind the ringers was identified as at the west end of the south aisle at St Paul's, not far from the tower entrance. It is believed to be a picture of a Sonning Deanery Branch band that rang a peal of Grandsire Triples at St Paul's on 25th January 1923.

Frank Lush and Bill Brooks rang at All Saints (Bill had become Foreman two years earlier). Bill Paice learnt to ring at All Saints, but at this time he rang at Finchampstead. The others rang at St Paul's. William Houlton was Foreman at St Paul's, and had called the first local band peal at All Saints in 1907. George Cole was in the pre-war All Saints band, but moved to St Paul's in the 1920s. William Boyles, who moved to Wokingham in the early 1900s, spent many years unattached to any tower, rang at All Saints for a year, and eventually joined St Paul's.

Wokingham, St Paul
Oxford Diocesan Guild (Sonning Deanery Branch)
On Thursday 25 January 1923, in 3 hours 5 minutes
A peal of 5040 changes of Grandsire Triples
Composed by Rev. E Banks James

H William Boyles	Treble	William J Paice	5
George Cole	2	Samuel C Adams	6
William J Brooks	3	John Rance	7
Frank Lush	4	William Houlton	Tenor

Conducted by WJ Paice
Rung on the Feast of the Conversion of St. Paul the patronal festival of the church. The conductor's 40th peal.

Figure 35: The 1923 peal band

Between 1927 and 1935 only visitors rang peals at All Saints, in 1932 and 1933. There must have been at least one local attempt, since Branch minutes in 1934 mention unsuccessful peal attempts at Finchampstead & All Saints Wokingham.

Finally, in June and November 1935, came two locally organised peals, undoubtedly the work of GilbertThurlow[10], who had recently arrived as curate, and was a far more experienced and widely travelled ringer than any of the locals. Both peals were Major (8 working bells), whereas for twenty years, all peals with local ringers had been Triples (7 working bells). The first was Kent Treble Bob Major, to commemorate the 25th anniversary of the Rector's ordination, and Gilbert's own ordination the previous month. The second was Double Norwich Court Bob Major. Three of the ringers had All Saints connections: Bill Brooks (the Foreman), Bill Paice (son of a previous Foreman, who learnt here) and Gilbert. The rest were outsiders.

---

[10] See page 59.

During the eighteen inter-war years there were only eight peals – half as many peals, in twice as many years, as before the war.

Quarter peals – Only three quarter peals are known during this period, see Table 7, far fewer than in the pre-war period. The band should have been capable of ringing quarters. We saw in the last chapter that quarter peal ringing declined during the few years before the war. The two rung in 1919 looked like the start of a recovery, but seemingly they weren't, since there is a complete absence of quarter peals from 1921. That was the year in which Bill Brooks became Foreman. Was he not in favour of them? Were they rung but he didn't report them[11]?

Date	Dedication
22 February 1919	Half muffled, with a short service in the tower beforehand
6 July 1919	Prior to thanksgiving service
25 January 1936	Death of King George V (fully muffled, see page 64)

Table 7: Known quarter peals between the wars

Interestingly all three of these quarter peals marked events of national significance, for which the ringers surely had to make an effort. In fact the band considered the one in 1936 to be so special that they recorded it along with peals in the All Saints Peal Book, see Figure 36. It was special in another way too, because it was rung fully muffled, which is rare. To understand why needs an explanation.

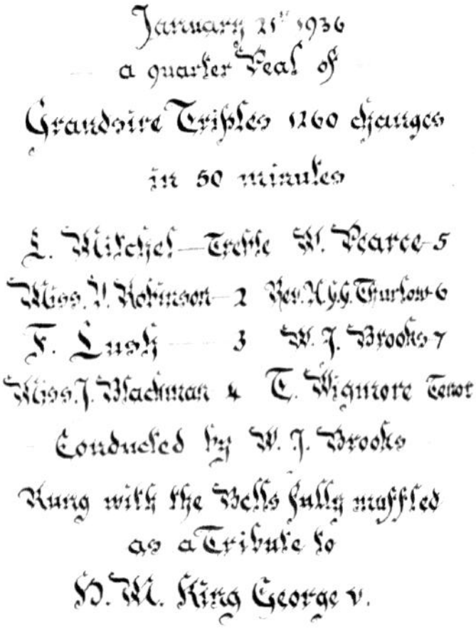

Figure 36: Quarter peal for the death of King George V, in the Peal Book

Muffled ringing – Normally the metal clapper strikes the metal bell, giving a loud, bright sound. Fitting a leather pad to the clapper ball makes the sound quieter and softer. Since the clapper strikes the bell on alternate sides, it is possible to muffle one side only (half muffled) or both sides (fully muffled). 'Half muffled' ringing gives alternate sequences of loud and soft notes when the bells ring together, as shown in Figure 37 (top). It is commonly done for Remembrance, for funerals, and in some places 'for the death of the old year' just before midnight on New Year's Eve.

---

[11] See chapter 7.

Fully muffled ringing is very rare, and is traditionally reserved for the death of a sovereign. In fact, 'fully muffled' ringing often means that all bells except the Tenor[12] are fully muffled, with the Tenor only half muffled so it rings 'open at backstroke', which is what happened on this occasion[13]. With the Tenor always ringing last in each row (which it did in this case, because they rang Triples[14]) the effect is shown in Figure 37 (bottom). The gaps in the sequences in Figure 37 are the characteristic pauses of 'open handstroke' ringing[15].

Figure 37: The effect (upper) of half muffled ringing and (lower) of full muffled ringing, with Tenor open at backstroke [black = loud, grey = soft)

Most towers have a set of muffles (one per bell), which they use for regular half muffled ringing. Assuming that All Saints was the same at the time, then they would have had to improvise the extra seven muffles needed for this performance. Maybe they had some old ones that were still usable for one occasion.

6.4 Meetings and things

The Parish Magazine reported tower AGMs periodically up to the early 1920s[16] but was then silent, which seems odd. It contained several reports of Sonning Deanery Branch AGMs during this period[17]. The earliest known minute book starts in 1935. We may speculate about what happened to tower AGMs in the intervening decade. If the post of secretary had been dispensed with after Brooks became Foreman[18], did meetings suffer a similar fate a few years later?

What did the ringers discuss in the meetings that are recorded? The early Parish Magazine reports had been mostly limited to who was elected, with periodic expressions of gratitude for services rendered. Occasionally they mentioned discussions about remuneration (see below). But we can assume that meetings were far from mere formalities. The 1925 report enigmatically stated that 'Many points bearing on the ringers' work were discussed'. If only we knew what they were!

On the record – The 1935 and 1936 minutes (the first in the extant minute book) are more enlightening. The first was dominated by a revised set of rules, and mentions little else of substance. Revising rules suggests a 'new broom' doing some sweeping. This was the first meeting that Gilbert Thurlow attended, and he was probably the new broom. Perhaps it also explains the appearance of a minute book.

The 1936 minutes say that the Foreman's report 'was brief' – was that laziness of the minute writer or a veiled criticism of the report? It goes on to say that after some

---

[12] Lowest note.
[13] Confirmed by the Parish Magazine.
[14] Methods that only change seven bells.
[15] The rhythm has an extra, silent, beat every other row. This style of ringing is almost universal.
[16] 1906, 1913, 1914, 1917, 1920, 1921, 1924, 1925
[17] 1926, 1931, 1932
[18] See page 58.

discussion he proposed that 'the Double Norwich method[19] be studied with a view to ringing it'. This might have been inspired by the fact that Thurlow and Brooks rang in the peal of Double Norwich a couple of months earlier. The decision to learn a new method (or methods) would not in modern times be considered important enough to be raised at an AGM.

The meeting also agreed that 'the Churchwardens be asked to have the bell frame painted'. Contrast this with the 1980s decision that the ringers would paint the frame.

Then inexplicably, the record stops as suddenly as it started, until after the war. There should have been three more AGMs before war broke out in Autumn 1939. What happened? There was nothing obvious to cause a hiatus – the Rector and the Foreman were in post throughout. In particular, Gilbert Thurlow was still here until summer 1939, so if he had been responsible for stirring things up in 1935, one might not expect to see any lapse before he left.

Money – We saw in previous chapters how some form of payment persisted, even after the formation of the 'Society of Honorary Ringers' in 1873. The ringers received voluntary subscriptions from parishioners at Christmas, and we saw how they were concerned that this source of remuneration might be threatened by handbell ringers passing themselves off as being related to the church. The same concern was among the small number of topics that made it into print during this period too. Up to the first war, the ringers were still receiving money, both from the Churchwardens, and from a public collection. At the 1913 AGM, they had expressed their thanks to 'all those who have contributed to the Bell Ringers' Fund', and in 1920 we hear that:

> 'Previous to the war, the Churchwardens used to make a grant to supplement money collected as a very small honorarium to the ringers, in recognition of the great services they render. This was foregone at the wish of the ringers during the war. Though the amount fell short this year, they again unanimously desired, in view of the present need of money for Church maintenance, that no grant should be given by the Churchwardens. The Parishioners, who owe a very great debt to the ringers for the many hours they practise, and on Sundays, and in the spirit in which they give it, will appreciate very highly this action on the part of the ringers.'

The Rector must have felt this was the right balance, because the following year, while thanking the ringers, he added that he:

> '... always regarded their service as being voluntarily rendered for the Church, though a very small honorarium, collected at Christmas time, was divided among them'.

This stimulated discussion, the upshot of which was that:

> 'The members unanimously expressed a desire that the honorarium should be discontinued : and it is proposed to arrange for an excursion, in the summer, along the lines of that made by the choir.'

Note the coupling of the two items. Giving up the honorarium doesn't seem quite so generous when we realise that the choir outings they proposed to emulate were paid for by the church.

---

[19] Double Norwich Court Bob Major, a moderately simple but musical 8-bell method.

Finally in December 1935, near the end of this period, the spectre of rogue handbell ringers again reared its head. Presumably like their predecessors, they were passing themselves off as church ringers in order to raise money, but there was no explanation with this announcement in the Parish Magazine that came out of the blue:

'It is not generally known that the ringers who go round at Christmas time and call themselves "The All Saints Ringers" are not connected with the ringing at All Saints Church.'

Outings – We saw there were joint events between ringers and choir as far back as the cricket match in 1873 and the annual suppers in the 1890s. In 1929 we hear that 'Senior members of the Choir and Bell ringers and their wives met at the Rectory on 11 Feb ... [and] ... a very pleasant evening was spent'.

The choir also had an annual outing, and the ringers clearly liked the idea, as we saw above when they gave up their honorarium. At that time they were proposing to hold their own outing, but they must have decided later that joining forces would be more practical because in 1921: 'the choir & bellringers united in a happy Excursion to Portsmouth on July 16th'. The report of the outing also expressed 'gratitude to the subscribers', so it must have been subsidised.

Subsequent outings went to many places. In 1927, '22 people went to Bournmouth by motor coach', including a 'beautiful drive through many miles of the New Forest'. In August 1929 they also took their wives to Southsea for 'a most enjoyable day'. In 1934, the report of a 'very delightful day in Brighton' ends enigmatically by saying that 'none got lost'. Is that perhaps a coded allusion to the fact that someone did get lost the year before? In 1936 there was an even longer, almost blow by blow, description of the proceedings, ending with a statement of disappointment that 'owing to another engagement, the Rector was unable to join us'. The cost of running these outings was around £16[20].

These seaside outings, with their fresh air and fun, but not a hint of ringing, were a far cry from modern ringing outings, which didn't appear until after the second war, where our story picks up in the next chapter.

The Peal Book – The first peal in the book was rung in 1903, but the book itself seems to have been started in 1933. At the bottom of the title page is inscribed 'Donovan Watts, Wokingham, 4/9/33'. Donovan Watts was not a ringer, and at the time there were no ringers by the name of Watts, so he wasn't a family member either. Presumably he was a willing volunteer with a neat hand. All the entries up to peal number 24, on 23rd July 1932, are written in the same clear handwriting, see Figure 25 on page 48, which supports this view of when the book was created.

Watts may have volunteered for the initial task, but he did not continue. Peal number 25, was rung a few months before Watts completed his task, on 10th May 1933, but it has a footnote 'AEP, Wokingham, January 1947'. That entry, and all others up to peal number 29 in June 1945 are written in a somewhat less legible gothic script, see Figure 36 on page 64. The second of them uses less ornate lettering than the others, and so might perhaps have been written by someone else.

---

[20] Equivalent to around £370 in modern currency.

Pearl Gibson inscribed all peals from number 32 on 26th June 1982 to number 65 on 29th January 2000. The footnote at the bottom of the first of these (number 32) says 'P.J.Gibson, October 1998', but slight variations in style and ink suggest that she did not wait sixteen years to write them all. After all, she rang in the 1982 peal. Peals number 66 to the present were inscribed by Jane Mellor in 2008. The peal book also includes a list of Foremen since 1880, and lists of the dates of various (known) significant work done to the tower and bells.

An old wooden cross – One other artefact from this period survives. In 1928, Frank Lush (described as 'young Frank' in Chapter 4, who rang throughout this period) made a small wooden cross to hang on the ringing room wall. The complete cross has not survived, but the inscribed plaque below it has:

> 'Made for the belfry in 1928 by F Lush, a ringer of this parish, from old oak removed from the tower in 1903.'

The oak would have been from the old 6-bell frame, which was replaced with an iron 8-bell frame when the bells were augmented in 1903, or perhaps an un-rotted part of a floor beam. Where it had been in the intervening twenty five years is a mystery.

Wokingham and Sonning Deanery – Wokingham continued to be the central point of the branch throughout this period, with the AGM held in Wokingham every year. The service alternated between All Saints and St Paul's, but the meeting was more often than not in Church House.

In 1930, things didn't go quite to plan:

> 'Some 90 members & visitors assembled at the Church House for the usual meat tea but the pies arriving somewhat late, the Chairman called upon the Sec to read the minutes of the last Annual Meeting which were confirmed and duly signed ....'.

The minutes don't record when the pies did arrive, but they must have done so because the minutes also say:

> 'The arrangements for the tea were carried out by a staff of ladies under Miss D Westcott, all of whom were heartily thanked by Canon Coleridge, who also expressed the thanks of the meeting to the preacher for his helpful address in Church'

Interestingly in 1931 the cost of the tea had to be doubled from 6d to 1/- 'owing to the decrease in Branch funds, due chiefly to the high cost of the Annual Tea'. Were the meals subsidised as a matter of policy, or was it just poor management of costs?

When Gilbert Thurlow[21] arrived in Wokingham in 1934, he too played a full part in Branch affairs and attended most meetings, no doubt exerting a strong influence on the ringing. Inevitably he was invited to preach at the AGM, and did so in 1936, when like those of his fellow clerics his words had an uplifting message. But Gilbert was no ordinary cleric[22], and rather than a high sounding theme or a biblical text, he chose the earthy sounding 'luke-warmness'. His address 'stressed the importance of being regular & punctual at times of ringing, of being keen to make progress in our art, & to keep it up to a high standard'.

---

[21] See page 59.

[22] In his later years he had a wry, engaging sense of humour, and I am sure he always had.

7 The mid 20th Century (1940 - 1979)

The war disrupted tower life, and killed a former All Saints ringer, Henry Cole, whose father George we met in previous chapters. Henry was elected in 1936 and rang for a couple of years. He served with 6th Battallion Grenedier Guards, and died in Italy on 30th January 1944, aged 23.

Ringing was banned for much of the war on the grounds that bells would be used as a signal in the event of an invasion[1], so there would have been no regular ringing at All Saints. Some bands rang handbells during the ban. All Saints had a set (and possibly two[2]) which they could have used for practice, but there is no evidence that they did[3]. The ban was lifted in August 1943, when ringing activity began again.

7.1 The band

Only nine of the eighteen pre-war members remained after the War but numbers soon reached pre-war levels and went on to peak at two dozen in 1953. Several new ringers began training in 1943 when the wartime ban was lifted, and by the time of the first post-war AGM in October 1945, three ringers (Gwen Crockford, Godfrey Moles and Ted Langley) were sufficiently competent to be proposed as Guild members. Walter Barrett also began learning in 1943, but wasn't proposed as a member until 1947. When asked about this unduly long apprenticeship, his wife said 'Wally Pearce was a very strict task master and learners were not let loose on open bells until they were considered to be fully competent after numerous practices on tied bells.' Even so, four years is an incredibly long time to reach basic proficiency.

Turnover – A total of eighty five people joined the band between 1945 and 1977. Most of them would have been newly trained ringers, and only half lasted more than three years, with twenty only remaining for a year. The Foreman, Walter Pearce, thought that this required action, but his solution focused not on trying to improve retention (or even on selecting trainees who might be more likely to make the grade) but on avoiding people becoming Guild members for so short a time. At the 1963 AGM, he proposed that newly trained members should only be put forward for Guild membership the year after they were elected to the band, when 'loyalty and efficiency have been proved'. He claimed it would save a lot of wasted effort, but the administrative effort would surely be tiny compared with the effort invested in their training. Maybe he was more concerned about money. The tower was probably paying Guild subscriptions at the time, at least for younger members[4], which most of the trainees would have been. The meeting agreed to the delayed election scheme, and it ran for a decade, during which time many still dropped out after a year of membership, lasting long enough to be elected, but giving up after another year.

---

[1] There are doubts about whether this would ever have worked, since there would not necessarily have been ringers available to ring the bells, and any bells left 'up' (see pages 7-8) would have been dangerous and possibly lethal if non-ringers had attempted to ring them.

[2] A set was bought in 1873 (see 30) and by the 1980s there were two old sets in the tower.

[3] Change ringing in hand is normally performed with two bells per ringer (one in each hand) which requires distinct additional skills. Most handbell ringers are also tower bell ringers, but relatively few tower bell ringers ring handbells.

[4] In 1975, the AGM agreed to 'continue to pay' the Guild fees for school children.

Even more recruits were lost during training, before becoming members. Trainee numbers were high whenever mentioned (8 in 1957, 10 in 1962, 12 in 1966, 4 in 1969, 7 in 1973). Comparing them with the number of new members in the same or following year suggests that most were lost, and that the success rate was lower during the early years (when Walter Pearce was teaching recruits) than it was in later years (when Bob Begrie took over), but it is a tenuous comparison.

The four trainees who started at the end of this era in 1978 do not fit this this pattern of high loss – they are all still ringing. But by 1978 things were already changing as a precursor to the modern period covered in the next chapter.

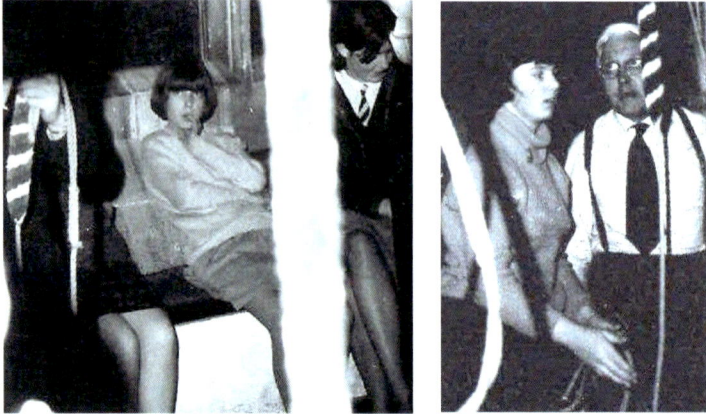

Figure 38: (L) Waiting to ring – Jane Saunders and Sarah Hutt
(R) Under instruction – Ann Barfoot and Bob Begrie

Ringers wanted – It seems that word of mouth could not provide enough recruits to be trained (and lost) during this period. Between 1945 and 1958 the Parish Magazine had no fewer than seven advertisements for new ringers. The first said 'Mr Brooks, Foreman of the Bell-ringers, will be glad to welcome new candidates for bell-ringing'. The formula varied a bit over coming years. In 1948, he added that recruits could be male of female, but in 1949 he was having second thoughts: 'We would be glad to welcome one or two men as Bellringers'. This probably wasn't an attempt to turn back the clock on sex equality (almost equal male and female recruits since the war) but a desire for some stronger adults to supplement the youngsters. In 1952 he specified stature rather than age: '... of any age, male or female, not less than 4ft 2in'. Brooks advertised three more times, in the autumn of 1954, 1955 and 1958. The last included a rather odd throw away comment:

'The Bells of our Church are being rehung, and we should like to hear from anyone who would like to learn the art of Bellringing. We are short of ringers at the moment and will welcome anyone who would like to try this important work for the Church. I will be in Church on Monday evenings, and will be glad to talk to anyone who wants to come along and see me.'

This is the only public mention about the bells being rehung, which seems surprising, since it was considered to be such a big improvement at the time (see page 90).

The Rector must have taken up the cause after the 1955 appeal, because at the next AGM we read:

'The Rector's appeal for recruits had generated 8, of whom 5 remained'

Walter Pearce followed in Brooks' footsteps, with several recruitment notices in the Parish Magazine. In 1965 and 1967 he said 'anyone from the age of twelve upwards (male or female)'. In 1968, the age reduced to eleven, and his language was florid: '... a chance to start training in the noble art of Campanology, and to acquire a skill needed to pull with one of the keen and competent bands of Berkshire ...'.

Honorary members – None of the successive versions of the rules[5] mention honorary members, but three examples of them are on record. Bill Parker joined the band some time during 1966, having previously been at Sandhurst. He was elected a member at the 1967 AGM, and when he announced a year later that he was leaving to become Foreman of Yorktown, he was made an honorary member. He was a former Branch Ringing Master, and must have made a strong impression on the band. He seems to have had itchy feet, because he moved on again, and Guild records in later years show him as 'unattached'.

The following year, 1969, Mrs White and Mr Howitt, both Finchampstead ringers, were also made honorary members 'in view of their invaluable help'. In later years the help was to be reciprocated, when Winifrid White relied on a group of All Saints ringers driving to Finchampstead after morning ringing to make up numbers there.

In the same era (the mid '70s) All Saints also relied on several of St Paul's ringers to help with Sunday ringing. Keith Begrie and Ross Dick were as regular as All Saints' own ringers, but they never seem to have been made 'honorary members'.

Dormant members – One might assume that most members rang regularly. Why else be a member? Of course there were exceptions, for example Bill Brooks was too ill to ring during his last couple of years. But it seems that by the late 1970s, many members had become completely inactive. This came to a head at the 1978 AGM, which agreed that adult members[6] should pay their Guild subscriptions. If the tower (or the church) had been paying all subscriptions, then there would have been little incentive for those who couldn't be bothered to turn up for ringing to end their membership. The secretary was instructed to write to the 'non participating members' to inform them that by default they would cease to remain members.

The upsurge – At the very end of this period, membership rose dramatically, fuelled by a combination of experienced ringers joining the band, and much more successful training of new ringers. One example of this renewed vigour was the training course in 1978, when the band invited tutors from the Diocesan Guild in for the day to lead the course. The photograph of participants in Figure 39 clearly shows the burgeoning numbers in these last few years, which laid the foundations for what was to come later, as we shall see in Chapter 8.

---

[5] See Annex C.

[6] Not those in education, who would still have their subscriptions paid, with free Guild badges.

Figure 39: Training course in 1978 (L-R) (Back) Dave Dewar, Terry Scott, John Harrison, Francis Moore, Audrey Moore, Pam Vassie, Evan Kozakiewicz, (Middle) John Scott, Angela Chapman, Alison Moore, Ruth Hosken, Pearl Gibson, Simon Tomlinson, Sarah Chapman, Betty Tomlinson, (Front) Stewart Gibson, Martin Hosken, Walter Pearce, Nellie Pearce, Chris Gibson

End of the closed shop – Ever since the formation of the Society of Honorary Ringers in 1873, there had been an official limit to the number of members. It had changed over the years and latterly was 16. The 1979 AGM finally abolished the fixed upper limit, but agreed to a limit 'at the discretion of the Foreman'. What this really meant is unclear. We saw above that the band was experiencing rapid growth. Would they really turn away new competent ringers moving into the Parish? Perhaps it was a concession to the Foreman, who was facing changes that were out of his control. The minutes go on to record:

'Further although 3 people were keen to join they will be delayed by at least 9 months; and also no new (learner) members could join until the foreman gives his permission. We would start a waiting list & the secretary would report this in the magazine.'

There was a lull in training that year, but given the vast numbers of recent trainees still being absorbed into the band, that was probably no bad thing.

7.2 Notable ringers

'**Eddie' Whittingham** rang at All Saints from 1903 to 1968, longer than any one else. He was a carpenter by trade, and saw active service during the 1914-18 war. He was an unexceptional ringer, and only rang the most basic of methods. He finished in fine style, ringing literally to the end of his life on the evening of Monday 20th May 1968. Here is how the Rector described it in his July letter:

'It is not given to many people to be a regular Church bellringer for more than sixty years, but this was the record of Mr. Edward[7] John Whittingham who passed from this life in the latter part of May.

Some years ago Mr. Whittingham decided that he had reached an age when he must give up ringing. I remember making a presentation to him on behalf of his fellow ringers. Soon after this, as an early stage of our plans for the restoration of the Church, the bells were taken away to Whitechapel[8] for repair and re-tuning. They were then brought back and rehung in a more modern manner on ball bearings.

One day Mr. Whittingham tried one of the bells again and found that he could manage it with ease. From then on he resumed his customary place in the belfry and so continued until the actual moment of his death for he passed from this life actually in the ringing chamber at a normal Monday evening practice. It is a wonderful record.'

His life also ended with an error. He was baptised Edgar John, on June 17th 1883, but for most of his life was simply known as Eddie. When he died, six years after his wife, no one seems to have known that his real name was Edgar. The powers-that-be must have considered that 'Eddie' was too informal for a burial record, and assumed (wrongly) that his name was Edward, as his tombstone shows.

Figure 40: Edgar Whittingham – misnamed in death

George Wigmore probably had a longer ringing career than any other All Saints ringer, though he only rang in Wokingham for 45 years. He learnt to ring at the turn of the 20th century, aged 11, but was 40 when he joined the band at All Saints in 1929. He rang regularly until Christmas 1973, a total of almost 74 years, and he died the following September. He was a hire car chauffeur with Herrings (and later Brimblecombe) and at one time he became the preferred driver of Hon. Mrs Corfield, a former Mayor. He lived in Peach Street, and in the 1930s had the distinction of having Gilbert Thurlow[9] as a lodger during his curacy at All Saints. In his final years, George moved to Sale Garden Cottages.

---

[7] This was not his baptised name, see subsequent paragraph.

[8] He was mistaken – the bells were not removed from the tower, see page 89.

[9] See page 59

Figure 41: (L) Eddie Whittingham and (R) George Wigmore[10]

William James Brooks (Bill), whom we met in Chapter 6 as Foreman for most of the inter-war period, was approaching sixty when the war ended. He suggested standing down, but was persuaded to stay on, and led the band into his seventies. He was very much respected and liked as a person, which is probably why the band persuaded him to continue as Foreman. He was not a forceful individual, being happy to go with things as they were, as long as ringing kept ticking along. He was very encouraging though, for example cycling with the younger more keen ringers to ring at other towers.

Walter John Pearce (Wally) learnt to ring in his teens, and became a member in 1925. He played a leading role throughout the post-war period, first as deputy to Bill Brooks from 1945-63, and then as Foreman from 1964-79. He was more outgoing and forceful than Bill, but he could be intimidating. Unlike most Foremen at All Saints, he came from a Wokingham family. 'The name of Pearce has long been associated with All Saints' said the obituary of his father (also Walter). He was a plumber by trade, and for many years he was also Sexton and Verger, living in one of the cottages next to the church. He later lived in Waterloo Road, and spent his final years in sheltered housing opposite the church where he had rung for nearly sixty years. The ringers helped in this final move, with a hired van. Walter died in August 1984.

---

[10] Picture reproduced courtesy of Wokingham Times

Francis Moore[11] relocated from Merseyside in 1971. He made friends with Bill Burkey, whom he succeeded as Industrial Liaison Officer with DTI in Richmond, and who suggested Wokingham as a good place to live. Bill was an All Saints ringer, and introduced the Moores to All Saints. Before long Francis, his wife Audrey, and their daughters Lindsey and Alison all learnt to ring. Francis succeeded Bill as Deputy Foreman in 1977 at a time when the Foreman, Walter Pearce, was becoming less able to play an active role, so Francis was mainly responsible for running the tower. He was also responsible for helping to foster much better relations between ringers and the church, and integrating the ringers into church life (see page 82). He gave up ringing after a back injury in 1979. Francis is a Chartered Electrical Engineer and a member of the Chartered Institute of Marketing.

Robert Begrie (Bob) moved to Wokingham from London to become Chief Engineer at Pinewood Hospital in 1961. Bob and his son Keith[12] both joined the band at All Saints. Bob was an experienced and competent ringer who rapidly made a significant contribution to the band, both as a ringer and a teacher. When Walter Pearce became Foreman in 1964, Bob would have been the obvious choice to become his deputy, but for some reason he wasn't elected to the post until 1966[13]. He then served in the role for the next nine years, until his early death in 1974.

William Burkey (Bill) rang at All Saints for ten years, holding one or more offices for most of those years. His wife and two daughters also rang. Bill holds the record for the number of tower offices held simultaneously – in the mid 1970s he was Deputy Foreman, Treasurer and Steeplekceper at the same time. He was a prime mover of the proposal to install a glass screen between the ringing gallery and the nave in the 1970s. He was a Production Engineer by profession, and later a lecturer at Slough College.

Mary Cole was one of the wave of ringers who learnt in 1943, after the wartime ban on ringing was lifted. She was a second generation ringer. We met her father George in previous chapters, and her brother Henry (mentioned at the start of this chapter) rang in the mid-1930s. Mary was an active member of the growing post-war band. She served as Tower Secretary for twenty years, from 1954 to 1973, and even after she gave up ringing, she continued to audit the accounts of the Sonning Deanery Bellringers.

---

[11] Picture reproduced courtesy of Middlesex Chronicle

[12] Keith later moved to St Paul's, but remained a supporter of All Saints into the 1970s.

[13] Keith Goddard, who held the post during the intervening two years, was unaware of any reason why Bob was not elected earlier [8].

7.3 The ringing

Although the state of ringing was not consistently reported, we can infer something of the ebb and flow of post war ringing. There was no Foreman's report until 1949, but from 1951 we start to see glimpses of what the ringing was like. There are increasing references to special performances, the quality of the ringing, progress with learning methods and the number of methods rung, as well as ubiquitous reports of discussions about outings[14].

Method ringing – Eight AGM reports mention specific methods, and they give us a flavour, if not the detail, of the band's method repertoire during this period.

For example, in 1952 'it was suggested that the young recruits were far enough advanced to begin to learn Stedman, and that other members should try Kent and Oxford[15] throughout the coming year.' 'Younger' probably means less experienced, assuming that most recruits were youngsters. It seems odd though. If they were advanced enough to learn Stedman, why exclude them from the team effort of learning to ring Kent? It is not significantly harder, and would have made them feel more involved with the band as a whole. They might have been able to help the older ringers, who after two years of trying, made 'no progress' with Kent, though they did make 'good headway' with Oxford Bob Triples. Maybe they just found ringing Triples easier, because it leaves the Tenor 'covering' (ringing continually in last place) and makes the ringing more stable. That would have been critical if, like Walter Pearce[16], they relied on memorising which bells to follow, rather than knowing their own places and being able to see what was happening around them. It is also possible that they didn't have anyone capable of competently turning in[17] the Tenor, which is heavier, and harder to ring well, than the other bells.

Methods were not mentioned again until 1964 when 'progress had been made' with Kent, and in 1965 'good progress'. The following year, Double Norwich 'had been attempted, but with slow progress'. Two years later that was downgraded to 'limited success'.   The final method mention was in 1971, when 'the older ringers were learning a new method – St Clements'.

Progress overall seems to have been slow and painful. The band was obviously struggling, and it seems that in the early years at least, only Bill Brooks really understood methods [6]. Added to all this, prior to 1958 the bells went badly, with plain bearings and no rope guides. Many visiting bands had great difficulty ringing them at all. So despite various attempts to be more ambitious, their staple diet remained Grandsire, Plain Bob, Stedman and Single Oxford [8].

Peals – During this period, the local band rang no peals at all, though there were unsuccessful peal attempts in 1950, 1952 and 1953. There were also only four peals by visitors. These were truly lean years.

---

[14] See page 79
[15] Kent Treble Bob Major and Oxford Treble Bob Major, respectively.
[16] I remember him once reciting to me the sequence of bells to follow in Grandsire.
[17] Changing places along with all the other bells.

Quarter peals – We can't be sure how many there were, because the band wasn't good at recording them. One rung after Bill Brooks died in 1963 [8] was neither published in *The Ringing World* nor mentioned in the Parish Magazine. Many others went unrecorded, rung on the spur of the moment if the right people turned up for service ringing [25]. In 1952, the new Rector, Fred Steer, sensed the significance of these performances, and felt that the band ought to keep records of them. This comment came after the chairman's (ie the Rector's) report, but we don't know whether there was any discussion on the topic. Even if there was, no one seems to have taken his advice, since there are no known tower records for this period. As a result, our knowledge is fragmentary (see Table 7) and drawn from several sources:

- The Foreman's reports, as recorded in the minute book [4]
- Articles published in *All Saints Parish Magazine* [3]
- AJ Buswell's records based on *The Ringing World* publication (post '66) [23]
- Cards records held by the Oxford Diocesan Guild (ODG) [22]

Year	AGM	Buswell	ODG	Magazine	Year	AGM	Buswell	ODG	Magazine
1945					1963	occasional			
1946						attempts			
1947					1964	eight		5	2
1948	several		2		1965	fewer		2	
1949					1966	numerous	2	1	
1950	several				1967		0		
1951	five		2		1968		3		
1952	six				1969		1		3
1953	several				1970		1		2
1954	several		3		1971		1		
1955			1		1972		1		
1956					1973		2		1
1957	none				1974		1		2
1958					1975		1		
1959					1976		0		
1960					1977		0		
1961					1978		2		3
1962					1979		7		4

Table 7: Evidence for quarter peals rung between 1945 and 1979

The methods and dedications of known quarter peals are in Table 8. Grandsire Triples still dominates (almost two thirds of them, 19) with Oxford Bob Triples next most frequent (6). Oxford Bob was Walter Pearce's favourite method, and accounted for a third of the quarters rung while he was Foreman. There were only three of Major (all 8 bells working), all rung after the rehang on ball bearings. This may reflect a shortage of good 'back enders'[18], able to ring the Tenor well to Major.

---

[18] Ringers competent to ring the heavier bells properly.

Date	Method	Dedication
24 May 1948	Grandsire Triples	Half muffled tribute to Bertram Long[19]
19 September 1948	Grandsire Triples	
12 March 1951	Grandsire Triples	Half muffled tribute to Dr E Ward, churchwarden
25 August 1951	Plain Bob major	First quarter by a local band
28 December 1953	Grandsire Triples	Half muffled tribute Fred Langley, Sexton/Verger
11 June 1954	Grandsire Triples	
2 August 1954	Grandsire Triples	
30 July 1955	Stedman Triples[20]	For the marriage of Rev AGG Thurlow
8 February 1956	Grandsire Triples	To mark the birth of Christopher Newton[21]
28 August 1958	Grandsire Doubles	Half muffled, in memory of WJ Paice
April 1963	Unknown	In memory of Bill Brooks [8] [22]
29 March 1964	Grandsire Triples	Easter Day
August [23] 1964	Plain Bob major	Farewell to Miss RE Rowarth[24],
20 September 1964	Oxford Bob Triples	Farewell to Rev J Bromley
27 September 1964	Grandsire Triples	Welcome to Rev AG Millard
4 October 1964	Grandsire Triples	For Harvest Festival
24 January 1965	Grandsire Triples	In Memory of Sir Winston Churchill
30 January 1965	Grandsire Triples	In Memory of Sir Winston Churchill
21 August 1966	Stedman Triples	Farewell to Muriel Longhurst
2 October 1966	Oxford Bob Triples	For Harvest Festival
24 November 1968	Oxford Bob Triples	For confirmation
7 December 1968	Grandsire Triples	For the dedication of the organ
30 March 1969	Oxford Bob Triples	Palm Sunday
19 October 1969	Oxford Bob Triples	Farewell to the Rector
24 May 1970	Oxford Bob Triples	90th anniversary of Sonning Deanery Society
31 October 1970	Grandsire Triples	Eve of All Saints Day. Sheila Cameron marriage
8 October 1972	Plain Bob major	For Harvest Festival
14 Oct 1973	Grandsire Triples	Farewell to Rev Christopher Hewitson
18 November 1973	Grandsire Triples	Wedding Princess Anne & Captain Mark Phillips
10 February 1974	Grandsire Triples	Walter Pearce 50 years member Diocesan Guild
23 November 1975	Grandsire Triples	18th birthday and engagement of Wendy Burkey. Farewell to the Ellsworths

Table 8: Known quarter peals at All Saints during this period

Two quarters were of Stedman[25] Triples. The one in 1955 set out as a peal attempt to mark the wedding of Gilbert Thurlow[26], but when the peal failed they rang a quarter peal instead. Only half of the band were All Saints ringers, the others being more experienced outsiders. In contrast, the one in 1966 was rung by the local band, and

---

[19] Former Rector, see Chapter 5.
[20] After an unsuccessful peal attempt.
[21] Son of Walter and Barbara Newton, former members.
[22] The quarter wasn't published.
[23] The exact date wasn't published.
[24] She rang in the quarter peal, but doesn't appear to have been a member.
[25] More difficult than Grandsire, but very musical and popular.
[26] See page 59.

was the culmination of a considerable effort to master Stedman, a method that is notoriously easy to lose[27]. They had attempted Stedman in 1963, but failed.

The commonest dedications (8) were for clergy or ringers arriving in or leaving the Parish. Next came special services (6) and deaths (6). It is interesting that very few performances had no dedication. The one in September 1948 was on a Sunday, so presumably was rung for a service. The one in August 1951 – the first by an unaided All Saints band – was on a Saturday when there would have been less pressure or constraint than when ringing before a service. The two in 1954 (Friday and Monday) were presumably rung simply for the satisfaction of doing so.

Practices – A weekly ringing practice is almost universal among ringers – often from 7-30 to 9-00 on a weekday evening. The 1935 rules stated that the practice was on Monday at 7-30 pm. Whether those pre-war ringers turned up promptly at 7-30 we don't know, but their post war successors seem to have had trouble doing so. In 1951 Harry Dyer reminded members that 'practices started at 7-30, not 8-00 or 8-15'. Punctuality was also discussed the following year. In 1960 John Watts complained about practices starting late, and after discussion the meeting agreed to move the start to 7-45. This probably just shortened the practice, with no corresponding change to the finish time. It can't have been a success, because the next year, the start time was moved back to 7-30 'to give learners adequate practice'.

In some years, practices were disrupted. While one of the nave pillars was being replaced in 1955, ringing was suspended completely for fear that the vibration might cause the church to collapse. In the severe winter of 1962-63, practices were suspended for several weeks because of extreme cold, and the AGM (which was held in the tower) did not take place until 11th March, whereas it was normally in January.

1965 saw more disruption, with confirmation classes in church on Monday evenings. We don't know how many practices were lost, but the 'preliminary talk' to candidates was at 7pm on 9th March, they 're-assembled' in Church on 14th September [after a summer break?] and the confirmation was on 22nd November. Perhaps practices started late instead of being cancelled, but even so, they were disrupted for over half a year. Confirmation must have been popular though, because there was another two months later, on 25th January 1965 – another Monday!

Outings – The seaside excursions with the choir, which had begun in 1921, were revived briefly after the war. In 1947 they went to Southsea, where some of them watched county cricket as well as the usual seaside activities, but that was the last. In later years they went on what is now the normal type of 'ringing outing' – where the main activity is ringing, travelling between several towers to ring a while at each.

In 1948, 'Mr Whittingham raised the question of an outing'. The Foreman was left to organise it, and invite St Paul's to join in. Another was proposed the next year, with almost identical words, duly seconded and carried. This pattern of formal proposal and 'details left in the hands of the Foreman' continued for many years. Only in 1964, after Brooks died, was the outing relegated to 'any other business'. Outings

---

[27] Its structure is different from most methods, and it is very easy for one trip to escalate with several bells going wrong at once.

feature in the record of 16 AGMs. Often the minutes record the destination (in several cases 'after some discussion'). Were there competing views about the merits of different places? Did they have to brain-storm likely venues during the meeting?

Considering the state of post-war road transport, some destinations were ambitious, for example to Kent, Dorset and Gloucester. Early outings were whole day affairs. They rang at four towers, with lunch at the second and tea at the last. Venues for lunch and tea were recommended by the local ringers. Outings were always by coach[28], always full, and with ringers wives, etc making up the numbers. In 1956, there was an extra half-day autumn outing, which suggests a stronger, active band.

Figure 42: Outings (names left to right)
(L) 1949: Pat Newport, Mary Cole, Gwen Crockford, Barbara Crockford, (front)
Walter Newton. (R) 1952?: (back) Walter Pearce, Robin Pearce[29], Walter Newton,
(middle) [??], [??], Keith Goddard, Ted Langley, Harry Dyer, Tom Langley, [??],
Len Woodason, Ernie Pearce, John Watts, (front) Bill Brooks

Figure 43: More outings (left to right) 1954: Harvey Mitchell, Len Woodason,
Harry Dyer, Bill Brooks, Barbara Newton, Gillian Piggott, Mary Cole. Late 1950s:
Bill Brooks, Keith Goddard, Frank Tomlinson[30], George Wigmore, Jane Huckings,
Walter Newton, Len Woodason, David Tomlinson, John Watts, Walter Pearce, [??]

---

[28] Brimblecome in Mary Cole's time. George Wigmore, see page 73, was one of their drivers.
[29] Not a ringer
[30] Frank and his son rang at Binfield

The 1960 outing to Sussex had to be cancelled for shortage of ringers, and there was no outing in 1961. A half day outing in 1962 was successful so they agreed to another in 1963, but it was not to be. In his first report as Foreman the following year, Walter Pearce said there had been no outing 'because of an expanded demand for ringing for weddings'. Were there really so many weddings? Could the band not have agreed in advance with the church that for one Saturday in the whole year there would be no wedding ringing? Could they not have arranged for ringers from other towers to cover during their absence, as is often done today?

Half day outings, with 'tea' but not 'lunch', and ringing at only three towers, became the norm until July 1978, which was the last half day main outing, and also the last outing by coach. In December that same year, there was an additional, whole day outing by car to Hertfordshire and Essex, which was the forerunner of much greater outing activity in the future, as we shall see in the next chapter.

Generally the ringers paid for their ringing outings, unlike the earlier joint outings with the choir, which had been paid for by the church, but they still recieved a subsidy. In 1963, a Mrs Knapp sent a donation towards the cost, and in 1964 the AGM decided to ask the PCC for a grant. In 1965 (while asking for an increase in wedding fees) the Foreman proposed that the additional 5/- should be put towards the cost of the outing. Again in 1971 he asked the (new) Rector to approach the PCC for a grant towards the outing, and a £10 grant ensued. Whether it was repeated in 1972 we don't know, but at the 1974 AGM, the Treasurer reported that the PCC had not been asked for a grant, and the following year it was reported that organising an outing was becoming more difficult 'for financial reasons', though the minutes don't provide any details to support the assertion. Soon afterwards the idea that the church should subsidise ringing outings must have been permanently consigned to history, because it was not mentioned again.

Quality of the ringing – The casual reader of the AGM minutes might notice many comments about the quality of ringing. There were comments about good quality in 1952, 1962, 1965 and 1974 and about deterioration or the need to improve in 1955 and 1957. On the other hand, that only adds up to six mentions of quality in 33 years, the same as the number of comments about the quality of the outing and/or the tea!

A more interesting discussion took place at the end of this period, during the 1979 AGM. The Foreman (as it turned out in his final year of office) reported that the standard of ringing was increasing. That view wasn't shared by the recently joined experienced ringers, who were concerned that the standard was far from good. Theresa Scott proposed quarter peals on Sunday evenings to help encourage better striking. She was supported by Francis Moore (Deputy Foreman) Bob Chapman (future Deputy) and John Harrison (future Foreman) but the Foreman opposed the motion 'on the grounds of restricting ringing'. In fact it would have created considerably more ringing (but it wouldn't have been done with other people sitting around waiting to ring). There were 'numerous arguments for and against' and the motion was carried. The record then enigmatically informs us that 'the officers were charged to organise the ringing.'

One thing that should have helped to improve the quality of ringing was the work done on the bells in 1958[31]. After half a century of use, the plain bearings would have deteriorated. It is noticeable that peals rung after replacement with ball bearings were generally faster than those before[32]. The new rope guides would also have helped. Before, there was over twenty feet of free rope in the ringing room, which coupled with the fact that most of the ropes ran out of true, would have made them prone to snaking sideways in the hands of any but the most careful ringers.

7.4   Ringers and the Church

With complete AGM minutes, as well as articles in the Parish Magazine, we get a better view of how the ringers related to the church. Ringing spans two worlds. In its own right it is an engaging field of human endeavour, with a rich heritage, culture and infrastructure. At the same time it provides a closely integrated service as part of the worship and traditions of the Church. In Chapter 4, we saw how in the 19th century the Church actively promoted change ringing, which had evolved as a mainly secular activity. In some ways, this relationship is similar to that between classical music and the Church's liturgy – separate but closely inter-twined.

Out of sight, out of mind – At All Saints, the relationship between church and ringers has generally been good, and mutually supportive, but it was not always so. In the early 1970s, ringing was not well regarded. In part this might have been because ringers tend to be less visible than some other groups. They perform out of the way in the tower. Some of them don't stay for the services, and even those that do come through the door like anyone else, and are not immediately identified as ringers. Contrast that with the choir, whose members are much more visible, and which at this time was extremely successful, with very full ranks and high standards.

The ringers' poor image changed dramatically after Francis Moore gave an illustrated talk to an open meeting of the PCC in 1978 on ringing and its place in the ministry of the Church. The talk generated great interest. Along with the interest came greater understanding, and invitations to participate more widely. Francis followed his talk with a series of regular articles in the Parish Magazine, summarised on pages 86-7.

The 'wrong kind of ringer' – We can see an example of the occasionally awkward relationship between the church and ringers just after the war when the band desperately needed new recruits. It transpired that two young trainees, progressing to the point where they would want to become full members of the band, were Methodists[6]. At the 1945 AGM 'the Rector spoke of the high office which ringers hold in the Church and expressed the view that ringers should be members of the Church of England'. After some discussion, the minutes record that 'whether any one who was not a member of the C of E should be encouraged to come to practices was left to the Rector to refer to Canon Coleridge'. Coleridge was Master of the Oxford Diocesan Guild at the time, and the answer was no, which displeased the band since they were short of ringers. Brooks' advertisement in October that year concluded by saying:

---

[31] See page 89.
[32] See page 141.

'Needless to say, bell-ringing is a great privilege, and the qualification for membership is that candidates must be members of the Church of England. This is the rule of the Diocesan Guild of Church Bellringers[33].'

Things had definitely changed by 1977. The report of ringing for the Queen's Silver Jubilee had a very different tone:

'As part of our Jubilee thanksgiving, the people of Wokingham were summoned to a United Service for the Town by an ecumenical band of ringers comprising non-conformists as well as representatives of neighbouring C of E towers.'

And a report about shortage of ringers in the Parish Magazine included:

'... At present our bells are only kept ringing for the main services of the church as a result of the generous support we receive from our members who are of a non-conformist persuasion, and regular visitors from neighbouring towers. I am sure that it is good that our bells should be used to provide a link with other churches, but surely our congregation has an obligation to think seriously about its own stewardship of the cultural and physical heritage the bells represent. As our Rector reminded us last month, the parish church building is not a museum, and we may well ask ourselves "What, precisely, is our parish strategy?" ...'

Different Rectors – Three Rectors presided over this period: Gordon Kenworthy, Frederick Steer and Kenneth Martin. Each seems to have had a different relationship with the ringers. They all chaired (almost all) tower AGMs, something that to this day helps to underpin a good working relationship with the church.

Gordon Kenworthy only chaired six post-war meetings but seems to have been very aware of ringing matters. For example when the Master of the Oxford Diocesan Guild was ill, he suggested sending a letter of sympathy. He also used to give each new ringer a basic ringing book. We don't know for how long he did this, but it was mentioned in 1948 when Walter Pearce asked the Rector whether those who had given up ringing ought to return the books. (After some discussion on the matter, the Rector decided that they could keep them.)

Fred Steer's interest in the ringers seems to have been at a more functional level: a request for better punctuality, pleasure at seeing more youngsters, suggesting a longer period of ringing before evensong, concern for the surrounding houses at Midnight on New Year's Eve, a 'noticeable improvement in striking and punctuality for service ringing', and so on. One interesting insight is a report of the 1964 AGM that appeared in the Parish Magazine. Steer was the only non-ringer present, so presumably wrote it. It surely couldn't have been written by a ringer:

'The Annual Meeting of the Ringers was held in the Ringing Chamber on Feb 3rd, Once again, we were able to thank them for an unbroken record of ringing on all occasions when their services were required throughout the year and also to congratulate them on the progress made in mastering ringing methods. We are also able, and we deem it a matter upon which we can offer our congratulation, that every member of the Band was present at the Annual Meeting.'

---

[33] That requirement disappeared when the Guild rules were revised in 1958.

Ken Martin seems to have been particularly keen for the ringers to integrate into Parish life. In 1971, he hoped the ringers would come to a social gathering in the Rectory garden in the summer. In 1974 he passed on remarks from the congregation about the quality of the ringing, and also asked for two ringers to read lessons at a Deanery service. He repeatedly urged the ringers to contribute to the Parish Magazine. That request took a while to take effect, but when it did it yielded spectacular results, particularly from 1977-1979 (see below).

He was keen for the congregation to know more about ringing too. He asked for a copy of *The Ringing World* to be displayed on the magazine rack in church, and felt that a ringer ought to be on the PCC. Presumably he encouraged Francis Moore's seminal talk to the PCC mentioned above. On a more practical level, when Ken Martin first arrived in the Parish, he heard that the ringers were trying to get the PCC to buy a new carpet for the ringing chamber, and offered to provide a suitable one himself. Perhaps he had some spare ones, having recently moved in.

Moving meetings – The venue for AGMs moved around quite a lot. Before the war the AGM had been held in the Rectory, but afterwards it moved into the tower. Gordon Kenworthy was still Rector for the first six of these meetings, so what had changed? Was it inconvenient for him to host them, or did the ringers want the meeting on their own ground? Meetings continued in the tower during Fred Steer's time, but when Ken Martin arrived in 1970, they returned to the Rectory. Only briefly though – the following year he apologised that he couldn't host the meeting because there were too many ringers, and it moved to Church House. It was held in the vestry in 1974, and then in the Annex from 1975-77. Finally in 1978, the meeting was held in the home of one of the ringers, as it has been ever since.

Moving ringing – In 1966, the Parish introduced a new service at 9-00am on Sunday morning, as well as the long established 11-00 service. In 1974 the new service moved to 9-30am. The 1976 AGM discussed a request to ring for what had become the most attended service. There was a complaint that it was 'too early, hence the lack of ringers' (presumably a prediction, since it it hadn't yet happened so they wouldn't know). The band continued to ring at 10-30 for the 11-00 service, but for most of them it was 'ringing after the 9-30 service', which they attended. The inevitable change had to wait another six years to happen.

The Parish Magazine – During this period, the ringers visibility in the the Parish Magazine varied dramatically. From 1943 to 1976 there were 37 articles about bells or ringers, just over one per year (even lower than the 1.2 per year average from 1900-1940), see Table 9. Apart from quarter peal reports, the most numerous articles were the continual pleas for more ringers, already discussed. Then in the late 1970s came a surge of 24 articles in just over a couple of years, see Table 10.

Vera Robinson, whom we met in Chapter 6, and who gave up ringing shortly after the war, continued to feature in the Magazine. In 1955, she wrote an obituary for Alice Walker, with whom she learned to ring nearly forty years earlier. In 1961 she wrote a report of the Diocesan Guild Festival in Oxford. Not surprisingly, she linked the lesson 'Let us now praise famous men' to her father and the other founders of the

Oxford Diocesan Guild, and reminded her readers that the first idea of founding the Guild was at a meeting in Wokingham.

The Rector mentioned Vera twice in his letters, even after she left Wokingham in 1965 to look after sick relatives, for example in 1967:

'Miss Vera Robinson has sent a further gift of £40 to add to her former gift of £100[34]. This was a cause of joy to me not only for its own sake, but also because two letters written in connection with its transmission almost brought the sender before my eyes.'

In 1972 Vera wrote an article about the death of Rev Lionel Edward Lydekker, who had been curate at All Saints from 1909-1914.

	1943-49	1943-49	1960-69	1970-76	Total
Death, marriage, departure, ...	1943, 1945,		1966, 1968		4
Recruitment	1945, 1948, 1949,	1952, 1954, 1955, 1958	1965, 1967, 1968		10
AGM reports	1948,		1964, 1966,	1970	4
Guild events	1948, 1949,	1953	1961		4
Quarter peals			1964, 1966 (2), 1967 (2), 1969,	1970 (4), 1973, 1974	12
Report on the bells			1965		1

Table 9: Topics reported in the Parish Magazine: 1943-1976

In the summer of 1977, the Rector's repeated request for more articles about ringing took root, and ringing blossomed on the pages of the Magazine like a shrub that had remained dormant in the desert until the rains came. From summer 1977 to autumn 1979, no fewer than 24 articles appeared, many of them being quite substantial. Francis Moore, who had recently been elected Deputy Foreman, was the main instigator, but many other ringers contributed articles as well.

Table 10 lists the twenty four articles in the late 1970s, and shows the diversity of what there is to say about ringers and ringing, when someone gets round to saying it.

Figure 44 shows illustrations from the articles for January and October 1978. The tune, known as 'Whittingtons' is said to have originated when Dick Whittington heard the sound of Bow Bells calling him back to London. The lion's head appears on bells cast by Roger Landen, who ran Wokingham Bellfoundry in the mid 15th century. It also appeared on All Saints ringers' T-shirts, see Figure 58 on page 109.

Figure 44: (L) Whittingtons (wrongly printed[35]), (R) Roger Landen's lion emblem

---

[34] For the Parish Centre Fund.

[35] The first three and last three notes were interchanged. The tune should rise and then fall.

July 1977	Sound as a bell	All towers in Sonning Deanery were to be open for the Diocesan Guild Festival. 'Many people will probably wish to visit the town and if you happen to see any lost ringers in the street, please give them a welcome and direct them to the appropriate tower'.
August 1977	Jubilee Bells	Historical introduction about Elizabeth I's liking of bells, with report of ringing for the Queen Elizabeth II's Silver Jubilee celebrations
September 1977	Ringing News	Departure of ringers. Welcome to Andrew Hodgson on sabbatical from the University of Rhodesia. Congratulations to Salisbury (Rhodesia) ringing the first 10 bell peal in Africa for the Jubilee ...'prayers and blessings for the problems of the future'
October 1977	Ringing News	Ex Wokingham ringer Stephen Skates, who had joined the Army Catering Corps, and excelled in his training in Aldershot (where he also rang) was being posted to Germany[36].
November 1977	Ringing News	Loss of ringers from the congregation '... our bells are only kept ringing through generous support ... from our members who are of a non-conformist persuasion, and regular visitors from neighbouring towers'. ... 'change ringing is little understood by many laity and clergy' ...'bellringing offers opportunities to Serve God in his church, work together with others in a team of mutually dependent members, ... engage in healthy mental and physical exercise'.
December 1977	Ringing News	The significance of bells and ringing in Christian life and the community
January 1978	The Exercise	(In the pantomime season) ... Richard Whittington founded the 'College of the Holy Ghost and Hospital of God's House' from whose name is derived the Ancient Society of College Youths – one of the premier ringing societies. Explained the structure and working of 'The Exercise' (the ringing community) ... working together ... mutual dependence ...
February 1978	Ringing News	Change ringing as a peculiarly English art and science. Ringers have suffered at hands of cartoonists (like clergymen & school teachers) ... Describes the physical process, learning methods ...
March 1978	Ringing News	Report on 'well attended' AGM
April 1978	First Steps in Ringing	Author's description of what it felt like learning to ring (see page 88)
May 1978	Ringing News	Looking forward to the Ringers' Service on 16th April, at which five new members will receive Guild certificates.
June 1978	Ringing News	'You are invited to follow the Mayor of Wokingham up the tower of All Saints Church ...' description and invitation to attend the tower open day. Notice of outing. Congratulations to youngest ringer, commended by his schoolteacher for a poem.
July 1978	Ringing News	The joy of ringing to welcome the new Mayor to the Civic Service, and of ringing the same afternoon for a wedding. Reflection on the changes in the band's fortunes since writing about the lack of ringers 8 months before. Welcome to five more experienced ringers.

---

[36] He later served in the Falklands, and survived the attack on RFA Sir Galahad.

August 1978	Ringing News	Numbers up from half a dozen to over twenty ... shortage of space on practice nights ... plan carefully to give everyone a ring.. 'There is a great sense of community in the tower'. – Successful tower open day and outing. Alison Moore passed the 'interest' part of the Duke of Edinburgh Award (needed to conduct a touch of at least 120 changes). Quarter Peal for evensong to welcome new ringers.
September 1978	Ringing News	Farewell to Ruth Hosken, going to York University. Article about university ringing societies and their role in recreation of students.
October 1978	Ringing News	Article about Wokingham Bell foundry with picture of Roger Landen's 'lion' founder's mark (see page 85.)
December 1978	Ringing News	Report of outing ... Ringers practising to ring carols on handbells at Christmas – would welcome invitations to perform. Planning a training day (run by Guild Education Committee) for the 'many keen learners' – lectures followed by practical ringing at different towers.
January 1979	Ringing News	Training day successful. New Year a time to assess progress ... look forward to new challenges ... reflect on working together as a group ... role that the Church played in development of polyphonic music, drama, literature and change ringing ... prepare for AGM.
February 1979	Ringing News	Thanks for handbell ringing donations, given to charity. Quarter peal for carol service. Two young ringers being confirmed. Alison Moore achieved Queen's Guide award. Struck by good will and friendship shown to members by ringers who live outside Wokingham.
March 1979	Ringing News	Ringers to run white elephant at May Fayre. Report of AGM. Explanation of quarter peals: to mark special events, and as personal landmarks. Quarter peal for Wally 71, and a ringer for 50 years.
April 1979	Ringing News	Churches are often near pubs. In the old days ringers were paid in beer, or paid a penalty to their fellow ringers in ale for making a mistake ... 'rest assured ... a very sober band rings your bells ...' Ringing was almost severed from the Puritan church in 17th century because they considered enjoyment sinful – ringers enjoy ringing.
May 1979	Ringing News	John Harrison was elected chairman of Sonning Deanery Branch. Gloucester bells were restored – the Dean, Gilbert Thurlow[37] rings with us whenever in Wokingham ...'many may remember his stirring sermon at Mr Wigmore's funeral'. The ringers didn't know about the Editor's April Fool joke (see below) but it took in two local newspapers! Historical note about bells being rung backwards (up the scale) to sound an alarm such as a fire.
November 1979	Ringing News	Numbers depleted during the summer. Francis Moore injured his back and can't ring. Quarter peal for departure of Gordon Kendal (curate). Half muffled quarter peal for Vera Robinson[38]. Entered Branch striking competition and came 3rd.
December 1979	Ringing News	Bells rung for evensong on All Saints day. Quarter peal the following Sunday. Report of cycle outing .. rain ... puncture ... difficult bells ... but lovely wooded country and good food.

Table 10: Parish Magazine articles about ringing 1977-1979

[37] See page 59.
[38] See page 60.

Some of these articles are worth a closer look. for example Francis Moore's article:

First Steps in Ringing – It all looked so easy. I was watching a band of eight experienced bell ringers. They stood quietly in place in the tower, and at a given signal pulled their ropes in turn setting the bells ringing in a splendid splash of sound. I watched carefully and it seemed to me that little effort was needed to pull the rope, just a smooth easy rhythm, not too fast and not too slow. It shouldn't be too difficult to do.

My first lesson in handling the bell was memorable. The effort required to pull the sally down seemed enormous and far from pulling the rope with a slow easy rhythm, the sally and the rope jerked with what seemed an excessive speed before my eyes and the harder I pulled the rope the heavier seemed the bell. I felt hot and exhausted and knew the beginnings of despair. It was then I became aware of the wonderful support and encouragement that is constantly there in the tower. To my surprise my feeble effort was praised and I received constant encouragement and constructive criticism until gradually I began to gain control of the 3 cwt. bell[39]. The co-ordination of movement felt good.

It is the custom in the Tower that the newest recruit rings the 'minute' bell before the service is due to begin. When this honour fell to me I found it both moving and exciting to stand facing the main body of the church ringing in as steady a rhythm as I could manage until the entry of the choir from the vestry, when I had to stop or rather "stand" the bell. This was for me one of the more difficult operations as a beginner, and try as I would the bell would not stand, and by necessity I had to continue tolling. The choir processed steadily into the church, then into the chancel. Still I "toll". I was going to be there for ever. Thoughts of the Rector preaching his sermon to the everlasting toll of the No. 2 bell passed swiftly through my mind. Help at last. A quiet voice by my side telling me not to worry it would "stand" next time. It did – and all was well but not to be forgotten.

The June 1978 article advertising a tower open day didn't tell the whole story. The Mayor[40] was indeed the first visitor to climb the tower, but he was closely followed by the press, who interviewed both him and Francis Moore on the tower roof.

In 1979, the ringers were the butt of an April Fool by the editor, Gordon Kendal.

News from the Parish Organisations – The Bell-ringers at All Saints' have been invited to carry out a ringing tour of the Soviet Union next year. This is the first time that such a tour has been made by ringers from Wokingham, and they will be there for two months. About twenty of the ringers will be going. As there is a shortage of bell-towers in Russia, our ringers plan to take the All Saints' bells with them. "This will present a certain amount of difficulty, because of their weight", explained Mr. Frank Pearson, the foreman of the ringers, "but the parish transport scheme organised by the Stewardship Committee has come to our assistance". The tour begins in Leningrad on 1 April next year, and the ringers wall be active in a total of 23 different cities and towns, finishing on 31 May in Vladivostok, where they will ring a quarter peal before evensong in the parish church. The ringers will be accompanied by representatives of the choir, the Mothers' Union, the Men's Society, the Women's Fellowship and the Sunday school. Leaflets giving full details will be available in church on April the First, or contact Mr. Kendal (780820).

---

[39] He was misled. The lightest bell weighed 5½ cwt.
[40] Peter Johnson, who was also a churchwarden at the time.

'Intruders' – In 1945, in 1968, and again in 1975, Walter Pearce complained about non-ringers entering the belfry. This seems to have been a perpetual hobby-horse of his [6] so the minutes represent just the tips of an iceberg of continual friction. In 1945 he complained of the danger if any one 'interfered with' the bells whilst they were up[41]. In 1968 he said that an accident had been narrowly avoided, and in 1978 he complained about 'too many people being allowed into the belfry without special consent or reasonable excuse' and that 'various organisations had left it in a mess'.

A gallery at the back of the nave is an obvious place where other people will want to do things like sing solos, take photographs, and so on. Access must be controlled during ringing, but it was unreasonable to try to prevent all non-ringing access. A better approach would have been to manage it properly, as is done now, but that was not how Walter saw things.

He was right to be concerned about the danger though. For many years, the bells were always left up, with the ropes hanging temptingly where a non ringer might idly pull one. The obvious solution would have been to lower the bells when not in use and/or to draw the ropes up out of harms way, both of which are now routine, but that solution seems not to have presented itself to him.

His inconsistency on safety emerged in 1978. The new steeple keeper was alarmed to find what looked like a large fishing net between the wall and the bellframe in the bell chamber[42]. When asked about it, Walter explained that a friend used it to catch pigeons. He wanted all the pigeons caught, so they would stop being a nuisance. It's hard to think of anything riskier than wielding a net on a six foot pole while perched on a thin metal frame between upturned bells. One slip would be fatal. And how could anyone believe it would be possible to catch all the pigeons in Wokingham?

7.5 The tower fabric

Bellropes – An intriguing article appeared in the Parish Magazine in October 1953:

> Church Bell Ropes – We had the loan of a Barrel Organ and spent the day on Sat Sept 12th going round the town with it. The grand sum of £17-12-2 was collected. Our thanks are due to the enthusiasm and help of four young Bell Ringers. A special thanks to Mr H Dyer who so nobly pushed the Organ all day.

The author, SM Finch did not ring. Bill Brooks was a church warden at the time, which might explain the involvement of the young ringers. Bell ropes are not cheap, but their repair and periodic replacement are routine activities[43], so it seems odd to have had to mount a special fund raising activity to pay for them.

Rehanging – 'Rehanging' can mean anything from replacing the bearings, to complete replacement of frame and fittings. The work done in 1958 was at the lower end of this scale, with the old plain bearings[44] being replaced with ball bearings. The bells remained in the tower, each being lifted in turn while the new bearing

---

[41] Balanced mouth upwards ready for ringing, and dangerous for anyone not aware of the risk.

[42] Author's personal memory.

[43] Much less so since the advent of pre-stretched polyester top ends for bellropes, which are almost indestructible, but these were not used at All Saints until the 1980s.

[44] See page 21.

assemblies were fitted. The actual bearings are inside closed housings (to keep out the dirt), see Figure 45. They were fitted with greasers, but the need for this is questionable, and using them had the unfortunate side effect of bursting the seals round the gudgeons, so grease used to leak everywhere, some of which can be seen in Figure 45. The white patches are pigeon down sticking to the grease.

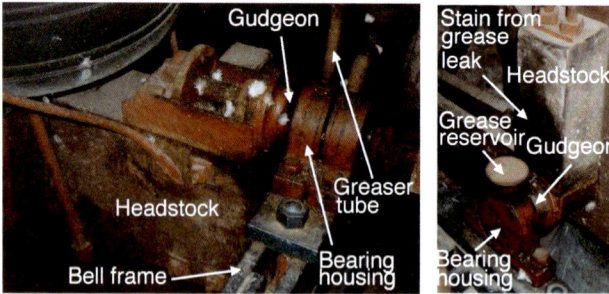

Figure 45: (L) Bearing assembly[45] (bell up), (R)

The new bearings made the bells easier to handle[46], and eliminated the chore of regular lubrication that plain bearings needed. Also a rope guide was installed, which as we saw earlier made the ropes less flighty and the bells easier to ring.

Perhaps the most surprising thing about this restoration is that it seems to have come out of the blue as far as the Parish was concerned. The first mention of it in the Parish magazine was after the work had been done, in a throw-away comment in a recruiting notice[47]. The 1957 AGM minutes mention a report by Mears & Stainbank, and record the Rector saying that the work would be included in the general appeal fund for restoration of the whole church, but we don't know who initiated it. The work cost under £400 – out of a total of around £6000 for the whole church restoration, which included replacing one of the chalk pillars in the nave.

There were two post scripts to this work. The first was in 1965, when the bell hangers were called back to investigate frequent mysterious failure of the 6th rope. Their inspection quickly revealed that there was little mystery. The rope had a tendency to 'flap out'[48] and catch the top of the 7th bearing, as 'proved by demonstration during the visit'. The cure was simple enough – fitting a 'flapping board', shown arrowed in Figure 46 (L), to limit the throw of the rope.

November 1971 saw a more dramatic result of a flying rope. Walter Pearce was teaching a learner to handle a bell, and clearly didn't have everything under control, because somehow the rope caught round one of the rope guide bosses, see Figure 46 (R), and partly ripped the steel bar holding it out of the wall. This was frightening for those present, and the repair cost £77-75[49].

---

[45] The picture actually shows two bearing housings belonging to adjacent bells.

[46] See the story of Eddie Whittingham on page 72.

[47] See page 70.

[48] At the speed a bell wheel rotates, 'centrifugal force' can lift a bell rope a few inches from the wheel, especially if any friction reduces the downward movement of the rope below.

[49] Equivalent to nearly £700 in modern currency

Figure 46: (L) Flapping board to limit throw of 6th's rope, (R) Rope guide

Lighting – In 1974, the ringers discussed the inadequacy of the tower lighting. That was hardly surprising, since at the time there was just a single dim bulb in the ringing chamber and no light at all in the clock room, the bell chamber or the stairs leading up to them. They requested a strip light for the ringing room, but their request got bogged down with the Finance Committee wondering what they really needed, and even questioning whether they needed anything at all! As a result, nothing was done.

Interference – Also in 1974, the ringers were concerned that the inevitable noise caused by tidying up after ringing before services was a distraction to members of the congregation who were preparing themselves for the service. Ringing from a gallery open to the nave helps the ringers to feel part of the church, but it has its drawbacks, of which this was one. The problem was partly solved by putting a carpet on the ringing room floor, but Bill Burkey offered a more radical solution of wrought iron windows[50] that could be swung shut during ringing. They were to be manufactured by the inmates of Long Larton prison, presumably at modest cost. The proposal progressed as far as obtaining a faculty, but then it fell through. As we will see in the next chapter, the problem of the open gallery didn't go away, and became worse.

Handbells – We heard in Chapter 4 of the set of handbells bought for the new Society of Honorary Change Ringers to practise. Their bells were the larger of the two sets still in the tower in 1978[51], where they had no doubt lain unused for many years. When they were brought down for use, both sets were found to be incomplete. It transpired that Walter Pearce had taken home a couple of bells from each set, since he believed that any prospective thief would not steal an incomplete set![52]

7.6 Sharing the load

During this period, the band progressively created more posts to share the tasks of running the tower. The Foreman was the only pre-war ringing officer, but by the end of this period, there were officers responsible for each different aspect of the work.

Secretary – The role of secretary had long since lapsed (probably in 1921, as we saw in previous chapters). At the 1945 AGM it had been 'vacant for a number of years'. Someone wrote the meeting minutes between 1935 and the war, but there is no record of who it was. Examination of the handwriting, suggests that the Foreman probably

---

[50] Presumably the wrought iron was a frame to contain glass, though that wasn't mentioned.
[51] Most were cast by William Blews of Birmingham, who made handbells from about 1865-1880.
[52] Author's personal memory.

wrote them, because when he took the chair in 1951 during the interregnum, and signed the 1950 minutes as chairman, his signature looks very similar.

In 1951 the band elected a secretary, Gwen Crockford. The minutes report no discussion, though one might have expected some reason to be given for creating a new post. Three years later, Mary Cole succeeded Gwen, and held the post for 20 years until 1973, although for much of that time she didn't ring[53]. Since then a further 15 ringers have held the post of secretary.

Deputy Foreman – The post of Deputy Foreman was created at the 1945 meeting, as a role for Walter Pearce after Bill Brooks failed to get him elected to succeed him as Foreman (see below). Walter continued as Deputy Foreman until he became Foreman in 1964. Since then, 19 more ringers have held the post.

Steeple Keeper – This post, initially called Tower Keeper, was first mentioned in 1957, as a combined post with Deputy Foreman, held by Walter Pearce. The minutes don't mention the post again until 1974 when Walter (who had been Foreman for a decade) announced that after 50 years of ringing, it was time to relinquish the role of Steeple Keeper (which he had presumably held unelected for 17 years). Bill Burkey was elected to take over from him, and this gave Bill three simultaneous offices (Deputy Foreman, Treasurer and Steeplekeeper). Since then, a further 11 ringers have held the post of Steeple Keeper.

Treasurer – The role of Treasurer emerged later still. There seem to have been minimal tower funds prior to 1966, and the money was kept in a box in the tower. We know this because the minutes noted that 'the tower box had been opened' to send a contribution of £2-10-0 to the Easthampstead appeal. Wedding fees had been increased, and money was 'mounting up', so the meeting agreed to open an account. That year, Mary Cole acted as Treasurer as well as Secretary, but in 1967 a separate Treasurer was elected. Sheila Cameron did the job until 1970 when Bill Burkey replaced her. The report in the Parish Magazine said that an additional post of Assistant Treasurer had been created[54], and filled by 'Mrs W Burkey'. It was still common to describe women with their husband's initials (though an article about a pantomime a few months earlier called her Jo Burkey) but did Bill really need his wife as an assistant, or was it just a misprint? When Bill stood down from the role in 1979, it was again combined with the post of secretary (until 2001).

Foreman – This key, long-established role, dating from at least 1873 when the Society of Honorary Ringers was founded, was the only post to exist throughout this period. At the end of the war Bill Brooks, then in his late fifties, had already been Foreman for twenty four years. At the first post-war AGM, he clearly thought it was time for a change, and proposed Walter Pearce to succeed him. Walter was 37 at the time, and had been very active training new ringers since the wartime ban was lifted.

But no one was willing to second Walter, so Bill was re-elected to the post. One can see that a hostile bid to oust the incumbent Foreman might have failed out of respect for the current Foreman, but why did the band refuse to support the Foreman's own

---

[53] She said she never rang with the rope guide, which was installed during 1958.
[54] But the minutes don't mention it.

Errata: p 150 – Add "Neil G Curnow 2008-2008" should be "Burlison & Grylls"

p 38 "Burkson & Gryffs" should be "Burlison & Grylls"

p 115, Figure 63 – "Bloundelle" should be "Bloundele"

proposal
been the
was a g
them?
characte
knowlec
an activ
Saints.

Bill ap
respon:
also a (

In 195
succee
clearl}
as a r(
he se(
as Fo
rathei

Bill's
and I
age (
good
fact,

This
duri
exp(
alte

Thi
act'
hac
wa
to\

It
of
m

T
f;
f(
N
c

or? We know that Bill was well liked by the band. He had [a]lmost all of them, and must have been like a father figure. He : true sense of the word. What alternative was he offering itgoing and energetic, but he had an abrasive side to his ne to upset people. Although competent, Walter was a less han Bill. Bill was also a more rounded individual who played vider ringing fraternity, whereas Walter did little outside All eason, the band chose to stay with the Foreman they knew.

delegated teaching learners to Walter, while he retained r aspects of running the tower. For most of this time, he was so he provided a natural link with the church authorities.

year) Bill again asked the band to think about someone to man. He stood down as churchwarden that year too, and was)ut his advancing years. Again the band ignored his request, and ed Foreman until his death in 1964. For his last couple of years en completely absent, with Walter running the tower, and acting it name. The minutes even record a 'Deputy Foreman's report' n's report.

the way for Walter to become Foreman after 19 years as Deputy, : for 16 years. In 1973, he told the AGM that 'he had reached the as quite happy to carry on as Foreman as long as his health was aid he would teach no more ringers because of failing eyesight. In ed almost entirely on his deputy, Francis Moore, to run the tower.

ideal situation, and the band became increasingly unhappy with it ly of the members were recently joined experienced ringers who be properly managed. But no one wanted to offend Walter, so no in was proposed, and Walter was again elected at the 1979 AGM.

head a few months later when an injured back put Francis out of uggled on manfully, but was incapable of running what by that time busy practices. Most of the band were more competent than he /ocal members (in 'The Metropolitan' after practices, not in the to leave unless something was done.

derable trepidation that I approached Walter the following week and im run the ringing. To my surprise and relief, he warmly accepted ninded me sharply that he would stick his oar in when he felt like it.

d. I leant over backwards not to upset Walter, and we rang his d (Oxford Bob Triples) quite often. I remember once, with a tower ringers, I decided we would ring a course of Superlative Surprise <pecting Walter to veto it. But he didn't, and when we finished he s on how nice it sounded.

---

one of the 'Standard 8' Surprise Major methods, and considerably more complex ng than the much simpler methods that Walter was able to ring.

This interim arrangement solved the immediate problem, but was not a permanent solution. A few weeks before the AGM in January 1980, the secretary (David Dewar) posted a notice in the tower with spaces for nominations for officers ahead of the meeting, something that had never been done before. Behind the scenes, the ringers consulted the Rector, who had managed a similar situation with an elderly organist in a previous parish. "Leave it to me. I will talk to Walter." he said.

At the AGM, Walter stood up and read his report in his usual terse style. After covering the year's events, he announced that he had decided to stand down as Foreman, making it very clear that it was his own decision, and nothing to do with the 'nonsense' of putting notices up in the tower.

With the change made, and the load of trying to run the tower lifted from his shoulders, Walter settled happily into the role of being a 'senior citizen'. The band elected him 'Foreman Emeritus for life', and shortly afterwards presented him with a certificate and a gift of a portable radio, see Figure 47. He was absolutely delighted.

The end of an era – Walter was the last of the old guard, and his retirement from office was the end of an era in many ways. It was the culmination of changes that had begun over the previous couple of years, and which laid the ground for the band to develop in new ways over the coming decades. In terms of age, a generation separated Walter from the oldest of the rest of the band. In terms of background, he was almost alone as a craftsman among professionals. In terms of service, he had rung at All Saints for over half a century, whereas most of the others had only arrived or been trained within the previous few years.

Figure 47: End of an era – presentation to Walter Pearce in January 1980
L-R: Terry Scott, Betty Tomlinson, Pam Vassie, Rev Ken Martin, John Harrison, Dave Dewar, Stewart Gibson, Walter Pearce, Pearl Gibson, Bob Chapman, Nellie Pearce, Angela Chapman, Sarah Chapman, Evan Kozakiewicz, Jane Chapman, Simon Tomlinson (half hidden), John Scott.[56]

[56] Picture reproduced courtesy of Wokingham Times

8 The modern era (1980 - 2008)

The years around 1980 saw major change, whose seeds had been sown in the preceding couple of years. A sustained influx of new members[1] over a few years had a transforming effect, and within a short time the band had been almost completely renewed. By 1982, the only remaining members of the pre-1977 band were Walter Pearce, and his wife Nellie, neither of whom rang any more. The active band grew quickly to around two dozen ringers, of whom just under half had come to Wokingham as experienced ringers, with the rest being locally trained during those few years. For all practical purposes, it was a new band. and it was exciting to belong to one whose numbers and capability were rapidly growing.

The events of the early 1980s set the scene for the next couple of decades, with the band's goals neatly summed up by the newly elected Foreman in 1980:

'Good striking, Good atmosphere, Good methods'.

The brave new world had its down side though. The new band had little collective memory of its history, or of how things were done before. It was so excited by the future, that it overlooked the past. For example, Vera Robinson had died in 1979, just as the new band was emerging, and although the band rang a half muffled quarter peal in her memory on 4th September that year, few of the incoming ringers had any idea of who she was. In Chapter 6 we saw that she was one of Wokingham's first women ringers, and the first Wokingham woman to ring a peal. Through her father, she was our last link to the genesis of the modern ringing era. Through her own life, she had made a considerable impact in the Parish. Her passing ought to have been a major landmark for the ringers, but for most of us it wasn't.

Nevertheless, the band prospered, and the next quarter century was a full one. There were more changes, but none as dramatic as in those few years around 1980.

8.1 The band

Growth – The number of ringers doubled between 1976 and 1985, from a low point of 16 to a high of 33, all of whom were new, as noted above. Numbers subsequently fell back, with another peak in the late 1990s, and a slight rising trend after 2000.

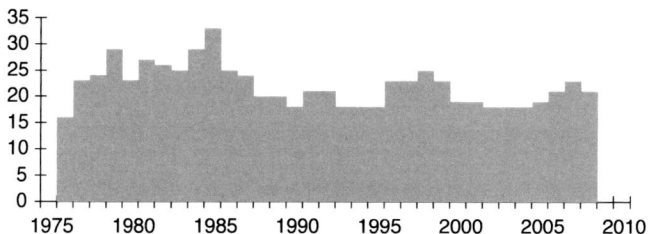

Figure 48: Membership

---

[1] By coincidence, I joined the band in the summer of 1977, at the start of this influx. I had rung briefly at All Saints in the late 1960s, but not become a member, and hardly rung at all during the intervening decade. I remember vividly those first few weeks in the summer of 1977, and the contrast with what followed.

Figure 49: Some of the band in 1983 (clockwise) Richard Woodward, Phillipa Moon, Alex Nelson, Eve Reader, John Scott, Sheila Williams, Louise Clements, Martin Layley, Pearl Gibson, Stewart Gibson[2]

Training – Eleven new ringers had already been trained in 1978 and 1979 mostly in ones and twos, but in 1980 the training machine went into mass production. Seven recruits were trained in 1980, all of whom went on to be elected members in 1981, though three of them only lasted a year. A further six were trained in 1982, of whom five became members. A similar number followed the next year, and another six in 1986. Of around two dozen people trained, about half continued to ring, a few moved away, and the rest gave up within a couple of years. That is fair record compared with ringing in general.

The pace of training reduced in the 1990s. Most ringers were trained one or two at a time, and most of them (17) went on to become members, but as before, about half gave up after a year or so. Fewer ringers have been trained in recent years, and it is notable that of the seven local trainees to become members after 1998, five were the children or god-children of members of the band.

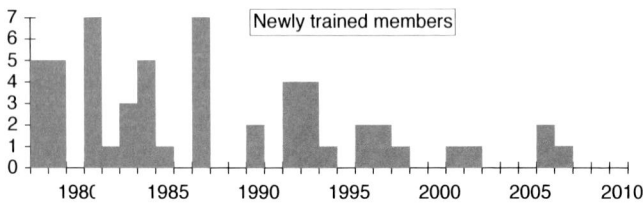

Figure 50: Newly trained members

Officers – In the previous period, the band had increased the number of officers to Foreman, Deputy Foreman, Secretary/Treasurer and Steeplekeeper. These were incorporated into the 1990 rules[3], with only small changes since then. In 2001, Secretary and Treasurer were split, and in 2008 the post of Ringing Master (responsible for running the ringing, as distinct from tower management) was

---

[2] Picture reproduced courtesy of Wokingham Times
[3] See Annex C.

separated from Foreman. At the 1985 AGM, a 'non-executive' role of archivist was proposed, reflecting the amount of material that the band was accumulating for its scrap books (begun in 1978). After some discussion about whether the secretary ought to do the job, the archivist role was agreed, but on an unofficial basis. The post has been held at various times by: Christine Roper, Eve Reader and Jane Mellor.

In 1980 the band adopted a rule that officers would not normally serve for more than three years in the same post. This was motivated by a desire to avoid the situation where someone gets 'locked into' a role, as seemed to have happened in the past. It was just another way that the band felt the need to modernise itself, and with the change made just after Walter Pearce stepped down as Foreman, there was no sense that it was intended to remove anyone from office.

Figure 51 shows the considerable diversity of office holders since 1980. No fewer than twenty three separate people held one or other post at some time during this period, that is one in three of all members who rang here for more than a year.

In fact, with more ringers, and with more activity, very few ringers who took office even did a full three year stint, and those that did were generally happy to stand down when their turn came. In only four cases, has the band invoked the 'normally' clause to override the restriction when no obvious successor was willing to take a post. Julie Branson (now Goodchild) was secretary for four years from 1990-1993, Arthur Moss was steeple keeper for ten years from 1996-2006, Stephen Smith was Deputy Foreman for four years from 2003-2006, and John Harrison was Foreman for ten+ years from 1999-2008+.

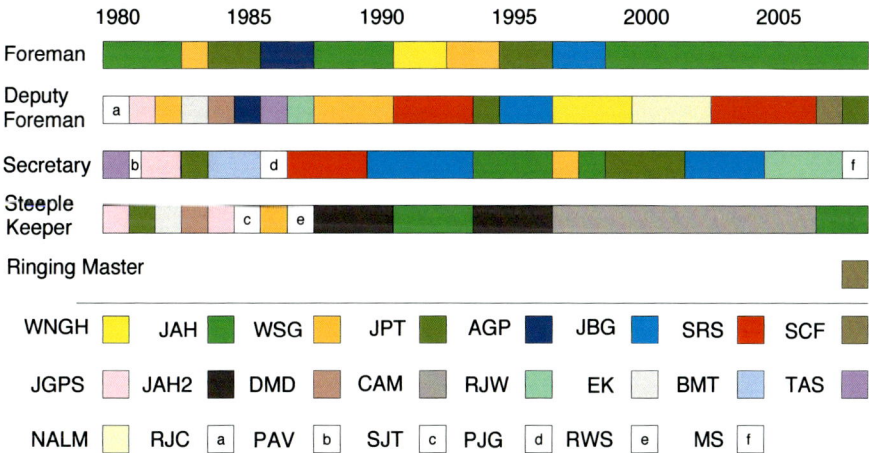

Figure 51: Diversity of office holders since 1980

There is a list of all known officers from 1880 on pages 136 and 138.

8.2 Notable ringers

Six people served as Foreman, with ten changes in twenty nine years, compared with just four changes in the previous hundred years.

Stewart Gibson was Foreman in 1983 (the shortest term apart from Fred Mattingley in 1920) and from 1993-94. He served four years as Deputy, and a year as Secretary. He learned to ring at Boyne Hill, Maidenhead after meeting his wife Pearl who was a ringer, and he served two years there as Tower Captain. From 1971 to 1977, he was Tower Captain at Morpeth, Northumberland, where he and Pearl re-established change ringing after a long period of only chiming and curfew ringing. He joined All Saints in 1978. He was at times Sonning Deanery Deputy Ringing Master, Vice Chairman and Chairman, and he and Pearl represented the Deanery in the ODG General Committee from 1995-97. After retirement, he moved to Fladbury, Worcestershire. From 2002 he was Peal Secretary of the Worcestershire and Districts Change Ringing Association. He died in January 2008.

Julie Goodchild (nee Branson) was All Saints first woman to become Foreman. She was also the only home-grown Foreman to serve in the modern era. She learnt to ring at All Saints in 1986 while still at school, and has rung here ever since, apart from a break for university where she rang with both the York University Society and the York Colleges Guild, serving as secretary of both. After graduating, she became Tower Secretary from 1990-1993 and a few years later was elected Foreman, from 1997-1998. Her husband was not a ringer when he met her, but learnt to ring soon afterwards. Julie is a chartered accountant by profession.

John Harrison grew up in Kirkby-in-Ashfield, Nottinghamshire (then with a 5-bell tower) where he learnt to ring in 1959. He was tower captain briefly before studying and ringing for three years in Cambridge. He married and moved to Wokingham in 1967, and despite having been extremely active up to that point, gave up regular ringing soon afterwards until summer 1977. Since then he has rung continually at All Saints. He was Foreman from 1980-82, 1988-90, and 1999-2008+ and has held most other tower offices in between. He is a member of the Central Council of Church Bellringers (1989-2008+) and chaired its Education Committee from 2000-2007. Locally he is Training Co-ordinator for Sonning Deanery. As '*Tail End*' he wrote a monthly column on training in *The Ringing World* from 1999-2007. He has written seven books on ringing, as well as producing other training aids. He received a Civic Award from the Mayor of Wokingham in 2006 for services to the community through bellringing. John is a Chartered Engineer and a Registered Ergonomist.

Nigel Herriott learnt to ring at Wonston near Winchester during his final year at school, and he subsequently rang at Winchester Cathedral. His ringing developed rapidly at Oxford University, particularly under the influence of David Brown. He rang his first peal and over 100 more while there, and served as the Oxford University Society's steeplekeeper. He moved to Birmingham, where he became a proficient 12-bell ringer, and then to Warwick, where he was tower captain. During his captaincy he developed the band's 10-bell method ringing repertoire and conducted the Warwick band in the national 12-bell striking competition. He moved to Wokingham in 1990 and served as Foreman from 1991-92. He devised Wokingham Surprise Major[4]. Nigel is a Chartered IT Professional, a Freeman of Berwick-upon-Tweed, and a member of the Ancient Society of College Youths.

Tony Pullan learnt to ring at Whitchurch in Devon, and rang at Windsor before moving to Wokingham. Although he only lived here for five years, he played a very active role in developing the band. He was Foreman in 1986-1987, having served as Deputy Foreman the previous year. He and Jon Tutcher between them led the band though its years of peak performance. Tony is seen here holding the trophy for the Guild 8-bell striking competition in May 1986. Tony was as active outside the tower as within. He was secretary of East Berks & South Bucks Branch from 1981-1983 and General Secretary of the Oxford Diocesan Guild from 1984-1988. When he married, he moved to Wanborough, Wiltshire, where he played an active role in getting the bells restored some years later. Tony is a member of the Ancient Society of College Youths.

Jon Tutcher was All Saints' youngest Foreman since Albert Hill in 1880 – he was 28 when first elected to the office, not quite as young as Albert who was only 24. Like Albert, Jon came from the West Country (Somerset not Wiltshire). He learnt to ring in 1967 at Ilminster (a heavy eight) 'on a diet of Grandsire Triples and call changes'. He studied at London University where he rang for a couple of years as a member of the University of London Society of Change Ringers. Jon moved to Wokingham in 1977 and started ringing with the Wokingham All Saints band in 1979, becoming a member in 1980. He was Foreman in 1984-85 and 1995-96, and has held every Tower Office at one time or another. Jon is a Chartered Engineer.

---

[4] A new method, rung in the peal for the church's 800th anniversary – see page 105.

Others who made significant contributions to ringing or the church outside All Saints:

Elizabeth Barter (Liz) rang in Wokingham between 1998 and 2006. From 1999-2001 she was also Director of Music, thus ensuring good lines of communication between ringers and choir, something not always easy to achieve[5].

Pearl Gibson rang at All Saints from 1978-1999, and was secretary in 1986. She was Branch representative to the Oxford Diocesan Guild from 1985-87, and is currently secretary of the Southern Branch of the Worcester & District Association.

Charles Herriott learnt to ring at All Saints aged 9. He served as Master of the University of London Society of Change Ringers in 2006-7.

Theresa Scott (Terry) rang at All Saints from 1978-1992. She was secretary in 1980 and Deputy Foreman in 1986. After leaving Wokingham she was ordained priest. From 1994-2001 she was at Drayton, Oxfordshire, following in the eminent footsteps of Rev. FE Robinson, who we met in Chapters 4 and 5. In 2005, Terry became Area Dean of Maidenhead, and an Honorary Canon of Christchurch Cathedral Oxford. In 2008 she moved to become Team Rector of Bicester.

Andrew Smith (Andy) learnt to ring at All Saints in his teens, and while at Cambridge University served as Assistant Master of the Cambridge University Guild.

Simon Tomlinson learnt to ring at All Saints in his teens (along with his mother). He served as Master of the University of Bristol Society of Change Ringers from 1986-1987, and called his first peal (appropriately of Bristol Surprise Major) on the eve of his 21st birthday. He went on to become Ringing Master at Christ Church and All Saints in Bristol, and later deputy ringing master at Westbury-on-Trym.

John Wells came to Wokingham as an experienced ringer, and rang here from 1986-1987, before returning to the Reading area. He called the 1990 peal of Wokingham Surprise Major[6]. He subsequently became first the Secretary (from 1991-1996) and then the Master (from 1996-2002) of the Oxford Diocesan Guild of Church Bellringers. He then chaired the Guild's Education committee for six years.

8.3 The ringing

From the low point in the late 1970s, things could only improve, and they rapidly did. In 1977 the band had been struggling. It had a limited method repertoire, poor striking, and relied on ringers from St Paul's to make up the numbers on Sunday mornings. With the influx of new ringers, the band quickly expanded its repertoire, and achieved higher standards of performance. Inevitably there was some waning and waxing after the initial peak in the 1980s, but even through the lean times, the repertoire remained much broader than it appears to have been in former years.

Common sense prevails – Chapter 7 ended with the band still ringing for the mid-morning service, rather than the much more popular one at 9-30, which most ringers attended anyway. That clearly didn't make sense, and in 1980 morning ringing moved to 9-00, for the 9-30 service. The move deprived the few parishioners who

---

[5] See page 116.
[6] See page 105.

attended the later service of hearing the bells, so it was agreed to ring for Matins on major festivals. That didn't last long though. By 1982 it was only done at Easter and Christmas, and in 1984 it stopped altogether.

Stretching times and shrinking times – Half an hour had always been long enough to ring for services, but with growing numbers in the early 1980s, people became dissatisfied because everyone couldn't get a fair turn, especially on Sunday mornings. In 1981 the band discussed starting earlier but decided not to change because of recent complaints about ringing from local residents. The problem didn't go away, and it came up again two years later, after the sound control had been installed. The sound level on practice nights was reduced, and complaints had stopped. There was 'heated discussion' of a proposal to start ringing at 8-45, and the eventual compromise was an 8-50 start, with evening ringing also changing to 5-50.

But no sooner had the ringers gained extra time at the start of ringing, than they lost it at the finish. The Musical Director wanted a period to play the organ before the service. With an open gallery, ringing and organ playing don't mix, and he wanted the ringing to stop early. The Worship Planning Committee arbitrated on the dispute, and ruled that ringing should finish five minutes before the services, ie at 9-25 and at 6-25. Some years later the organ rarely used the five minutes. The Foreman and (a different) Musical Director agreed to end ringing three minutes before the service. This lasted until 1998, when (yet another) Musical Director decided that three minutes was not enough, and the five minute rule was re-introduced.

Baptisms – voting with their feet – The idea of ringing for the monthly Sunday afternoon baptisms was first mooted in 1983, and began in 1986 with the concession of no evening ringing on the same day. The following year the Foreman reported that 'changes to baptism services had caused planning difficulties', but that 'Sunday evening services were now supported by the learners'. The planning difficulties probably relate to uncertainty over which weeks had baptisms, but the comment about learners supporting evensong ringing seems a little premature, since the first record of evening ringing on a baptism day was in March 1987, two months after the AGM at which the statement was made. The band rang for ten baptisms that year, and the Foreman again expressed concern about manning them. In the ensuing discussion people complained that afternoon ringing was inconvenient, but most of them recognised the value of ringing for baptisms, which were well attended by non-churchgoers, to whom the church wanted to extend a particular welcome. So the debate hinged on whether to ring for evensong as well. In fact, there was no evening ringing at all on two of the ten Sundays with baptisms in 1987.

The following year, the Foreman reported a 'continuing policy of trying to ring for all baptism services', and then the topic slipped quietly off the agenda for a decade. At the 1998 AGM, the Foreman reported that the number of baptisms they had rung for had 'fallen from 11 to 7'. Discussion of a written motion produced pleas of hardship from many present, a repetition of why it was worth doing, and a comment by the Rector that it was not reasonable to expect ringers to turn out, but that if it was feasible then they should ring. People were thanked for airing their views, but there was no conclusion. There followed an equally inconclusive discussion in 1999. In

2000 the Foreman reported trying to raise a band for all baptisms, but failing to do so for any. The ringers had voted with their feet to drop an innovation that the much stronger band of the mid 1980s had willingly introduced.

The vexed question of Holy Week – Ringing in Holy Week is a topic of perennial discussion among ringers. Holy Week is the Church's most solemn period, with many extra services during the week, and several on Good Friday. Ringers respond by foregoing their weekly practice. One might also expect them to make an effort to ring for the extra services, and to mark Good Friday with half muffled ringing[7]. In some places this happens, but in others, including much of the Oxford Diocese, there is a tradition of no ringing at all during Holy Week. The subject was raised at the 1982 AGM, but the Rector 'wished to continue the tradition of not ringing during Holy Week rather than change to half muffled ringing on Good Friday'.

Time to practise – With more trainees coming on stream, the band needed more practice time. It inherited the widespread custom of a 7-30 to 9-00pm practice (on Monday). The band had already reclaimed bank holiday Mondays for practice (in 1978)[8], but they wanted more. After sound control shutters were installed in spring 1982, they extend practices until 9-30pm, which would have been unthinkable before. The extra 33% proved valuable, but the band still wanted more, especially for the learners (who paradoxically get less ringing than more experienced ringers because to make the ringing stable round them, only a few of them can ring at once).

In 1984, the band began holding occasional extra practices on Thursday, with either basic ringing for learners or quarter peals to give the more advanced ringers sustained ringing. By 1985, Thursday had become a regular ringing evening, and it remained so for several years. When numbers declined steeply in the late 1980s, Thursday practices were harder to sustain. The Rector suggested releasing Thursdays for other use in 1988, but the band was reluctant to abandon them. For a couple more years the band used them to teach bell handling, and there were occasional Thursday practices in the mid 1990s, but they disappeared around the turn of the century.

Practice time was on the agenda at the 1996 AGM, but for a different reason. Ringers were turning up late. Practices rarely began at 7-30, and sometimes were as late as 7-50. One person (presumably a late-comer) justified it on the grounds that people might be 'concerned they might have to wait outside if the key holder is late'. All four officers had keys, and it seems unlikely that they were all regularly late. But an extra basic set of keys was provided to be held by someone who would be sure to be on time. Punctuality hardly improved, and practices still began late.

The officers resisted the suggestion of a later start, on the grounds that people would probably just come later than the new time, making the practice shorter still. In 2000, the start time was moved to 7.45, and as predicted, the lateness moved to a later baseline with practices still starting around ten minutes late. A few years afterwards the time moved again, to 8.00. So the band was back with the hour and a half weekly practice that it had sought so hard to extend a couple of decades earlier.

---

[7] As rung for funerals, Remembrance Day, and other sombre occasions.

[8] In later years, too few people were available on bank holidays, so practices were dropped again.

Who's in charge? – In 2001 the band introduced a rota for running practices. This idea emerged from a discussion about the growth of the Foreman's responsibilities, and the difficulty of finding volunteers to take on the role. The rota did share some of the responsibility, and provided considerable variety of style, but at the cost of coherent development. It was dropped in 2007, when Simon Farrar took over running the ringing. A year later, the band created a separate post of Ringing Master.

Mutual support – 2000 saw the introduction of special Surprise Major practices every other month. The aim was to invite visitors from the Branch for mutual benefit, and to be able to ring more advanced methods than would otherwise be possible. This meant a third of the band (who didn't ring Surprise) lost a practice. At first, other events were organised for them, but after a while they lost interest and just took an evening off. The Surprise practices were discontinued in 2007.

Quarter peals – Quarter peal ringing flourished, with over 400 rung, an average of nearly 14 per year – ten times the average of under 1.5 per year from 1966[9]-1978.

Many quarters were rung for services, normally on Sunday evening but also weekday services like Christmas Eve, All Saints Day and Ash Wednesday. Many other performances marked weddings, births, national events and so on. There were several in 1980 to mark the centenary of the foundation of the Sonning Deanery Society, and more in 1981 for the centenary of the Oxford Diocesan Guild.

Some quarter peals didn't commemorate anything, but were just rung for enjoyment and skill development. 40-50 minutes of settled ringing on the same bell permits a level of concentration and refinement that is hard to achieve with the usual stop-start, 5-10 minute touches of a typical general practice or service ringing.

It is interesting to look at the days of the week when quarter peals were rung, shown in Figure 52. Sunday performances (shown orange) appear throughout, and give a crude indication of which were rung for services (an under estimate, because of mid week services). Of the other days, Thursdays stand out as a regular ringing evening during the late 1980s and early 1990s.

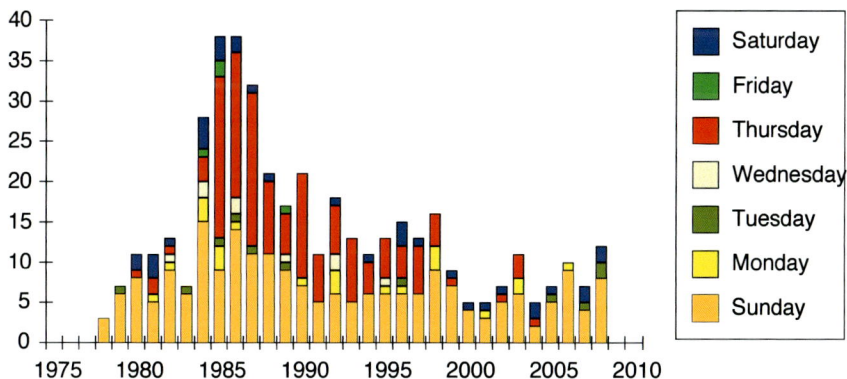

Figure 52: Quarter peal activity during this period

---

[9] AJ Buswell's quarter peal analysis goes back to 1966. Prior to that there are no indexes or lists.

During the mid 1980s peak, when All Saints was the leading quarter peal tower in Berkshire, over a third (28 out of 76 performances in 1985 and 1986) were rung on Thursday. Regular Thursday quarter peals disappeared after 2000. The three Thursday performances in 2003 included one to mark the enthronement of the Archbishop of Canterbury and two training quarters – Charlotte Kozakiewicz's first quarter peal, and then her first inside[10].

What the band rang was very different from what they rang in earlier periods. Over half of the performances were of 8-bell methods (Major) compared with only 10% in the previous period. The band rang more varied methods as well, with over a third of quarters being of Surprise methods[11]. Figure 53 shows the overall breakdown.

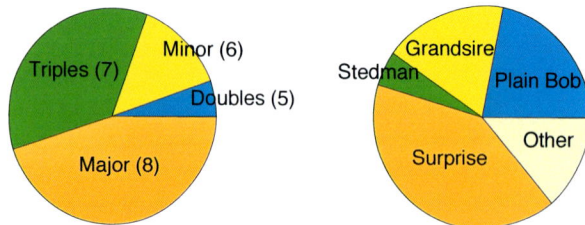

Figure 53: Quarter peals (L) number of working bells, (R) methods rung

Date touches – A date touch is a performance with as many rows as the year in which it is rung. Ringing date touches is a minority activity, and even bands that ring them tend only to do so at New Year. John Harrison had rung and composed several in his youth, and introduced the idea to All Saints. The first was rung on New Year's day in 1984, and eleven more have been rung since. 1984 was a good year to start, because it is divisible by 32 (the number of rows in a lead of a Surprise Major method). The lengths needed for other years can be more awkward to achieve, and generally needed unusual mixes of different types of method, see Table 11.

Date	Year	Length	Method(s)
1 Jan	1984	1984	Yorkshire Surprise Major
18 Jul	1985	1985	Plain Bob Major
31 Dec	1985	1985	Plain Bob Major
31 Dec	1986	1986	Yorkshire Surprise Major
1 Jan	1987	1987	Original & Plain Bob Major
1 Jan	1989	1989	Plain Bob, Reverse Canterbury & Original Major
1 Jan	1991	1991	Plain Bob Major & Grandsire Triples
1 Jan	1992	1992	Little Bob Major
1 Jan	1996	1996	Yorkshire Surprise & Gainsborough Little Bob Major
30 Jan	1999	1999	Yorkshire Major & Plain Bob Triples
1 Jan	2004	2004	Plain Bob & Bastow Little Bob Major
10 Jul	2005	1945*	Grandsire Triples (* 'backdated')
17 Jan	2006	1881*	Plain and Little Bob Major (* 'backdated')
1 Jan	2008	2008	Plain & Little Bob Major

Table 11: Date touches rung at All Saints, Wokingham

---

[10] Ringing a fully working bell, rather than the Treble, which rings a simpler path.

[11] A class of method more complex and challenging to ring, aspired to by many ringers.

Stretching the concept further, in July 2005 and in January 2006, there were two non-standard date touches to mark anniversaries of historic events, with the length 'back dated' to match the original event. The first (of 1945 rows) marked 60 years since the end of the war in 1945, and the second (of 1881 rows) marked 125 years since the founding of the Oxford Diocesan Guild of Church Bellringers in 1881.

Peals – Peal ringing also revived after 1980, with a total of 43 rung in under thirty years, well over half of all the peals ever rung at All Saints. More significantly, two thirds of them included local ringers, reflecting the strength of the modern band.

St Mary, Hurst, Berks			
On Saturday 14th June 1980, in 2 hours 52 minutes.			
5056 Plain Bob Major			
Sheila M Williams	Treble	*John GP Scott	5
*Sarah L Chapman	2	Robert J Chapman	6
§Theresa A Scott	3	§Melvyn J Freeman	7
*Ian LT Barber	4	John A Harrison	Tenor
Conducted by John A Harrison			
* First peal, § First of Major			

Figure 54: The first peal by a Wokingham band for half a century

The first peal by the modern band was in June 1980 at Hurst (so as not to inflame the noise complaints in Wokingham[12]). It was the first peal for three of the band, and the first of Major for two more. It echoed the first peal by the band after World War 1, also at Hurst, which also including many personal firsts.

The first peal at All Saints since the 1960s was in June 1982, after installing the sound control. Another first, in 1990 for the Church's 800th anniversary, was the first peal ever of Wokingham Surprise Major. No such method had been named[13], so Nigel Herriott searched among un-named methods for a fairly musical one, within the band's capability. They rang a quarter peal of it the previous week, and then the peal on 4th November, at the conclusion of a ten day long festival in the Parish.

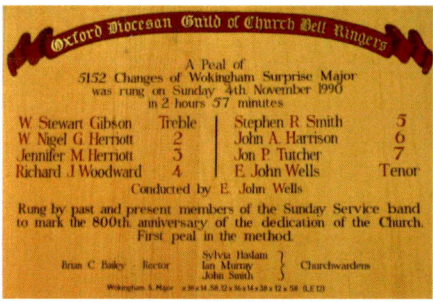

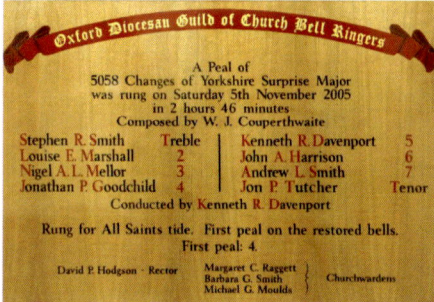

Figure 55: Peal boards: (L) 800th anniversary (R) First on the restored bells

---

[12] See page 122.

[13] A few years earlier the name 'Wokingham' was used in a controversial multi-method peal that was disallowed by the Central Council of Church Bellringers, thus freeing the name again.

Unsuccessful peal attempts don't normally find their way into the record books, but one is worthy of mention. 9th August 2006 was the centenary of FE Robinson's 1000th peal, and to celebrate this momentous achievement[14] another peal was planned at All Saints, using the same composition that he called in 1906. Sadly it was unsuccessful, but the band rang a quarter peal instead. An earlier peal in February 1990, 80 years after FE Robinson's death, was successful. Figure 56 shows the ringers on both occasions by his grave (incomplete in the case of the 1990 band).

Figure 56: Bands that rang in memory of FE Robinson, by his grave:
(L) 80 years after his death: John Harrison, Peter GC Ellis, Geoff Dodd,
Steve Smith II, Helen Piper, (R) 100 years after his 1000th peal: Anthea Edwards,
John Harrison, Philip Saddleton, Nigel Mellor, Ken Davenport, Jonathan Goodchild,
Andy Smith, Steve Smith I

In Chapter 5 we saw that a band rang peals at both Wokingham towers on the same day in 1912. That feat was repeated nearly a century later on 10th May 2008, this time by a local band, see Figure 57. Neil Curnow, John Harrison, Nigel Mellor, and Jon Tutcher are All Saints ringers. Chris Cole, Geoff Cooke and Ken Davenport, are St Paul's ringers. Richard Johnston, from Yateley, rings regularly at both towers. A few months later, a Reading band (including four ex All Saints ringers) did it again.

Figure 57: Twin peal band (back) Geoff Cooke, Neil Curnow, John Harrison,
Richard Johnston (front) Nigel Mellor, Jon Tutcher, Ken Davenport, Chris Cole

---

[14] He was the first person ever to ring 1000 peals, see pages 53-56.

Table 12 lists all peals since 1980 that had a specific dedication[15]. All Saints' complete peal ringing history is covered in Chapter 9.

Date	Method	Dedication
26 Jun 1982	Plain Bob Major	Birth of Prince William
18 Sep 1982	Stedman Triples	In Memoriam FE Robinson
1 Feb 1986	Yorkshire Surprise Major	Christening Jennifer Elise Field
23 Jun 1986	Yorkshire Surprise Major	Wedding of Prince Andrew & Sarah Ferguson
6 Apr 1986	Cambridge Surprise Major	Silver wedding of Pearl & Stewart Gibson
31 Jan 1987	Rutland Surprise Major	Tower dinner day
12 Apr 1987	Cambridge Surprise Major	Marriage of Louise Clements to Mike Cole
6 Feb 1988	New Cambridge Surprise Major	Tower dinner day
4 Feb 1989	Amsterdam Surprise Major	Tower dinner day
15 Apr 1989	Vale of the White Horse Surprise Major	Marriage of Tony Pullan to Nicola Jones[16]
18 Feb 1990	Stedman Triples	80th anniversary of FE Robinson's funeral
4 Nov 1990	Wokingham Surprise Major	800th anniversary of dedication of the Church
26 Jan 1991	Yorkshire Surprise Major	Tower dinner day
25 Jan 1992	Superlative Surprise Major	Tower dinner day
30 Jan 1993	Cambridge Surprise Major	Tower dinner day
29 Jan 1994	Spliced Surprise Major	Tower dinner day
17 Apr 1994	Yorkshire Surprise Major	Ordination of Catherine Dyer and Theresa Scott
15 May 1994	Rutland Surprise Major	Wedding of Jonathan Goodchild & Julie Branson
27 Jan 1996	Double Norwich Court Bob Major	Tower dinner day
12 Apr 1997	Pudsey[17] Surprise Major	Induction of Rev. David Hodgson as Rector
5 Oct 1997	Yorkshire Surprise Major	Ordination of Colin James
31 Jan 1998	London Surprise Major	Tower dinner day
29 Jan 2000	Superlative Surprise Major	Tower dinner day
5 Nov 2005	Yorkshire Surprise Major	First on the restored bells, for All Saints tide
7 Jul 2007	Yorkshire Surprise Major	Ruby wedding of John & Anne Harrison
1 Nov 2008	Yorkshire Surprise Major	All Saints Day

Table 12: Notable peal dedications, 1980 - 2008

Striking competitions – Modern striking competitions have come a long way since those organised by Wokingham's 18th century inn keepers. Now as then, the aim is to ring with a perfectly even rhythm, and now, even more so than then, teams compete mainly for the honour of winning. But there the similarity ends. Modern competitions are run by the ringing societies[18], and not by commercially motivated outsiders. Almost all competitions[19] are for change ringing, though many local competitions allow inexperienced bands to ring rounds or call changes[20].

---

[15] The seventeen peals with no specific dedication are not included here.

[16] Nicola grew up in the Vale of the White Horse, at Stanford in the Vale, where she was a ringer.

[17] The method was chosen because the Rector grew up in Pudsey.

[18] Mostly set up in the late 1800s to promote improved standards in ringing, see Chapter 4.

[19] Apart from some in Devon and Cornwall.

[20] Periodic changes, called by the conductor, rather than continual changes.

Modern competitions have a much lower public profile than their 18th century predecessors, and are rarely publicised. People passing by can hear the ringing, but they are unlikely to take much notice of it, or of the groups of ringers in the churchyard, chatting or listening carefully to the bells.

Sonning Deanery Branch ran its first annual 6-bell competition in 1961, and added an 8-bell competition in 1975. The first suggestion that All Saints should enter a team was during the period covered in the previous chapter. Bill Parker, a former Branch Ringing Master who had just joined the band, suggested it at the 1967 AGM. Four years later (after Bill had moved on) Mary Cole made the same suggestion, but they never entered a team [6] until many years later.

All Saints' first entry was in April 1979, in the 6-bell contest. Four of the six ringers in the team had recently joined the band. The team that rang in the 8-bell competition that September, was all 'new' members. Every year since then, All Saints has entered both Branch striking competitions[21], with more than one team quite often during the high membership 1980s. Performance was not impressive at first, but it improved. In 1982, when the team came second in the 8-bell competition, the judge commended them as 'one of the few teams with a good basic rhythm'.

The first win came in the 1984 8-bell competition. This was held at All Saints, and had it been a one-off, it might have been put down to familiarity with the bells, but the same year the band entered the Guild 8-bell competition, and won against stiff opposition on the difficult bells at Olney in North Bucks. Had they not won, the day would have had a really miserable ending. They rang late in the running order, and when they went into the hall for tea while awaiting the results, all the sandwiches had gone and there was only one piece of cake between eight of them. Victory assuaged their hunger though, until a meal at an inn on the way back, where they made excited calls home with the good news (this was before the advent of mobile phones).

Far from being one-off events, these performances began a run. The band won the next Branch 6-bell competition, and so went on to represent the Branch in the Guild 6-bell competition at Radley. Here they faced a far higher standard of ringing, and came a creditable 3rd by the tiniest of margins – 7½ faults[22] against the winner's 6.

For a few years, success became the norm, with the band expecting to win every competition entered. They developed a routine – a team practice a few days before, and then one on the morning of the competition. Most Guild competitions involved travelling some way, so they booked a practice tower en-route, and had a picnic lunch together (no alcohol before the contest). The team spirit went even further when they wore team T-shirts, with a design by Pearl Gibson, based on the lion motif, as used by Roger Landen at the Wokingham bellfoundry, see Figure 58(R).

---

[21] Except 2003, when the Branch didn't hold an 8-bell competition.

[22] Most striking competitions are scored by counting the number of 'faults', ie deviations from the ideal, perfectly even rhythm, so the team with the fewest faults wins. These scores show the standard. Each team rang about 270 rows, each of which could potentially have gained one or more faults if not rung perfectly.

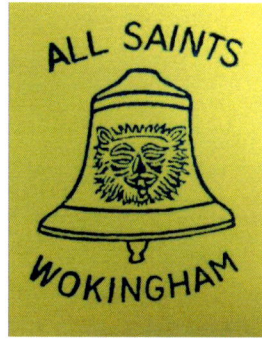

Figure 58: (L) The winning 8-bell team May 1986[23], (L-R) Sheila Williams, Terry Scott, Stewart Gibson, John Harrison, Tony Pullan, Jon Tutcher, John Wells, Steve Smith II, (R) Team logo on T-shirt worn for some competitions

Success couldn't last forever. The first failure came in the Guild 6-bell competition at North Leigh in October 1987. The team easily qualified for the final, and confidently began the test piece. But a minor trip a couple of minutes in, and a collective lapse of concentration, quickly led to a major 'pile up'. The conductor decided not to go on, and stopped the ringing. This was a controversial decision to say the least, with accusations of being unsportsmanlike, and 'only playing to win'. It was a bitter blow to the team members, but perhaps a salutary experience, since they had begun to consider themselves invincible.

At the Guild 8-bell competition at Quainton the following year, the bells were rung from the ground floor, and were difficult to hear. The team never got into its stride, and only came third. The band had one final moment of glory later that year, in the Guild 6-bell competition at Bradwell (appropriately in North Bucks, where the winning streak had begun). The team won by a clear margin, ringing Norwich Surprise Minor[24].

After that, All Saints never won a Guild competition. The team only won the Branch 6-bell competition 6 years out of 18, and so rarely earned the chance to compete in the Guild 6-bell competition[25]. For most of the period the band could not raise a team to enter the Guild 8-bell competition either, but All Saints ringers formed the core of a Sonning Deanery team for a few years[26].

Figure 59 graphically portrays the rise and fall of All Saints performance in both Guild and Branch competitions. It only shows placings in first, second or third (and Hon Mentions in the most recent Guild competitions[27]), and does not show those where All Saints was unplaced.

---

[23] Picture reproduced courtesy of Wokingham Times

[24] A more musical, but less conventional method than those rung by the other teams.

[25] The Guild 6-bell competition is limted to towers representing their branches. In Sonning Deanery the winner of the Branch competition.

[26] The Guild 8-bell competition is open to any tower or branch team.

[27] The Guild introduced Hon Mentions in 2004.

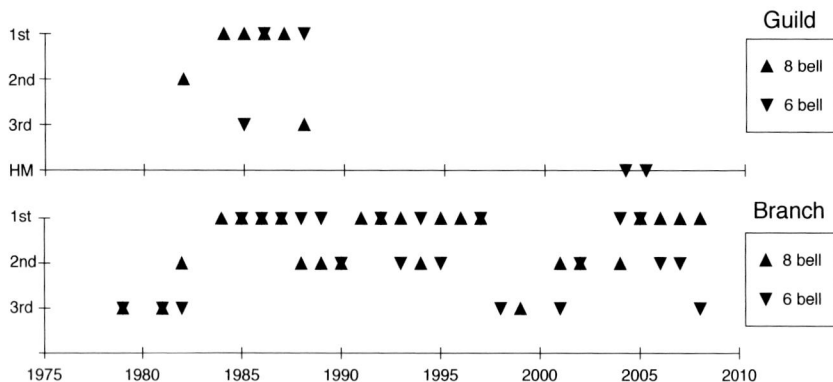

Figure 59: All Saints placing in Branch and Guild striking competitions, 1978-2008

The band entered other competitions, notably in 1988, when an All Saints team represented the Oxford Diocesan Guild in the 10-bell competition for the Tewkesbury Shield. It came an honourable second to Coventry, which was a crack band. When they heard about the Richmond Festival ringing competition, All Saints entered it, from 1988 to 1993. This was unlike most ringing competitions. The festival was for the performing arts (singing, playing, dancing, etc) but it also included a bellringing section with three classes: change ringing on tower bells, change ringing on handbells and tune ringing on handbells. The Wokingham team won the tower bell section every year that it entered (though in the later years, it was more a 'Wokingham & friends' team). Several times they also put a team (1 All Saints + 3 friends) in the handbell change ringing section, which they won in 1990. The All Saints (tune ringing) handbell group[28] also competed up to 1995, and often won, but All Saints never managed the hat trick with a win in all three classes in the same year.

Wokingham and Sonning Deanery – Having described the band's success in competitions, it is appropriate to reflect on the band's more general relationship with the local ringing community. We saw in Chapter 4 that Wokingham played a key role in the formation and early years of the Sonning Deanery Society of Change Ringers, and as late as 1970, Branch[29] AGMs were held in Wokingham (alternately at the two churches). We might expect that the invigorated modern band at All Saints would also have been a driving force in the Branch, but the record says otherwise. Although a few individual members were active in Branch affairs, supporting ringing events and serving as officers, the 'average member' seemed ill inclined to participate. Successive Foremen criticised this: '...not attending Branch practices, despite being a leading band' (1981), 'drifting further from the Branch – almost a self contained community, but we should be part of the church, the Branch and the Guild' (1985), 'no great change in the relationship between the Branch and the tower' (1986), 'we should accept that our own tower can't provide for all our needs, and support Branch and Guild events' (1990).

---

[28] See page 114.

[29] The Sonning Deanery Society became a branch of the Oxford Diocesan Guild in 1881.

110

Part of the problem was that, in narrow technical terms, the band could indeed provide much of what its members needed. The incentive of ringing methods that they could not ring in their own tower might encourage members of a weaker band to venture out to Branch practices, but it just didn't exist at All Saints. Despite their reluctance to go to Branch events, All Saints ringers were always very welcoming to other ringers, and for many years enjoyed the presence of regular visitors at their practices, which is a good indicator that they were lively and friendly.

The Branch itself declined during this period, with fewer people from all towers attending events, and fewer bands strong enough to enter competitions. Even those who took part often just turned up to ring, and left before the results were announced, rather than listening to the other teams, and socialising. The Branch varied the time to make it easier for teams with other commitments, but with little success. At one point, All Saints acquired the unfortunate reputation of expecting to pick a 20 minute slot, turn up, ring and go away, rather than be there at the start for the draw.

On a more positive front, as we saw on page 103, for several years the band offered to dedicate its Monday practice every couple of months to Surprise Major ringing, and to invite Branch members to join in. This was for mutual benefit – to broaden what All Saints could ring alone, and to offer a Surprise Major practice to Branch members who might not otherwise have the opportunity to ring it.

A very tangible contribution to the Branch was made when John Harrison of All Saints made a pair of matching engraved trophies for the 6-bell and 8-bell competitions, and presented them to the Branch at the AGM in February 1988. Each trophy is a cast bronze replica of a bell, with an inset relief of two ringers, mounted on a turned mahogany base.

Figure 60: (L) Sonning Deanery 6-bell competition trophy (R) Winning team in 2006 competition: Steve Smith, Richard Woodward, John Harrison, Katie Tutcher, Jon Tutcher, Barbara Smith

Quality of the ringing – Good striking[30] was the first goal mentioned by the new Foreman at the 1980 AGM. Did the band live up to that expectation during those heady days of change and in the coming years?

Striking appears in the record of around half of the AGMs since 1980, and was clearly of concern to successive Foreman. In 1981 there was a 'need to focus on striking'. In 1984 it was 'poor', but in 1985 'much better', and in 1986 'mixed'. This last comment needs to be taken in context, since it was the period when the band was winning almost every striking competition in sight, and the Foreman's aspirations were understandably high. In 1992, 'methods were being rung at the expense of striking'[31] and in 1993 there was 'improvement but a long way to go'. In 2001, the Foreman, who had been trying to focus on striking since taking office in 1999, reported that the 'general standard was better than two years ago', but as ever, there was 'some way to go'. The band was under considerable pressure at that time, with numbers down and the added effort of raising funds for the restoration project, so it is hardly surprising to hear the following year that 'we rarely achieve good striking', and perhaps worse 'we might be getting used to it'. In 2005, the striking had 'improved on the new bells', but for several years the message was a variable mix of good rhythmic ringing and distinctly less good performance, for example:

'We sometimes produce very pleasant ringing, but on too many occasions it is uncomfortable to listen to.'

What does all this tell us? The leader of any group of performers is rightly concerned about quality, and some chiding as well as encouragement is to be expected, but was this band any different from others? As we saw above, the band's peak performance (of its competition teams) hit some really high levels during this period, so why was the performance of 'bread and butter ringing' of continual concern?

The bells were not the easiest to strike, which was one of the main motivations for the 2004 restoration, but good ringers could strike them perfectly well, as was apparent when visitors from Farnborough (whose bells were out of action) swelled All Saints practices in the early 2000s. To end on a positive note though, at the very end of this period, in 2008, the band's overall performance was distinctly improving.

Outings – We saw in Chapter 6 that All Saints began ringing outings[32] in 1948, but they waxed and waned, with some years having no outing at all. Things were very different in the period we are looking at now, with at least one main outing a year, normally by car, and sometimes more than one. Cycle outings featured quite often, with the first in 1980, and there were several walking outings, usually between three adjacent villages, but also in Bristol and Oxford, which have many bells in the city.

There were a few smaller and larger scale outings. In years when there were a lot of new ringers, the band ran half day 'mini outings' to nearby towers. In 1999 and 2000 Nigel Herriott organised whole weekend outings (one in Somerset and one in Dorset).

---

[30] An even rhythm, ie high quality ringing.

[31] People were putting effort into learning more complex methods, possibly over-stretching themselves, and as a result not putting enough effort into striking them properly.

[32] In the modern sense, based around ringing rather than just sightseeing and socialising.

Figure 61: Outings – Top (L) 1984: Tony Pullan (on grass), Dave Dewar, Helen Mahoney. (Centre) 1986: Charles Herriott, John Harrison, Jonathan Goodchild, Nigel Mellor, Nigel Herriott, Jenny Herriott, Helen Herriott, Steve Smith 1. (R) 2006: Jon Tutcher. Bottom (L) 1986: Stewart Gibson, Simon Tomlinson, Pearl Gibson, Martin Mahoney, Betty Tomlinson, Helen Mahoney, Julia Clack, Paul Wells, John Scott, John Wells, Steve Smith 2, John Harrison, Sue Lambert, Sarah Scott, Terry Scott, Nicholas Scott, Tony Pullan, Jon Tutcher, Alison Moore, Ian Barber. (R) 1987: Jane Marlow, Sheila Williams, Julie Branson, Jo Wells, John Wells, Kevin Lovell, Dave Dewar, Terry Scott, Linda Williams, Jon Tutcher, Steve Smith 1, Simon Tomlinson, Rachel Longley

8.4 Handbell ringing

Over the years, there has often been an intermittent link between tower bell ringing and handbell ringing. We saw in Chapter 3 that handbells were sometimes given as prizes in 18th century ringing contests, and in Chapter 4 that a set was bought for the new Society of Honorary Change Ringers to practise (and they 'gave a clever specimen of change-ringing' at a dinner in 1874). Their bells, which had lain unused for many years, were in use for most of the modern period, first in an ad-hoc way, and then for regular tune ringing.

Carols – Long before this period, at the 1952 AGM, Mary Cole had suggested forming a team for handbell ringing at Christmas time, but nothing came of it. Then in late 1978, the ringers (with no knowledge of this earlier history) decided to ring carols around the parish. A group got together to teach themselves to ring simple carols, and practised until they were proficient enough to perform in public. In the run up to Christmas, they went round the town ringing in the old-fashioned way of carol singers – standing under a street lamp to see their music[33], while one of their number knocked on doors of adjacent houses to ask for donations. On their first outing, it even snowed gently, adding a picturesque Dickensian touch, but it didn't put them off. They collected £100 for the Church of England Children's Society.

For the next few years they did the same, but with a gradual shift from ringing outside houses to ringing in pubs and other gathering places, which yielded higher donations for the time spent ringing.

The Handbell Group – Most of the band were now moderately competent to ring tunes in hand. The repertoire had been extended with some slightly more ambitious home-grown arrangements including 'Hark the herald angels sing'.

In 1981, Stewart Gibson asked if handbell tunes could be rung for two events during the year. This provided the seed for another innovation, and an 'enthusiastic handbell group' was formed. In fact the group was so enthusiastic that they asked the 1982 AGM to consider recasting one of the handbells. The meeting agreed to consider refurbishment, which eventually resulted in the smaller set of 12 bells being sold to Taylors as payment for refurbishing the larger set of 15 bells (the 1873 set), including replacement of the cracked one. Most of the initial group were young, as Figure 62 shows, and all were trained tower bell ringers.

With the handbell group established as a separate entity, and not just a seasonal activity for the tower bell ringers, it began to develop on its own. New members joined from outside the tower, and gradually the proportion of tower bell ringers declined to the point where the group was completely separate, apart from reporting each year to the AGM. As the sole user of the Church's bells, the group looks after them, and had them refurbished in 1999. The group performs regularly in old people's homes, and for other charitable organisations. Its highlights include ringing for the Townswomen's Guild Christmas service at St Martin in the Fields church in London, and ringing for Snowdrop Sunday at Swincombe in Oxfordshire.

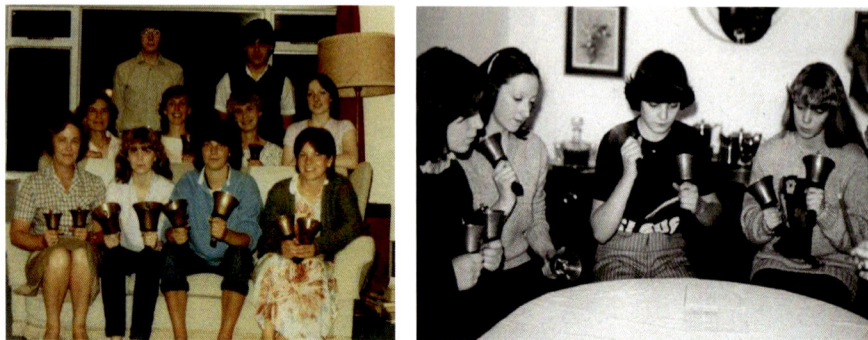

Figure 62: The early 1980s handbell band (L) (left to right, back to front) Simon Tomlinson, Evan Kozakiewicz, Sue Nelson, Helen Domm, Eve Reader, Louise Clements, Betty Tomlinson, Hilary Moss, Clare Lovatt, Briany Ilot; (R) in action.

---

[33] They didn't use proper musical scores – the tunes were written using a numerical notation.

Change ringing in hand – To a ringer, 'handbell ringing' means ringing changes not tunes. Tune ringing is more familiar to the public, since it is often performed to an audience, whereas change ringing is almost always performed in private, and only rarely seen by non-ringers. There is little evidence of change ringing in hand at All Saints before this period, though the post-war band tried and didn't get very far [6]. Perhaps Vera Robinson's group (mentioned above) rang changes. She might have learnt from her father, possibly even before she learnt to ring a tower bell.

About half of the current band have rung changes in hand at some time or other (many while at university) but few of them regularly ring handbells.

For a short while in 1986, a small group (including Tony Pullan, John Harrison and his 9 year old son, Stephen) used to to ring handbells on Sunday afternoons. A team representing All Saints (but including several 'friends') competed in the handbell section of the Richmond Music Festival competition, which they won in 1990[34]. In later years, three or four of the band occasionally rang in the streets to entertain the crowds at several Wokingham town fairs.

By the end of this period there were more active handbell ringers in the band, and November 2006 saw the first known quarter peal in hand (1260 Plain Bob Minor) by an All Saints band. Shortly afterwards, the annual dinner in January 2007 set a new precedent with a performance on handbells (see page 131), repeated in later years.

There were two public highlights for handbell ringing at All Saints. The first was during the 2001 'bell concert' which was held to raise funds for the restoration project. It included a brief explanation of bell music, followed by a performance of Plain Bob Major rung in hand, see Figure 63 (R). The other was during the restoration in 2004, when the tower was silent because the bells were away, and the band offered to ring handbells for weddings, see Figure 63 (L).

Figure 63: (L) Handbells for a 2004 wedding – David Struckett (Finchampstead), John Harrison (All Saints), Stan Scott and Steve Wells (Easthampstead)[35]; (R) during the 'Bell concert' in 2001 – John Harrison plus guest ringers Marcia Dieppe, Viv Bloundelle and Jenny Page[36]

---

[34] See page 110.

[35] Neighbouring towers often help each other with wedding ringing, and they did on the occasion

[36] Reproduced courtesy of Wokingham Times

8.5 Ringers and the church

In the last chapter, we saw how the ringers became more integrated into the life of the church towards the end of the post-war period. Two Rectors[37] presided over the modern period, Brian Bailey and David Hodgson, both of whom were very supportive in their different ways. At his first AGM in 1998, David Hodgson said that he believed 'real bells, rung by real people' were best.

Doing their bit – As well as ringing the bells, and winding the clock (a job probably acquired many years before) the ringers took on other tasks. There were 'one-off' jobs like the white elephant stall at the 1979 May Fayre, and some longer term jobs.

In 1991, the Rector persuaded the ringers to look after the Christmas tree. Ostensibly that grew out of the need to carry the decorations and crib figures from the clock room where they were stored. The ringers did this because they were more used to spiral stairs, down which the heavy and awkward figures had to be carried. They also took on the whole task of ordering, erecting and decorating the Christmas tree (and dismantling it afterwards). Trees delivered were often much longer than the 12 - 15 feet ordered (25 feet in one case) which meant sawing off a lot of wood to make it stable (in a plastic dustbin rammed full of earth). The job replaced a whole evening's practice, though there was normally time to eat mince pies afterwards.

In 1995 the Rector asked the ringers to take over flying the flag[38]. It only needs doing a dozen times a year, but is more onerous because in theory the flag should be raised and lowered during the hours of darkness.

The choir – Throughout this period, All Saints had a very active choir, which sought and achieved a high standard. Every summer, the choir would spend a week singing the services at a cathedral. In two years (1986 in Chichester and 1987 in Bath) the ringers travelled to ring for the final service of the choir's cathedral week away[39].

There is a natural affinity between the choir and ringers (both music-making groups) as we saw with joint outings in earlier periods. During this period there were no regular joint events, but several skittles matches where choir and ringers competed for an engraved wooden spoon (currently hanging in the tower), see page 132.

Back in church though, things were not so easy. The open ringing gallery caused problems, because playing the organ during ringing is distracting – it makes it hard to hear the bells, and hence difficult to ring them properly. Ideally ringing would continue until almost the start of the service, so most people can arrive to the sound of bells. But ideally too, they would hear the organ playing when they came into church. A compromise was needed, with ringing stopping early enough to permit a useful period of organ playing. Initially it was three minutes, but then five. At one point ten minutes was demanded. With some Musical Directors relationships were very good, but with others less so[40], especially when the choir began holding practices before Sunday evening services while the ringers were trying to perform.

---

[37] Apart from Ken Martin's final year
[38] In 1980, the previous Rector had included it in a list of things he thought they already did!
[39] This idea had been suggested and rejected a decade earlier, at the 1977 AGM.
[40] This saga was the inspiration for 'Oswald' who featured in 'third speeches', see page 131.

But there could be no compromise after a wedding. It would be inconceivable not to play the whole of something like the Wedding March, and equally inconceivable not to be ringing the bells as the happy couple emerged from the church. In 1988, this problem got worse with the installation of a more powerful organ, able to render the bells almost inaudible when it was in full flow. All that could be done was to ring rounds as carefully as possible, and hope that what the wedding party heard in the churchyard (but the ringers couldn't hear in the tower) would be acceptable.

Self sufficiency – The financial situation of the Church of England changed drastically during the late 20th century. On the big scale, the Church Commissioners no longer guaranteed to cover the church's cost from the proceeds of historic investment. This sent shock waves through the Church, with the Parish Share[41] inexorably rising over many years. At All Saints, as elsewhere, this meant increased levels of giving, and reduction of costs by taking jobs 'in house' that had previously been contracted out, for example production of the Parish Magazine.

In 1986, the contract for maintenance of the churchyard ended. Upkeep of a large churchyard had been a major call on the church's finances[42], and the PCC decided to switch to using volunteer effort. It made an appeal, not just for people to volunteer to work, but for groups to consider 'adopting' a particular area. The ringers agreed to look after the strip between the wall and path running east from the Annexe[43] to the 'bier shed' in the middle of the graveyard. It wasn't a randomly chosen patch – half way along this strip are the graves of Rev. FE Robinson and several of his family[44]. In the event, the ringers only looked after the whole of this strip for a few years, but a ringer has kept the two graves clear of weeds ever since.

A decade later, the ringers made another contribution towards self sufficiency. The steeple keeper (and others) had always looked after routine maintenance and small scale repairs in the tower, passing on the cost of materials, new ropes, etc to the PCC, but the 1996 AGM agreed to make annual donations to the PCC to offset the whole cost of the previous year's maintenance, providing there had been no abnormal costs. Typically the sum involved was under £100, but it could easily be much higher, for example if several ropes (£100+ each) needed replacing at the same time. In 2003, they changed this retrospective grant to give the officers approval to absorb 'normal' maintenance costs, and pass on any 'extraordinary' costs to the PCC.

The mid 1980s also saw the ringers begin weekly collection in a charity box, with donations each year to various charities. For many years this alternated between general social charities and bell restoration appeals.

The Parish Magazine – The burst of Parish Magazine articles in 1978 heralded a much greater willingness of the post-1980 band to tell the rest of the Parish about life in the tower. There were 130 articles during the 27 years 1980 to 2006, an average of four and a half per year. This is lower than the burst of activity in 1978-79, but far higher over an extended period than at any previous time.

---

[41] Each parish's payment towards the cost of clergy pay and pensions, and central expenses.

[42] It had been £1300 per annum in 1974, when volunteers had previously been requested.

[43] The 1960s building that preceded The Cornerstone.

[44] See pictures on pages 55 and 56.

The output varied somewhat, as Figure 64 shows. The 1980 peak was the tail end of the 1978-79 burst and the 40 articles in the early 1980s were when the band was growing and developing. The late 1980s had 24 articles, when the band was starting to decline. Only 22 articles in the whole 1990s suggests a more inward rather than than outward looking band. The restoration project caused peaks around 2000 and 2004, but with a significant dip in 2002-2003, when both numbers and attendance were suffering. The rise in 2008 bodes well for the future.

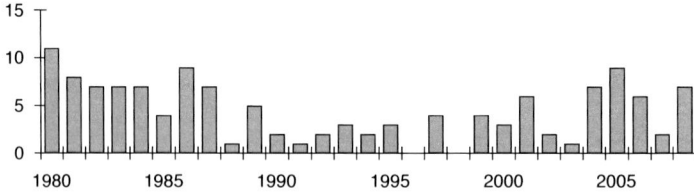

Figure 64: Rise and fall of ringing articles in the Parish Magazine

What did the modern band write about? Quarter peals feature most often. They are the ringers' most conspicuous non-routine activity, and the majority of quarter peals were rung for services, festivals or other church-related events. Peals come much lower in the list because there were far fewer of them even though they were more likely to be reported. Outing reports are an easy thing to write about, and were often delegated to a younger member of the band. Likewise, reports of life events, work on the bells, AGMs, and social events are all obvious 'news' items, the stuff on which a Parish Magazine thrives. Figure 65 shows the prevalence of different topics[45].

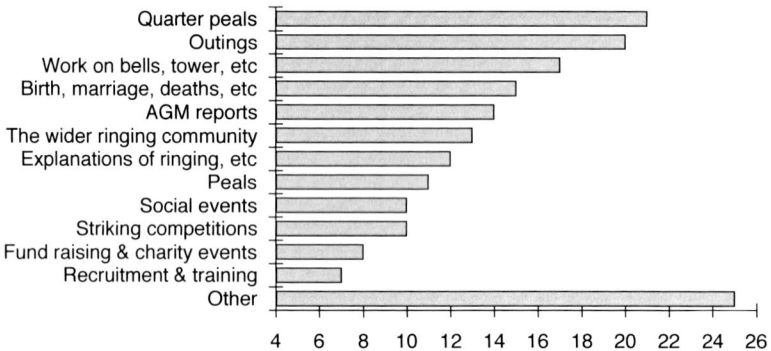

Figure 65: Subjects of Parish Magazine articles after 1980

Of particular interest are the articles explaining aspects of ringing to the layman, which had not featured prior to 1978. Most ordinary folk know very little about ringing, and are largely unaware of the existence of a wider ringing community. So for example, articles on striking competitions, though nominally 'news', often included a strong thread of explanation as well. The fact that the ringers sought to open windows on their world suggests a different attitude from that of their forebears.

---

[45] The total is more than the number of articles, since some covered several topics.

'Other' included tower open days, changes to service ringing, radio interviews, and special ringing – for royal events, dedication services, ordinations, and so on.

8.6 Ringing and the community

In 1984, the Rector invited the ringers to be represented at a meeting to discover common objectives of people in the community. There is no record of whether or not they responded to the invitation, but a decade later some of them took part in 'Find out Fortnight', when various church activities, including ringing, were on show.

Complaints – The band's encounters with the community at the start of this period were not entirely happy. Complaints from nearby residents were first recorded at the 1977 AGM, and in 1978 the Rector read a letter of complaint, and then offered his support if there were any more.   Such things can start with an over sensitive individual, but then spread and get quite heated. There were letters and phone calls. One call to the Foreman at 4am, was to 'see how you like being woken up', and on Christmas morning, a woman stormed into church cursing and swearing.

What had changed? Ringing at 6-30am for service on Christmas and Easter morning had revived after a thirty year lapse. Likewise, ringing the daily curfew had been revived – after a decade of lapse claimed to be due to to 'domestic pressures'[46] Dave Dewar now rang it every night. Even with these changes, ringing overall was far from excessive, but it was clear that something had to be done. The expanding, active band needed more ringing time, which would be likely to inflame things. Someone suggested sound control, and the Rector asked the ringers to investigate.

The band was advised to keep a written record of all ringing, in case a complaint led to legal action. This record was kept from November 1978 onwards, and although it was never needed for its original purpose, it has provided a valuable historic resource, especially with the inclusion after April 1986 of the number of people ringing.

In 1982, the band installed variable sound control – shutters that can open for services and be closed for practices, etc[47]. There was just one complaint the following week – from someone who liked listening to the bells on practice night!

Ringing for early services[48] on Christmas and Easter day, which had been suspended since 1978, resumed and caused no problems. Over the next 25 years there was only the odd isolated complaint. In 1990, the Rector took a call (about special ringing, not services) from someone who wouldn't identify himself. Then in 2005 a woman who was sympathetic to the bells, rang to ask why they had to ring until 9-30pm on Mondays, which upset her. That seemed odd. For a quarter of a century practices (with shutters closed) had ended at 9-30. Nothing had changed – or so the ringers thought. In fact, the lead cladding on the roof was removed for renewal a couple of weeks earlier. That let the sound out, and it was reflected down by the temporary cover above. So although the shutters were closed for practices, the bells were still clearly audible outside. A week later, the new lead covering was installed.

---

[46] The record doesn't say whose domestic pressures. It was probably Walter Pearce, who was Foreman and Verger at the time.

[47] See details of the installation on page 122.

[48] Now changed to 7-30 ringing for 8-00 service.

Looking outward – The ringers had always enjoyed being part of 'two families' (the parish community and the wider ringing community) and during this period they developed stronger links with the local community in Wokingham as well. Initially it was intermittent, with periodic tower open days, but two things brought this wider relationship into special focus. One was the bell restoration project, which had a high public profile, and the other was the church's own increasing focus on its role within the local community. The two became directly linked when the bell restoration project was brought under the umbrella of the 'Celebrating Community' project[49].

In 2002, Rev. Janet Lucas, arranged for a the Tower Foreman to give a short talk on ringing to the children of Westcott Infants School. The idea of a much more comprehensive programme of talks to other community groups emerged from a discussion at the 2004 AGM about doing more school talks. The Foreman agreed to do the talks, and Eve Reader undertook to seek out suitable groups. Over the next four years, the resulting programme of talks and conducted tower tours involved over thirty organisations and about 1600 people. Figure 66 shows two enthusiastic groups of visitors, one in the bell chamber and one in the ringing room.

Figure 66: (L) Enthusiastic young visitors (R) Steve Smith explaining to visitors

Tower open days – As we saw in the last chapter, there was a successful opening in 1978[50], which the Rector asked to be repeated for the 1980 May Fair. This continued for a few years. One event was said to produce a 'large influx of visitors'. A prominent feature of these events was the strings of red and white plastic bunting strung from the top of the tower to the gate posts opposite Rose Street. This bunting came to a sticky end – literally. After the ringers lent it to someone else in the late 1990s, it was returned and left in a box at the back of the church, but a vandal with a match got to it before the ringers did. They arrived for evening ringing to find flames licking up the wall, and the whole of the church full of black, acrid smoke. Needless to say, there was neither ringing nor service that day.

Interest in open days waned somewhat. In September 1996, the ringers tried a new venture, and opened the tower during National Heritage Weekend, along with other historical buildings, but numbers were disappointing. When they next opened for National Heritage weekend, in 2006, the ringers were more community focused and better at managing publicity. The event was an overwhelming success. In four

---

[49] See page 125.
[50] See pages 88-87.

hours, they hoped for 60, and planned to accommodate up to 90 visitors, so when 130 people turned up, they were very stretched. But a lot of visitors saw the bells and the splendid views from the tower roof, and went away very happy afterwards.

Figure 67: View from the tower roof towards the Town Hall

The website – In 2002, Andy Smith offered to set up a tower website, but despite his efforts the project didn't make great progress without a clear aim. That aim came from the community involvement over the next few years, and in 2005 John Harrison developed the current website drawing on extensive material from both the restoration project and the community talks. See allsaintswokinghambells.org.uk

8.7   Enhancing the fabric

During the 1980s and 90s, the ringers put a lot of effort into improving and renewing the physical assets, as shown in Table 13. In addition, they progressively upgraded the ropes to have pre-stretched polyester top ends, thus eliminating the traditional problems of natural fibre ropes: springiness, shrinking in damp weather, and regularly wearing out. There was also the once-a-lifetime bell restoration project.

Year	Work done
1980	Tower rewired and lighting provided to upper levels
1981	Safety rail added to low wooden rail overlooking the nave.
1982	Sound control shutters installed (see page 122)
1982	Rope spider provided[51] (see Figure 68)
1982	New notice board installed
1985	Modern locks fitted
1988	Bell frame cleaned and painted
1989	New carpet laid in the ringing room
1989	More boxes[52] made
1994	Clock weight shaft extended (see page 123)

Table 13: Enhancement of the fabric after 1980

[51] To draw the ropes up to the ceiling, out of the way when not in use.
[52] Portable wooden platforms, typically 3-12" high, for short ringers to stand on. They avoid the need for long ropes, which make handling difficult for tall ringers, and can lead to poor ringing.

121

Most work was done as soon as the need was identified, but a few jobs took a long time from conception through to completion. For example, between the 1982 inspection that recommended re-painting the frame and 1988 when it was done every steeple keeper dutifully reported that it had 'not yet been done'. Installation of sound control took three years from concept to completion, and the bell restoration took five years, but these were quick compared with two other improvements: auto-winding of the clock, and improving the ringing room environment.

Figure 68: (L) Cast aluminium 'spider', (R) Ropes drawn up on the 'spider'

Sound control – In 1982, after several years of complaints[53], the ringers installed sound control: shutters to be opened for public ringing, but closed for practices, etc.

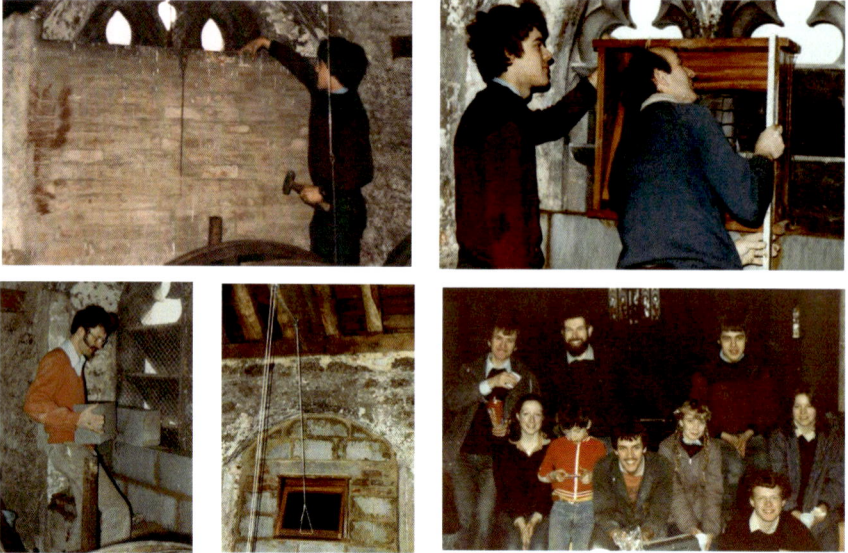

Figure 69: Installing the sound control in 1982: Evan Kozakiewicz about to remove the pre-existing bricking up; Evan & Bob Chapman fitting a frame; Dave Dewar laying blocks; A finished shutter and control cord; The workers (left to right, back then front) John Scott, John Harrison, Evan Kozakiewicz, Louise Clements, Stephen Harrison, Jon Tutcher, Hilary Moss, Martin Layley, Briany Ilot.

[53] See page 119.

At the time, sound control was very rare, so there was nothing to copy, and virtually no guidance. John Harrison designed a solution from scratch, calculating the expected performance of the shutters from basic physics, but the only way to find out whether it would work was to build it.

A previous generation had already partly bricked up the louvres, see Figure 69 (top left), but it was not practical to make opening shutters to fit the remaining space, so the walls were rebuilt with the shutters lower down. The aim was to maintain the previous sound levels when open, and to reduce it by 20 dB (ie to a hundredth of the power) when closed. Making the shutter area similar to that of the existing openings achieved the first aim. The second was quite demanding, but it was achieved.

The shutters and frames cost £300, and quotations for installing them ranged from £600 to £1500. That was unaffordable, so the band decided on a DIY installation, something that would probably not be permitted now. The total cost of all materials was £635, of which the PCC paid £400 and Sonning Deanery ringers granted £100.

Clockwork – For as long as anyone can remember, the ringers (usually the steeple keeper) have wound the clock by hand. It ran for little more than five days, so that meant a twice weekly task of climbing up to the clock, and cranking the handle to lift something like two hundredweight of lead up the tower.

In 1986 the ringers asked the PCC to allocate funds for automatic clock winding. The Standing Committee agreed that this would form part of the church's restoration project, and that 'action would be taken eventually'. The next few years saw 'no progress', until in 1995 a new steeplekeeper said that clock winding was 'less onerous now', and things went quiet. Interestingly in 2004, it was the same steeple keeper (a decade older) who stirred things up by saying that the clock 'should not need to be wound by hand in this day and age'.

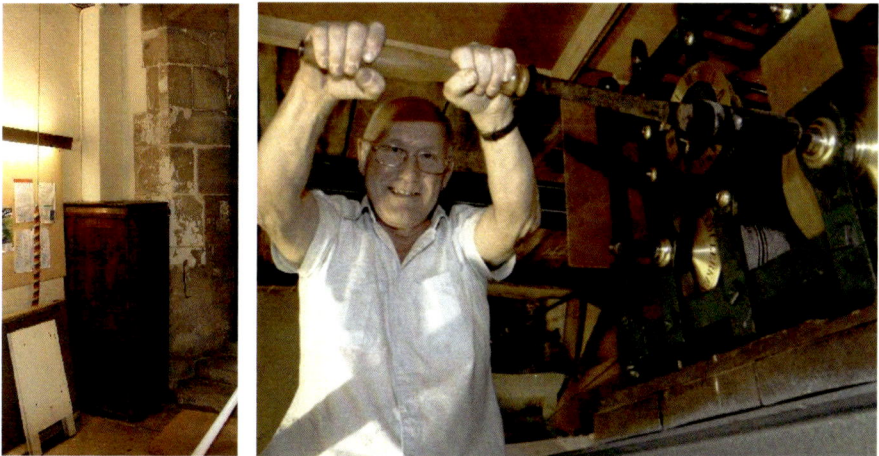

Figure 70: (L) Extended weight shaft, (R) Arthur Moss winding the clock[54]

---

[54] Reproduced courtesy of Totally Media (publishers of *Totally Wokingham*)

During this decade of delay, the ringers managed to make clock winding less onerous thanks to some detective work and a little DIY. They figured that if the clock weights could go right down to the ground, instead of stopping at the gallery floor, then the clock would run for a whole week. When they discovered that there was already enough wire on the winding drums to make this possible, the penny dropped. Almost certainly the clock would have run for a week when installed, but the fall of the weights had been curtailed when the gallery was renewed in the late 1870s. So they extended the weight shaft downward, see Figure 70(L) into a cupboard that might possibly have formed the base of the original 1817 weight shaft.

The clock became increasingly unreliable, and eventually stopped. In 2005 it was fully overhauled. Auto-winding was included in the faculty, but funds didn't stretch to providing it. Finally in 2006, thanks to a private donation, the clock was fitted with auto-winders, and the ringers' regular winding chore came to an end.

Tower lighting – It seems hard to imagine that as late as 1980 there was no electric lighting in most of the tower, and only a single bulb hanging in the ringing room. The ringers had complained about poor lighting in 1974, but it took another six years to get the problem solved. In the words of the July 1980 Parish Magazine:

> 'After yet another winter of winding the clock in the dark and fumbling up and down the staircase to the bells, it was decided that it was due time to re-wire the tower and install lighting on the stairs and in the clockroom. A group of ringers spent several evenings climbing on the bellframe, wedged across the stair, or balanced on the top of long ladders. Considerable quantities of old wire and conduit were removed and even greater quantities of new wire and fittings were installed. The new lighting has revealed some interesting stone mason's marks and other graffiti from the past.'

Ringing room environment – Improving the lighting was relatively easy, but other aspects of the ringing room environment proved to be much harder, and a more protracted problem to solve. As with the lighting, some of the problems were recognised in the mid 1970s, and there was an abortive plan to solve them, but the modern band was unaware of this when they were again discussed[55].

At the 1985 AGM, the ringers proposed to install a glass screen to isolate them from both the loud organ, and heat rising from the church. This was joined a year later by a proposal to install opening lights in the west window to alleviate excessive heat in the summer. Both schemes ran into the sand, but the problems were swept up later, along with other long-standing problems, in a report to the 1999 AGM on 'Ringers and the church building'. This led to the proposal to restore the bells, followed by installation of a glass screen in the nave arch, and a heat pump in the ringing room for summer cooling. The bells were restored in 2004, but other pressures delayed the environmental work for several more years[56].

Things that go bump in the night – The clapper of a bell is subjected to huge stresses every time it strikes. Broken clappers are mainly a problem with heavy bells, but can occur in any bell. So when the conductor of a quarter peal in 1988 heard a

---

[55] See comment at the start of this chapter about the band being unaware of its history.
[56] At the time of writing, the project is again being progressed.

loud bang aloft, he feared the worst. He listened, expecting to hear only seven bells, but all eight were striking. The ringers were all behaving normally, and none of them seemed to have a problem, so they continued ringing. In fact, the Tenor clapper had fractured, but not in the expected place – the flight had broken off, leaving the ball attached, which is why the bell kept striking. This was an unusual break – clappers usually break between the ball and shank (see Figure 71). The role of the flight is to act as a counterbalance and reduce the stress between ball and shank.

Expert advice on how to mend it was to drill holes in the ball and flight, to tap them to accept a threaded bar, and then to run a deep weld round the edge. The first repair failed the next year. A deeper weld lasted five years before failing. The third attempt lasted six years, and when it broke again in 2002, the ringers decided not to mend it, since the clappers would soon be replaced during the restoration anyway.

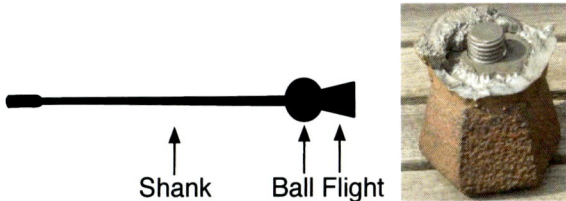

Figure 71: Tenor clapper flight after breaking the final time

Restoration of the bells – The decision to rehang the bells came out of the blue. The bells had never been easy to handle, and the sound was poor, but as they had always been like that, the ringers had got used to them. They knew that a rehang would be needed one day, but there was no immediate pressure to do it 'now'. But when the ringers were faced with the list of issues in the paper mentioned above, rehanging the bells emerged as their top priority, closely followed by the environmental work.

They were advised to 'get in quickly' before the Church Annexe[57] needed replacing, but in the event, the PCC decided to roll together the tower project, the new hall, and the churchyard development into an umbrella project called 'Celebrating Community'. The bell part was tiny compared to the new community hall (which eventually cost £1·2 million) but it was more advanced (fund raising started in 1999) and more visible, so bells played a prominent role in the main launch in May 2000.

The bells came out in May 2004, a few months after The Cornerstone (the new community hall) opened. Bells 1, 2, 3 and 6 were replaced, and the whole set tuned. They were hung on metal headstocks with new fittings, and an additional beam running north-south was installed under the existing east-west beams that support the bell frame. Figures 72-74 show various stages of the work as it progressed.

The restored bells rang for Remembrance Sunday 2004, and were rededicated by the Bishop of Reading at a special service on the afternoon of Sunday 23rd January 2005. The congregation was swelled by many former ringers and parishioners, VIPs, the bell hangers and civic dignatories.

---

[57] The life-expired hall adjacent to the church.

Figure 72: Removing the old bells (L) Bill Brindley (R) John Smith

Figure 73: (L) Casting new bells, (R) Bells in their moulds with Revd. David Hodgson, John Smith (warden), Arthur Moss, Anne Harrison, John Harrison

Figure 74: (L) Arthur Moss & David Welman fitting a wheel, (R) John Harrison tightening the new beam under the main frame

Bells are tuned by removing metal selectively from different parts of the inside, to bring the bell's different partial frequencies into line with each other, and to ensure that the eight bells form a true scale. The existing bells needed some tuning – not because they had 'gone out of tune', but because when they were cast, the science of bell tuning wasn't fully understood. Figure 75 shows the Tenor[58], which was lightly tuned, alongside one of the heavily tuned new bells, being lifted up the tower. The shiny areas show where metal has been removed.

[58] Bell 8, with the lowest note

Figure 75: (L) Lightly retuned bell (M) Heavily tuned new bell (R) Acoustic treatment in the clock room

Figure 76 shows a before and after comparison of the tuning. The match between ideal frequencies '+' and actual frequencies 'x' is much better after tuning.

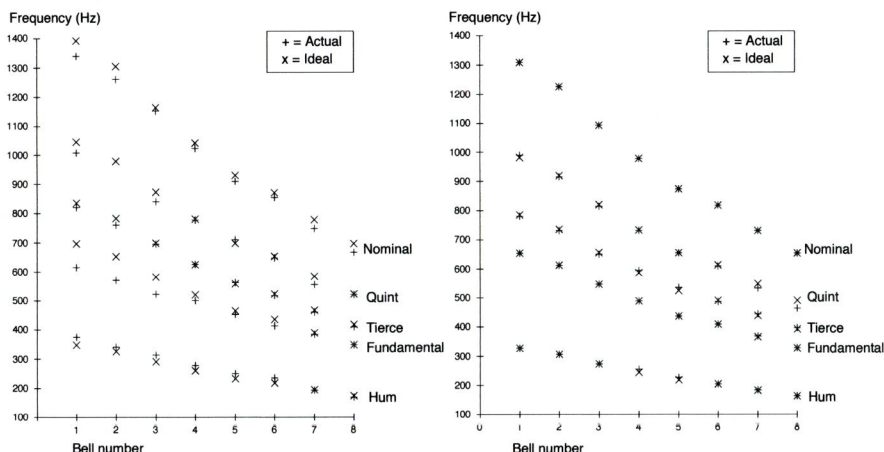

Figure 76: Bell partial frequencies before and after tuning

Internal acoustics – Ringers must listen acutely to ensure that each bell strikes at exactly the right time, but it is a difficult skill to acquire, and made harder if the strike of each bell is not distinctly audible above the reverberation of the bells. The ringers had recognised a problem around 1980, but it was only finally resolved in 2005, as part of the restoration project. The re-tuned bells had a richer, fuller sound, which though good in itself, made the reverberation problem even worse. The solution was simple and low-tech. Between the bells and the ringers, the sound passes through the clock room. Hanging soft material in front of its hard, reflective walls offered a simple way to reduce the reverberation. An appeal for old carpets got a massive response, and the walls are now hung with a rather garish multi-coloured 'tapestry', see Figure 75 (R), which produced a dramatic acoustic improvement.

Sound lantern – This could have been an improvement, but it never happened. When the bells were installed in 1704, the church stood at the edge of a small town, surrounded by open fields. The bells would have been audible over the whole of a smaller and quieter Parish. Some time during the intervening 300 years, the original large sound openings were partly blocked off[59] to reduce the sound to tolerable levels for houses next to the church. The bells are not audible over the whole of the modern Parish, which is an extended sea of houses bathed in traffic noise.

Prior to the 2004 bell restoration, much thought was given to whether the sound level could be improved at a distance, without deafening those who live next to the church.

In theory, it could be done using a 'sound lantern', which has large openings above the tower roof, so the parapet wall creates a 'sound shadow' near the church, but not at a distance. There are very few sound lanterns in existence, and it proved almost impossible to find one that could be heard in action. In the end, with no hard evidence that the long range sound could be increased[60], and to avoid the risk of further delay to the restoration project, the idea was abandoned.

Conservation and re-use – In former times, bells that were replaced were simply broken up and melted down, but the more conservation minded 21st century band sought to find new homes where their old bells could be re-used. One went to a church in Australia and two to a church in Yorkshire[61], all thanks to the Keltek Trust.

The old timber headstocks were also re-used, rather than having a big bonfire. The wood was turned into over 90 bell mementos to commemorate the restoration.

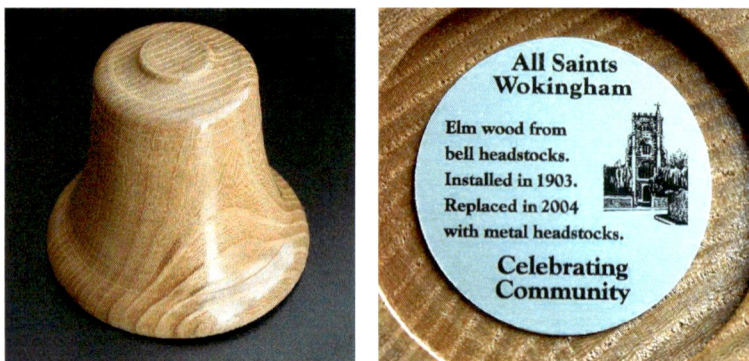

Figure 77: Wooden bell mementos from old headstocks

The tower walls – Ringers don't normally worry too much about the tower walls, but it had a big effect on them when the tower exterior underwent a major face lift. The business of the tower had to continue amidst the dirt and disruption. The most awkward time was when the west door was out of use, with access to the church via the south door. It was a mild inconvenience for the congregation, but it meant that

---

[59] See Figure 69 (top left) on page 122.

[60] As opposed to cutting down short range sound, which though very effective, was not the problem here, because of the inherited partial blocking of the louvres.

[61] At the time of writing, the other bell is earmarked for a chiming bell in an abbey near Worcester

ringers arriving to ring after weddings had to walk through the nave during the service. Even waiting outside, and entering as a group during a suitable hymn was distracting for the wedding guests, and distinctly uncomfortable for the ringers.

The work had to be done though. The tower is built mainly of puddingstone, a very coarse grain, iron-rich conglomerate – the layman might describe it as 'large pebbles held together with rust', see Figure 78(L). The pebbles themselves are very hard, but the matrix easily weathers[62]. For decades pebbles had fallen off and been swept away, but in 2003 the authorities decided this could not go on, and the erosion must be stopped. A loose stone could kill anyone unfortunate enough to be under it when it fell, and although the pebbles hadn't killed anyone in 150 years, luck was no longer deemed to be an acceptable protection. The tower was declared a safety hazard and fenced off. For a while there was a protective canopy to permit use of the west door, see Figure 78 (R), but during the work to restore the stonework, the tower was completely shrouded in scaffolding, as shown in Figure 79.

Figure 78: (L) Puddingstone, (R) Protective canopy, 2003

People had grown to love the deep brown walls that contrasted with the lighter limestone quoins, and did not want the appearance changed. Research suggested that the tower had been rendered prior to the Victorian restoration, so the modern appearance was not in fact 'original'. The sceptics weren't convinced, but proof finally came when the clock faces were removed, and revealed patches of the original render. The Victorians had indeed stripped off the protective surface, exposing the vulnerable puddingstone to the elements.

Several tons of loose material were removed before the new render could be applied, so there was no question about the whether the renovation was needed.

After many months, the tower emerged from the scaffolding and plastic sheeting, like a butterfly emerging from its chrysalis. Also like a butterfly, what came out was much brighter and more impressive than what went in. The tower now formed a much more prominent landmark, as can be seen in Figure 79.

---

[62] Unlike 'Hertfordshire puddingstone', which is a much harder conglomerate.

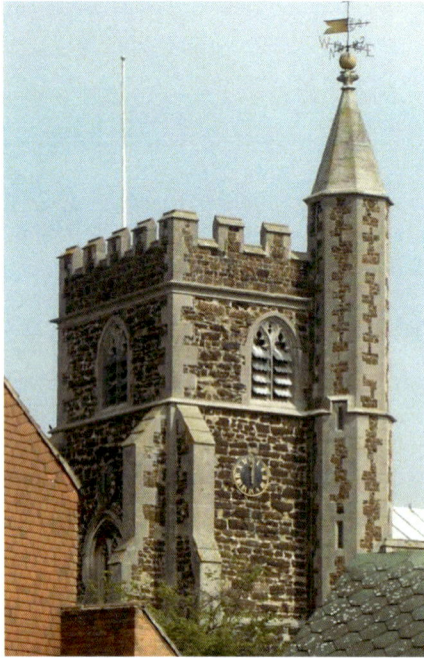

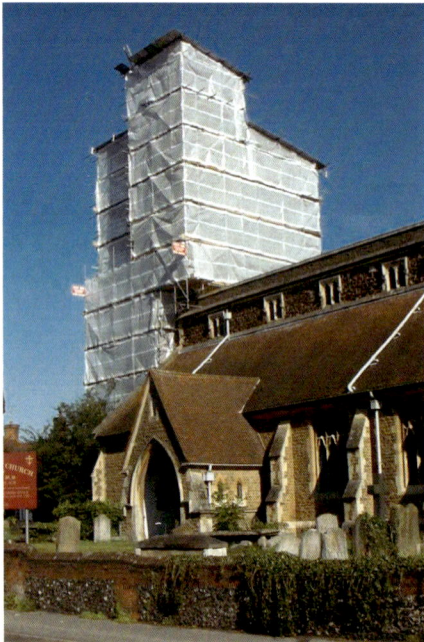

Figure 79: The tower before, during and after external restoration

8.8   Social life

Whereas we know little about the band's social life in former years, apart from the occasional joint dinner with the choir or St Paul's ringers, we know a lot about what the modern band did when they weren't ringing.   There are minutes, magazine articles, and six volumes of scrap books.

Annual dinner – The first annual dinner was on 3rd February 1984. Four years prior to that, a small group of four couples had attended a dinner dance at the Bull in Bisham but the 1984 dinner was the first event organised for the whole band.

That first dinner established the tradition of three speeches. The Foreman proposes the health of the guests, usually after some sort of light hearted review of the previous year. The principle guest replies and proposes the toast to the Band. Typically the guest is one of the clergy, a churchwarden or the Musical Director, with carte blanche to say (or sing) anything he or she thinks relevant. Then comes the 'third speech'. In the early years, delivering it was the booby prize for losing a game at the Christmas party, but in later years a name was drawn from a hat at the AGM. Third speeches have included poems, songs, recitals, mock quizzes and narrative, often lampooning members of the band, or other aspects of tower life.   A fictitious 'Oswald' once featured as musical director, in what were claimed to be extracts from the Foreman's private diary. Some years later a whole dynasty of Oswalds (ye first, ye second, and so on) appeared in what were claimed to be church archives from previous centuries.

In 2007 a handbell performance was added to the dinner routine. Andy Smith 1-2, Simon Farrar 3-4, John Harrison 5-6, and Nigel Mellor 7-8, rang a touch of spliced Plain and Little Bob Major on handbells before the speeches. Handbells feature at many 'higher powered' ringers' dinners[63], but it was a first at All Saints, and the tradition continued in subsequent years, see Figure 80.

Figure 80: Handbell touch at the 2008 dinner
(L-R) Chris Cole, John Harrison, Neil Curnow, Ken Davenport

[63] Including the annual dinner of Cambridge University Guild, to which three of the four who rang in that first touch belong.

Skittles – Good coordination of hand and eye to deliver a smooth straight movement. That could apply to handling a bell rope in the tower or to bowling in a skittle alley, so perhaps it is natural that almost the only 'sporting' activity in which the ringers engaged was skittles. They challenged both the choir (see page 116) and the PCC on several occasions for a trophy in the form of a wooden spoon.

Figure 81: (L) Stewart Gibson bowling, (R) The Wooden Spoon Trophy

Parties – We conclude this chapter with a look at the lighter side of tower life. Ringing is not all serious, and ringers do occasionally let their hair down. New Year's Eve parties began in 1980. Like the famous mints, and unlike most New Year parties, they had a 'hole' in the middle. Around 11.30pm proceedings were suspended while the ringers went off to ring the Old Year out (half muffled[64]) and ring the New Year in. Non-ringing partners and children amused themselves suitably until the ringers returned. The venue moved around members' homes, often hosted by whoever had the most children. Numbers at the parties began to dwindle around 2000, and a few years later the parties ceased, though midnight ringing continued.

Barbecue parties in the evening after ringing outings proved to be more durable institutions, and continued throughout the period.

A meal out instead of ringing practice on the Monday of Holy week also emerged as a common feature in the later years. It is traditional not to have ringing practices during Holy week[65] and so with Monday already free from other commitments, it was fairly easy to arrange a meal out together.

The story moves on – It is appropriate to conclude this last chronological chapter in party mood. Despite their dedication to the serious stuff of ringing, a band of ringers is a small community of friends, who share more than just the technical aspects of ringing.

We leave the ringers at All Saints as they move onwards into the future, but before closing, the final chapter will look back over the whole story, to see the big picture, and the underlying changes and trends over the years.

---

[64] See page 65.
[65] See page 102.

9 Retrospective overview

In this final chapter, we stand back and look more broadly at the All Saints ringers over the years. In previous chapters we looked at the trees in successive parts of the wood. Now we will try to take in the grand sweep of the whole forest.

9.1 The band

Numbers – How many ringers were there? Tower records are limited, but membership records of the Oxford Diocesan Guild go back to the 1880s. Figure 82 shows the number of All Saints ringers who were Guild members[1]. Figure 83 is derived from the earliest and latest mention of ringers in any record (tower, Parish or Guild) and assumes that people rang continually throughout. Aside from clerical errors, we might expect this to show higher numbers, because anyone who dropped out of ringing for a period and then took it up again would appear to have served continuously. The most notable example of this is the dip in Guild membership during the second world war. With a four year national ban on ringing, many ringers lapsed their membership, yet around ten of them rang again after the war, and so appear in Figure 83 as remaining ringers during the war.

What the graphs can't show is how many ringers were active. We know there were periods when some people remained members, but never rang. That speaks well of the band as a social institution, but it distorts the record of it as a functioning entity.

Until 1979 there was an official limit on the number of members, though why there should have been a limit on unpaid ringers is not clear. The limit was increased over the years, as shown by the dotted line on both graphs. It seems that the limit was regularly exceeded. Whether the rule was ignored, or whether some Guild members were not full tower members, we don't know.

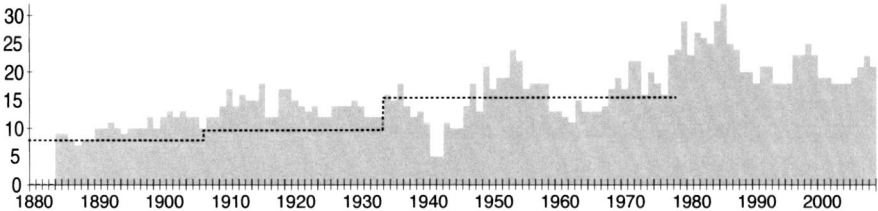

Figure 82: Oxford Diocesan Guild membership of All Saints ringers over the years

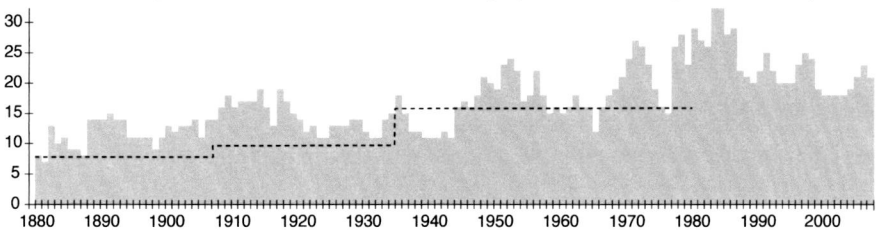

Figure 83: Numbers based on earliest and latest mention over the years

[1] Drawn from a combination of Guild reports and Branch subscription records. Neither covers the whole period, and where they overlap, there are a few minor discrepancies.

133

It is interesting to try to correlate the cold statistics – the rise and fall of the figures – with what we know about the band over the years.

All Saints entered the 1880s with just one change ringer and three probationer members of the Guild, as we saw in Chapter 4, but membership grew rapidly in the first few years under Albert Hill's guidance, and it continued to rise steadily under Sam Paice until around 1920. In the first two decades of the 20th century the band was very active, and rang several peals. It was also a time when the Rector, Bertram Long, seems to have taken a strong interest in the ringing[2].

Numbers fell back in the 1920s, at the start of Bill Brooks' long period as Foreman – the early part of which we know little about – with a small upsurge before the second war while Gilbert Thurlow was curate.

After the war, numbers grew. Bill Brooks was still at the helm, but now supported by Walter Pearce as deputy. Many new ringers were trained, and the band was active.

Numbers were already falling when Walter Pearce took over as Foreman in the early 1960s. They rose and fell briefly during the 1970s, though we need to interpret the figures for this period carefully, since many members didn't ring. The 1980 AGM reported that of 30 members on the books, 12 (40%) had scarcely been in the tower all year.

As we saw in Chapter 8, the whole band was replaced in the few years around 1980, and membership then rose to its highest ever level, with the band very active, and successful. Numbers reduced again, and the band became less active than it had been (though still doing more than in much of the previous hundred years). Membership figures slightly overstate the number of active ringers towards the end of the period, when only about 80% of members ring regularly.

Another interesting comparison is that for some reason, a lower proportion of the members attended AGMs in the last two decades than previously, as shown in Figure 84. Does this reflect a lower commitment in the modern ringer, or just the fact that people in modern day Wokingham live very busy lives?

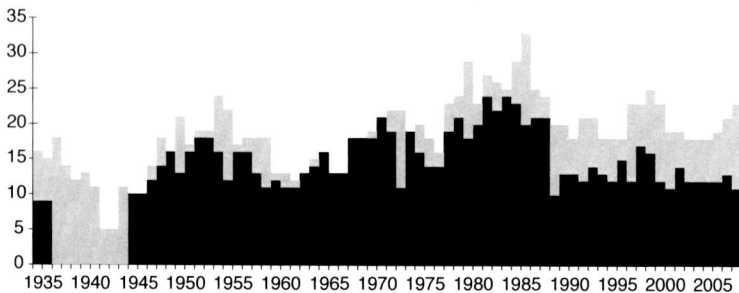

Figure 84: AGM attendance (black)[3] superimposed on number of members

---

[2] In Guild reports from 1905 to 1923 he was listed along with his ringers under All Saints, rather than separately with the Honorary members like the other clergy within the Deanery, though he did not ring.

[3] AGM records only exist for the years shown.

Length of service – Using the dates of first and last mention of individual ringers, we can also see how long ringers served at different times. In Figure 85 the vertical scale shows time, from 1880 to the present, and each vertical bar shows when an individual ringer was associated with the All Saints band. The horizontal scale doesn't represent time directly – it is the cumulative number of ringers, but approximate dates of joining are marked. They are not evenly spaced, because the number of new members joining varied over the years.

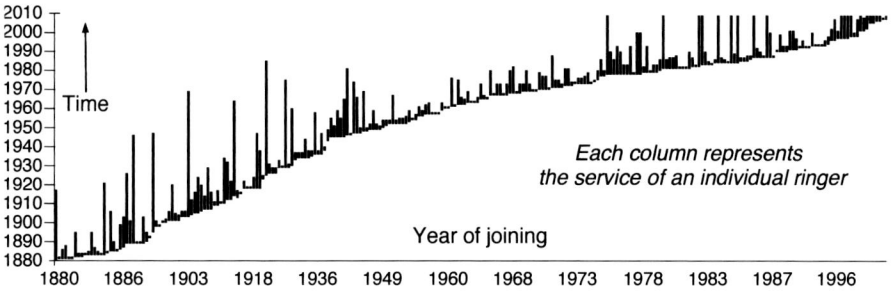

Figure 85: Length of service of individual members

Very broadly, the picture splits into three periods: from 1880 until the late 1940s, from the late 1940s to the late 1970s, and from around 1980 until the present day.

Recruitment for the first 70 years was modest (an average of 1.5 ringers per year) but many ringers from that era put in long service, with a dozen serving 30 years or more.

In contrast, the middle of the 20th century was a period of high recruitment (averaging 2.6 ringers per year) and low retention. No one who started in this period served for 20 years, and only a handful served for more than ten.

The final decades saw a slightly higher recruitment rate (averaging 2.8 ringers per year) but was again characterised by long service. Many of the current band have already served well over 20 years – and are still going strong. Only the future can tell whether they will serve as long as their predecessors did a century ago.

Another way to look at this information is in terms of the average length of service of members in the band at any one time. This is plotted in Figure 86.

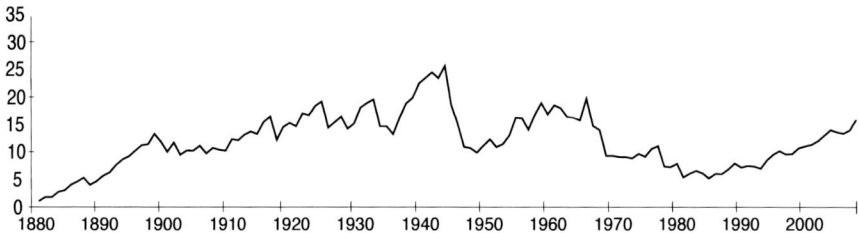

Figure 86: Average length of membership

135

The graph starts artificially at zero, because we have no records before 1880, and climbs steadily. By the turn of the century, the average length of service was 10 years. The graph then flattens out, so the lengthening service of the old timers was being offset by the early loss of other ringers. This was the time when the bells were augmented, and the band was achieving greater things. Perhaps that put off some of the less ambitious ringers.

Average service length continued to grow to a peak of almost 25 years by 1940, when a few ringers had clocked up 50 or 60 years. The drastic reduction of the average after the war reflects the influx of many new ringers. It rose again as this new cadre of ringers started to accumulate their years of service, but then declined as the old guard died. The major turnover and expansion in the 1980s took the average to a new low of 5 years, from which it steadily grew as the new band stabilised and aged.

Occupations – The change in occupations of Wokingham's ringers is very marked. Thirty one of the late 19th and early 20th century ringers can be identified in the 1901 census. Most of them were manual workers or craftsmen, with very few having 'white collar' jobs. Their occupations were: Carpenter (7), Baker (3), Labourer (2), Blacksmith, Bricklayer's labourer, Builder's clerk, Carriage trimmer, Circular sawyer[4], Coachman domestic, Farrier, Green grocer's porter, Life Assurance Agent, Solicitor's clerk, Messenger, Planer in sawmill, Plumber, Postman, Printer's compositor, Sawyer, Shop assistant, Smith & farmer, Wood machinist.

The contrast with the band of a century later could not be more marked. Almost all were white collar workers, and most were professionals. Of course the social demographic of Wokingham has changed, but it also reflects the way that ringing became more of a middle class activity during the latter half of the 20th century. Table 14 shows the trade or profession of all Foremen from 1880 to 2008.

	Foreman in years	Name	Occupation
Pre 1980	1880-1896	Albert Hill	Blacksmith (and later farmer)
	1896-1920	Samuel Paice	Postman
	1920	Fred Mattingley	Blacksmith
	1921-1963	Bill Brooks	Gardener
	1963-1979	Walter Pearce	Plumber
Post 1980	1980-1982, 1988-1990, 1999-2008+	John Harrison	Chartered Engineer
	1983, 1993-1994	Stewart Gibson	Industrial Chemist
	1984-1985, 1995-1996	Jon Tutcher	Chartered Engineer
	1986-1987	Tony Pullan	Professional Electrical Engineer
	1991-1992	Nigel Herriott	Chartered IT Professional
	1997-1998	Julie Goodchild	Chartered Accountant

Table 14: Occupations of Foremen – 1880 to 2008

Tenure of office – Table 14 shows another sense in which 1980 was a divide. The previous century was effectively presided over by four Foremen (discounting Fred Mattingley, who only held the role as caretaker for four months between Sam Paice's

---

4 Mis-transcribed in the 1901 census as 'Circular lawyer'.

death and the subsequent AGM). Since 1980, in little more than a quarter of a century, six different ringers have been Foreman, with ten changes of office. Of course the rule introduced in 1980 that officers should not normally serve in the same role for more than three years helped to ensure an increased turnover, but even so, it is notable that only one of the six modern Foremen has served three consecutive years – all the others served for only one or two years at a time.

Age – It is interesting to look at the age of Foremen over the years, which is shown in Figure 87. Albert Hill was 24 when he took over in 1880. Sam Paice was only a year younger, so the line keeps rising when he took over from Albert in 1896, until 1920 when he Sam died. Bill Brooks brought the age down to 32, but took it to a peak of 74 when he died in 1963. Walter Pearce took it nearly as high, to 71, and then after 1980 it fluctuated rapidly, including both younger and older Foremen.

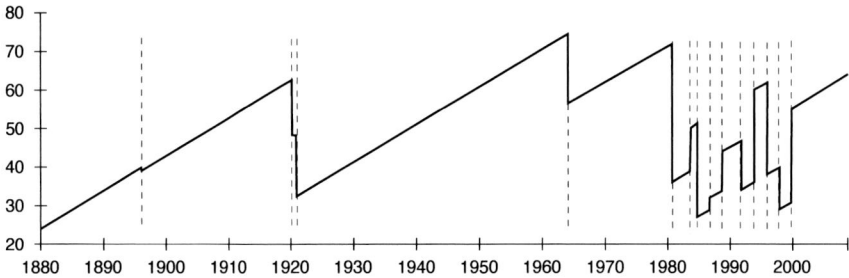

Figure 87: Age of Foreman

Imported talent – One interesting feature is that although large numbers of ringers have been trained at All Saints, many of the Foremen came from outside Wokingham. Albert Hill probably learnt to ring in Hampshire, Sam Paice learnt in Yateley and Bill Brooks learnt in Kent. Between them they were Foremen for 83 years of the century from 1880 to 1980. Walter Pearce is the notable exception, coming from a Wokingham family. (So did Fred Mattingley, but he was never elected, and only acted as Foreman for four months). After 1980, Julie Goodchild was the only home grown Foreman, though with Wokingham having a much more rapidly changing population it is less remarkable for recent Foremen to be incomers.

Other officers – When change ringing was introduced at All Saints in 1873, there were only two tower officers, the Foreman and Secretary. The post of secretary seems to have been held by the curate at the time (probably a non-ringer) until 1921. Then for the next three decades, there was no secretary. The post was re-introduced in 1953, since which time it has always been held by a ringer. For much of that time, the secretary also performed the treasurer's task, but sometimes there was a separate treasurer (and even an assistant treasurer).

The post of Deputy Foreman, created in 1945 when the band declined to elect Walter Pearce as Foreman, has always been held by a ringer. Initially the job included the duties of Steeplekeeper, but these have been separately held since 1957.

In 1985, an unofficial archivist role was created to maintain the scrapbook. Christine Roper, Eve Reader and Jane Mellor have held the role, but dates are not recorded.

In 2008, the band created a separate post of Ringing Master, responsible for running the ringing, but without the other duties associated with the Foreman (or Deputy).

(For a list of Foremen, see Table 14 on page 136.)

Years	Secretary
1873 -187?	Mr C Brooker
1879 - 1882	Rev John Frederick Eastwood
1886? - 1890?	Rev William Hyde Parker
???? - 1906	Rev Arthur Perronet Carr
1907 - 19??	Dr Nash (??)
1915? - 1921	Rev Frederick McDuff Christian Hare
1921 - 1950	(None?)
1951 - 1953	Gwen Crockford
1954 - 1973	Mary Cole
1974 - 1976	Wendy Burkey
1977	Janet Clarke
1978 - 1979	David M Dewar
1980	Theresa A Scott
1981	Pamela Vassie
1981 - 1982	John GP Scott
1983	Jonathan Peter Tutcher
1984 - 1985	Betty M Tomlinson
1986	Pearl J Gibson
1987 - 1989	Stephen Ralph Smith
1990 - 1993	Julie Belinda Branson
1994 - 1996	John Alexander Harrison
1997	W Stewart Gibson
1998	John Alexander Harrison
1999 - 2001	Jonathan Peter Tutcher
2002 - 2004	Julie Belinda Goodchild
2005 - 2007	Richard J Woodward
2008 -	Mary Spence

Years	Treasurer
- 1966	(Combined with secretary)
1967 - 1970	Sheila Cameron
1970 - 1978	William B Burkey
1979 - 2000	(Combined with secretary)
2001 - 2005	Jonathan P Goodchild
2006 -	Jonathan Peter Tutcher

Years	Assistant Treasurer
1970 - 1978?	Jo Burkey

Years	Deputy Foreman
1945 - 1963	Walter John Pearce
1964 - 1965	Keith Goddard
1966 - 1973	Robert Begrie
1973 - 1976	William Burkey
1977 - 1979	Francis J Moore
1980	Robert J Chapman
1981	John G P Scott
1982	W Stewart Gibson
1983	Evan Kozakiewicz
1984	David M Dewar
1985	Anthony Guy Pullan
1986	Theresa A Scott
1987	Richard J Woodward
1988 - 1990	W Stewart Gibson
1991 - 1993	Stephen Ralph Smith
1994	Jonathan Peter Tutcher
1995 - 1996	Julie Belinda Goodchild
1997 - 1999	W Nigel G Herriott
2000 - 2002	Nigel A L Mellor
2003 - 2006	Stephen R Smith
2007	Simon C Farrar
2008 -	Jonathan Peter Tutcher

Years	Steeple Keeper
1957 - 1973	Walter John Pearce
1974 - 1978	William B Burkey
1978 - 1979	John Alexander Harrison
1980	John G P Scott
1981	Jonathan Peter Tutcher
1982	Evan Kozakiewicz
1983	David M Dewar
1984	John G P Scott
1985	Simon J Tomlinson
1986	Martin J Mahoney
1986	W Stewart Gibson
1987	Richard Smith
1988 - 1990	John A Harding
1991 - 1993	John Alexander Harrison
1994 - 1996	John A Harding
1997 - 2006	Charles Arthur Moss
2007 -	Vacant (John A Harrison)

Years	Ringing Master
2008 -	Simon Farrar

Table 15: All known officers other than Foremen

9.2 Peals

Peals are special performances that stand out above the tower's routine ringing life of service ringing and practices. Ringing a peal is a significant undertaking[5], but a comparatively rare event for most ringers. Their rarity might seem to render peals of marginal interest, but two things make them particularly useful when looking back into history. There is a substantially complete record of all the peals that have ever been rung[6] (well over a quarter of a million worldwide), which doesn't exist for any other type of ringing. Even a band that does not regularly ring peals often makes particular efforts to do so to mark major local or national events.

The peal ringing context – To put All Saints' peal record into context, it helps to look briefly at the level of peal ringing activity in general over the last three centuries. The first recorded peal was rung in 1690, and the next in 1715. We saw in Chapter 3 that peals were rung in Reading, Farnham and other nearby towns not long afterwards. The graph in Figure 88 shows the the growth of peal ringing since then. Peals were rare until the late 19th century when change ringing was heavily promoted as part of the 'belfry reform' movement[7]. Since then, peal ringing has grown steadily, apart from dips associated with the two world wars.

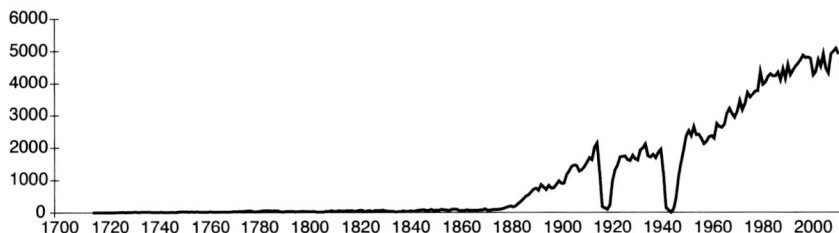

Figure 88: Peals rung per year, in all towers since 1715

Peals at Wokingham – Seventy four peals were rung at All Saints from 1903-2008. Prior to that there were none. We know that in the 1700s Wokingham ringers did not even practise change ringing, let alone ring peals. From 1873 when Bird introduced change ringing[8] it was nearly forty years before a local band rang a peal unaided.

The first peal in Wokingham was at St Paul's in 1864, the year that their bells were installed. It wasn't rung by local ringers, but by members of the Oxford Society of Change Ringers (founded in 1734). Oxford was a strong centre of change ringing, and it is quite common for peal ringers to travel to ring in other towers, especially if the bells are particularly good. St Paul's bells must have been considered good, since there were nearly twenty peals on them by the turn of the century, mostly by visiting ringers. Wokingham was definitely on the peal ringing map with its new ring of

---

[5] A peal is a continuous ringing performance of 5000 or more rows, typically taking 3 hours, and with strict requirements for the accuracy of the ringing.

[6] Canon KWH Felstead began a complete card index, drawn from all historical sources, which he bequeathed to the Central Council of Church Bell Ringers. The records are now available on-line.

[7] See page 25.

[8] See page 29.

eight at St Paul's, but not even the keenest of peal ringers seem to have had any interest in spending three hours ringing the lumpy old six at All Saints.

Restoration and augmentation to eight in 1903 changed that. As we saw in Chapter 5, the first peal came within a month of the rededication, and it was followed by a dozen and a half before the first war. There were some peals after the war, but they were far less frequent. After the second war they became even rarer, until the resurgence of activity around 1980. Table 16 shows the peal totals and averages in each period.

	1903-1914	*1919-1939*	*1944-1979*	*1980-2008*	*Total*
Local band peals	12	6	0	29	47
Total peals	**19**	**8**	**4**	**43**	**74**
Average peals per year	*1·6*	*0·4*	*0·1*	*1·5*	*0·7*

Table 16: Peals rung at All Saints in different eras

The distribution of peals at All Saints is very different from the general 20th century trend in peal ringing, as shown in Figure 89. The upper plot shows peals at All Saints, with active periods before the first World War and after 1980. There was much less in between, and nearly a fifty year gap in local peals (from 1935 to 1982).

For comparison, the lower plot shows the general trend in peal ringing during the 20th century – a more or less steady increase apart from the two wars.

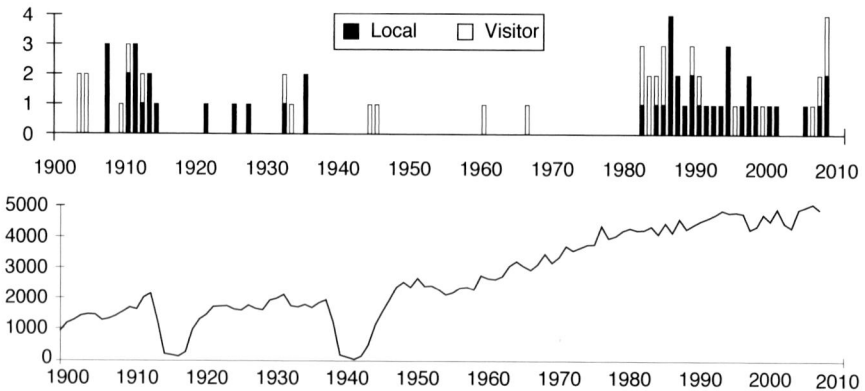

Figure 89: (Top) peals at All Saints Wokingham
(Bottom, for comparison) Peals per year rung globally after 1900

Figure 90 shows the split between peals of Triples and Major at All Saints. Triples is physically easier than Major, because the Tenor[9] doesn't have to be 'turned in'[10]. The more frequent incidence of Triples in the early part of the century might reflect that fact that the bells were hung on plain bearings then, and did not 'go' very well. In contrast, there have only been two peals of Triples since 1980, one of which was specifically chosen – Stedman Triples (FE Robinson's favourite method), to mark the 80th anniversary of his death.

---

[9] The heaviest bell.

[10] Varying the speed of the bell to ring changes requires more effort than ringing in the same place.

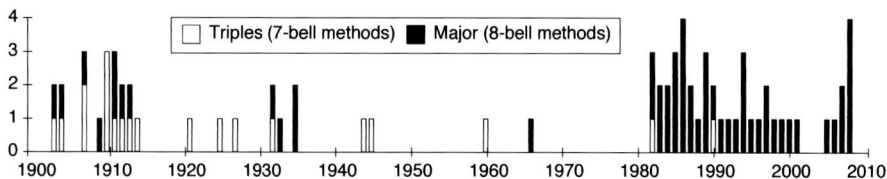

Figure 90: Seven and eight bell methods rung in peals at All Saints Wokingham

There is also a pattern in the time each peal took to ring, see Figure 91. Peals rung on plain bearings prior to 1958 were significantly slower than those rung on ball bearings in recent years – an average of around 3 hours 10 minutes, compared to an average of just under 3 hours. As one might expect, peals of Triples tend to be slightly faster than peals of Major. A few peals stand out from the general pattern, notably a very slow peal (3h19) of Surprise Major in 1966, and a very fast peal (2h32) of Stedman Triples in 1990. Both were rung by visiting bands[11].

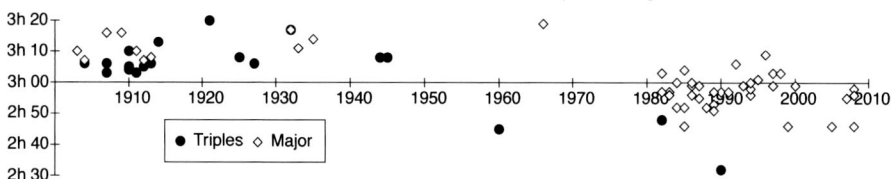

Figure 91: Peal times at All Saints

Dedications – As might be expected, many of the peals were rung to mark significant events in the Parish. Two peals marked the induction of new Rectors: Stedman Triples for Rev. Bertram Long in 1904, and Pudsey Surprise Major for Rev. David Hodgson in 1997. The latter was particularly apt since he grew up in Pudsey, West Yorkshire. Two peals marked ordinations to the priesthood: one in 1994 for Revd. Catherine Dyer (associate priest at All Saints) and Revd. Theresa Scott (former All Saints ringer), and one in 1997, for Revd. Colin James (curate at All Saints). Both were of Yorkshire Surprise Major.

Three peals were in memory of Rev. FE Robinson, all of Stedman Triples. The first was half muffled after his death in February 1910, the second was in September 1982 and the third was in February 1990, to mark the 80th anniversary of his death. A fourth peal attempt failed on 9th August 2006, the centenary of the day he rang his 1000th peal, so a quarter peal was rung instead[12].

Five peals marked weddings (mostly local people but also Prince Andrew in 1986) and four marked wedding anniversaries. Two peals celebrated births (including Prince William's in 1982) and four marked birthdays, notably the Rector's birthday in the early 1900s (probably nine, but the peal book does not say so in all cases).

Appropriately for All Saints church, seven peals were rung at All Saints tide: Grandsire Triples in 1910 and 1913, Double Norwich Court Bob Major in 1935, Wokingham Surprise Major in 1990 and Yorkshire Surprise Major in 2005 and 2008.

---

[11] I was the only local in the 1990 peal, and rang the 5th. I can confirm that it felt very fast.
[12] See page 106.

The 1913 performance had the extra distinction of being the first peal at All Saints in which a woman rang (something that is now routine) and the 1990 peal marked the Church's 800th anniversary.

Six of the 74 peals rung at All Saints are recorded on peal boards in the tower. Their pictures appear on pages 49, 62 and 105.

9.3 Quarter peals

The number of quarter peals rung at All Saints varied dramatically over the century since the first in 1904, but the figures must be set in context. Quarter peals are easier achievements than peals, and in modern times outnumber them (about 250 per week worldwide compared with 100 peals) but it was not ever thus. Quarter peals appeared much later than peals, and only became really popular in the second half of the 20th century. The bottom line of Table 17 gives an indication of of the overall level of quarter peal ringing in in each period[13]. From this perspective, All Saints appears pretty much as an average (inactive) tower between 1919 and 1979[14], whereas before 1914 it was ringing over ten times the average, and after 1980 around five times the average. So while the post 1980 achievement is indeed significant, the seemingly more modest numbers at the start of the 20th century show that the Edwardian band at All Saints was probably even more progressive in its day.

	1903-1914	*1919-1939*	*1944-1979*	*1980-2008*
Known quarter peals (All Saints)	14	3	37	401
Average per year (All Saints)	*1.2*	*0.15*	*1*	*15*
Comparator 'average tower' per year	*~0.1*	*~0.1*	*0.3 – 1*	*~3*

Table 17: Quarter peals in each era

Figure 92 graphically shows quarter peals rung at All Saints, compared with what the 'average tower' was doing.

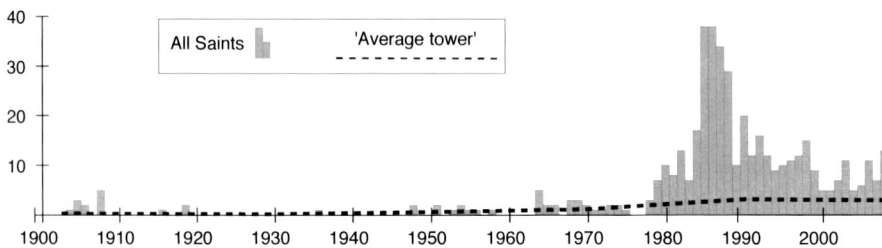

Figure 92: Quarter peals rung at All Saints (with comparator)

9.4 Tower, bells & fabric

Chapter by chapter we have seen how successive generations made changes and improvements in the tower. After 300 years of change, only the two heaviest bells remain from the original installation, and even they have changed. Their canons were removed in 1903, and their cast-in clapper staples were cut off, leaving iron stumps

---

[13] Based on approximate numbers published in sample years.
[14] Though the band rang more, unrecorded, quarter peals in the 1960s, see page 77.

that remained until they were removed in 2004. Iron stumps are the main cause of cracked bells, when they corrode. The crowns, over-thin when cast, and weakened when the canons were removed in 1903, were strengthened with resin in 2004. Finally, they were tuned to modern standards, along with the other bells. As a result they sound better now than they would have done when first installed.

Overall, the installation is much easier to ring than it would have been in 1704, thanks to the 2004 ball bearings and modern fittings, the 1903 iron frame lower in the tower, the 1958 rope guide and the improved 2004 rope runs.

The time-line in Figure 93 shows how the installation has evolved, with bells and their replacements colour coded by founder[15] and fittings coded by type. Note that the dark red bar (plain bearings) doesn't refer to a single set of bearings, since the bearings were replaced in 1903, and very probably also at the preceding minor rehangs. 'Bell work' and 'Tower work' show other things done at various dates.

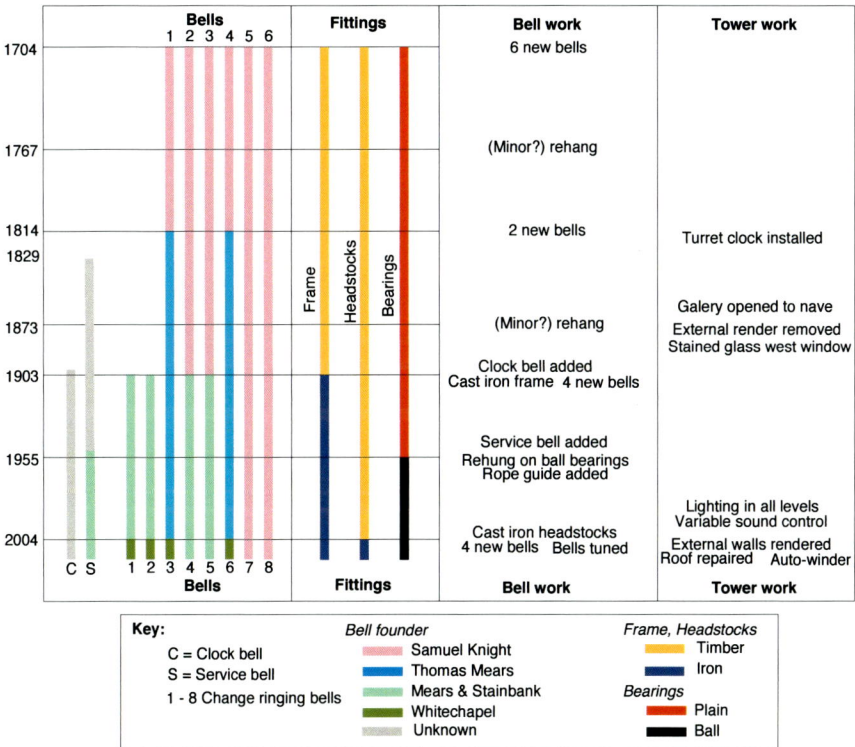

Figure 93: Time-line showing evolution of bells and fittings

The older bells have their history literally carved into them. Figure 94 shows the inner surface of the 7th, which was cast in 1704 and subsequently retuned at least twice. The rough vertical grooves at the top result from 'chip tuning', using a pointed

---

[15] Thomas Mears, Mears & Stainbank, and Whitechapel, all operated Whitechapel bellfoundry.

hammer, possibly done in 1903 to try to match it to the newer bells. The smooth horizontal grooves at the bottom were made by the tuning lathe, when the bells were tuned to modern standards in 2004.

Figure 94: Tuning – ancient and modern

Future development? – Generally, changes in the tower over the last three hundred years have been for the better. The bells sound better – there are more of them, and they are better tuned than they were in 1704. The installation needs less maintenance and the bells are significantly easier to ring than they were.

They had two narrow escapes from changes that would have made ringing much more difficult, when the money ran out for the misguided plan to extend the tower upwards in the 1860s, and later when the alternative of moving the ringers down to the ground floor was also abandoned.

Not everything is ideal though.

- Ringing from a gallery provides a positive link with the congregation, but the ringers suffer from the effects of both the church heating and a powerful organ. There is a project to solve this problem by installing a glass screen, but it has been very slow to progress since first being mooted in the 1980s, and being formally adopted in 1999.

- With the bells so far above the ringers, each ringer has to handle a lot of rope as well as the bell. Improving the rope runs in 2004 helped, but ringing will never be as easy as with a short rope draft.

- The tower's large arches[16] reduce its stiffness, so it moves more than it would otherwise, making the bells a little less predictable, and harder to control.

- Wokingham is bigger, more built up, and noisier than it was in 1704. That, coupled with the very reasonable measures to control excessive sound for the houses close to the church, means that however sweet the bells may sound, they are inaudible over much of the Parish. The idea of installing a sound lantern was abandoned in 2004 as too difficult. Maybe future generations will find a way to make the bells more widely audible, while still being a 'good neighbour' to those close by.

---

[16] See Figure 18 on page 38

Annex A: Glossary

Backstroke	Point in the cycle of full circle ringing when the bell is mouth up with maximum rope wound over the top of the bell wheel, and the ringer reaching up to hold the tail end of the rope (opposite to handstroke), see also page 7.
Bell chamber	Part of the tower containing the bells. Also called 'belfry' (though this term is sometimes used for the ringing room, qv).
Belfry reform	A movement inspired by the clergy in the 19th century to promote change ringing and to reform the behaviour of bellringers.
Call	Spoken command that alters the sequence of what is being rung
Call changes	Changing the ringing sequence by periodically calling a pair of bells to swap positions.
Change	Transformation between one row (qv) and the next.
Change ringing	Ringing where the bells strike in a continually changing order. In normal change ringing no bell moves more than one position at a time. The sequences are governed by a method, qv.
Churchwarden	Church officers with legal responsibility for matters of money and fabric in a church.
Churchyard bob	Derisory name used by 19th century change ringers to describe rounds ringing, also known as 'stony'.
Conductor	Person responsible for the conduct of a ringing performance, including calling any calls, and stopping it if it deteriorates.
Course	The natural length of a performance of a change ringing method, also called 'plain course' because there are no calls to vary it.
Date touch	A performance with one row for every year of the date when it is rung (or the year it was rung to commemorate).
Doubles	Generic name for methods with five working bells.
Double Norwich	A moderately simple 8-bell method (full name Double Norwich Court Bob Major).
Down	(of a bell) Hanging mouth downwards, safe but not ready for immediate ringing, see pages 7-8.
Exercise	Collective word for the ringing fraternity. Originated in the 17th century when young gentry rang bells for exercise.

Foreman	Local term for person in charge of the ringers, and responsible to church authorities. 'Tower Captain' is in more widespread use.
Garter hole	Hole in the rim of the bell wheel through which the rope passes to be tied to the spokes, see page 7.
Grandsire	A basic odd-bell method, widely rung, especially in earlier times.
Gudgeon	Metal pin on each end of the headstock, which fits into the bearing, thus allowing the whole bell assembly to swing full circle, see page 7.
Handstroke	Point in the cycle of full circle ringing when the bell is mouth up with rope wound under the bottom of the wheel, and the ringer reaching up to hold the sally, as well as retaining hold of the tail end (opposite to backstroke), see also page 7.
Headstock	The body of metal or timber to which a bell, its wheel, gudgeons and stay are attached, see page 7.
Kent	Kent Treble Bob, a method of moderate complexity.
Major	Generic name for methods with eight working bells.
Method	A named sets of rules that determine sequences of continual changes, with most bells changing place most of the time, see page 9.
Minor	Generic name for methods with six working bells.
Peal	A touch of at least 5040 changes (Triples and below) or 5000 changes (Major and above)
Plain Bob	A very basic method that can be rung on any number of bells.
Plain course	See 'course'.
Quarter peal	A touch of length equal to, or slightly more than a quarter of the length needed for a peal, ie 1260+ for Triples and below, or 1250+ for Major and above.
Ringing room	Part of the tower where ringers stand to ring. (Sometimes called 'belfry', thus confusing it with the bell chamber, qv.)
Rounds	Bells rung in a sequence of descending notes from Treble to Tenor, eg 123456 on six bells. Ringing performances normally start and end with rounds.
Row	Individual sequence, with each bell striking once.

Sally	Thick tufted woollen part of bell rope, at the position where the ringer grips it at handstroke, see page 7.
Single Oxford	A moderately simple method (full name Single Oxford Bob Triples) more popular in former times.
Slider	Bar beneath the bell against which the stay rests, and which can move to permit the bell to go just beyond the balance both ways.
Spider	Fitting with multiple hooks used to draw the rope ends up to the ceiling out of harm's way when bells are not in use.
Stay	Part of bell fittings – a wooden post attached to the headstock that permits the bell to be rested mouth up, but that is weak enough to break before any other component if the bell is mishandled, thus acting as a 'safety valve', see page 7.
Stedman	A popular, very musical odd-bell method.
Steeple keeper	Tower officer responsible for maintaining the bells and fittings.
Stony	Derisory name used by 19th century change ringers to describe rounds ringing, also called 'churchyard bob'.
Striking	The rhythmic quality of ringing. Perfect striking has the same interval between each successive sound.
Surprise	A more complex class of method, aspired to by many ringers.
Tail end	Lower end of the rope, held by the ringer while ringing, see page 7. The end is normally doubled up and tucked through itself to provide a better grip, and also to enable the working length to be adjusted.
Tenor	The lowest toned bell in a ring of bells, normally the heaviest.
Touch	A change ringing performance.
Treble	The highest toned bell in a ring of bells, normally the lightest.
Triples	Generic name for methods with seven working bells.
Up	(of a bell) Mouth upwards, set just beyond the balance point and ready for ringing, with its weight supported by the stay resting against the slider, see pages 7-8.

Annex B: Known All Saints ringers from 1880 to 2008

Dates are first and last mention. Some people may have rung longer, eg those who learnt at Wokingham would have started a year or two earlier than recorded. People may not have rung continuously between their dates. Anyone known to have returned after a period of absence, has separate entries marked with a *.

Name	Dates	Name	Dates
Rev Henry George Bird?	1873 - ?	F (Frank?) Pontin	1903 - 1905
Albert J Hill	1880 - 1916	Reginald Pontin	1903 - 1905
S Wynn	1881 - 1881	Edgar (Eddie) Whittingham	1903 - 1968
George Britten	1881 - 1885	William J (Bill) Paice	1904 - 1911
William Cheeseman	1881 - 1887	A (??Arthur) Wiggins	1905 - 1915
Herbert Watts	1881 - 1881	Arthur Price	1906 - 1919
Albert Jervis	1881 - 1881	JA (James Alfred?) Aldridge	1907 - 1913
Joseph Attewell	1882 - 1894	W (William) Jeynes	1907 - 1928
H Jervis	1882 - 1883	Samuel Frederick (T?) Paice jn	1907 - 1915
J Pocock	1882 - 1883	F (Fred?) Brooks	1909 - 1910
T Wynn	1883 - 1883	W Rhodes	1909 - 1916
George Chandler	1883 - 1884	HW (WH?) Boyles	1910 - 1910
Charles Cozens	1883 - 1894	E (Edward? Edwin??) Brant	1910 - 1933
Frank Lunn	1883 - 1886	G (George?) Green	1912 - 1931
Alfred Watts	1883 - 1884	Norman Carson Lawrence	1912 - 1921
G (George) Brant	1883 - 1883	William James (Bill) Brooks	1914 - 1963
Samuel Paice	1883 - 1920	Albert Victor Loader	1913 - 1916
Timothy Maidment	1884 - 1884	G (George?) Loader	1915 - 1915
FS (Frank) Mower	1885 - 1905	EC Clarke	1918 - 1921
E (Edward) Paice	1885 - 1889	Miss E Fielder	1918 - 1918
W Wilson	1885 - 1885	Miss M Fielder	1918 - 1918
W Loader	1886 - 1898	H Lovelock	1918 - 1923
Arthur Hosier (Hosler)	1887 - 1902	Miss M Vera Robinson	1918 - 1946
James Frederick Mattingley	1889 - 1925	Miss Alice H Walker	1918 - 1937
Arthur Jones	1889 - 1900	N Buckle	1923 - 1924
J (Jack) French	1889 - 1945	Walter J Pearce	1925 - 1984
W (Walter) Lush	1889 - 1900	H (Harry Charles MA?) Ingle	1926 - 1930
F (?Frank snr) Lush	1889 - 1889	F (Frank?) Nichols	1926 - 1928
H (Henry) Sargeant	1889 - 1902	E Ralph	1926 - 1928
E Bedford	1890 - 1894	G (George) Ford	1929 - 1932
H Marks	1892 - 1892	?? Saban	1929 - 1929
F (Frank jun) Lush	1895 - 1946	(T?) George Wigmore	1929 - 1974
C (Charles) Huckings	1898 - 1898	G (George Colin?) Wilson	1929 - 1930
G (?George) Mattingley	1900 - 1900	E (Ted) Langley	1930 - 1959
G (George) Paice	1900 - 1901	Miss M (Mable) Brooks	1933 - 1936
F (?Frank) Bacon	1901 - 1905	Miss A Baker	1934 - 1936
George Cole	1901 - 1919	Miss G (Geraldine) Baker	1934 - 1936
W May	1901 - 1904	Ernie (Harvey)* Mitchell	1934 - 1943
A Younger	1901 - 1903	Rev AGG (Gilbert) Thurlow	1934 - 1937

Joan Blackman (Rance)	1935 - 1937	Robert H (Bob) Begrie	1962 - 1974
Harry Dyer	1936 - 1957	Keith Begrie	1962 - 1965
Henry Cole	1936 - 1937	Miss Joan Salter	1962 - 1964
Mrs (P) Henderson	1936 - 1946	Harvey* Mitchell	1963 - 1968
Victor Bridges	1938 - 1939	Gerald Dance	1963 - 1963
David Watson	1943 - 1948	David Boshier	1963 - 1963
Gwen Crockford	1945 - 1954	Miss L (Lindy) Hope	1963 - 1965
Godfrey Moles	1945 - 1950	Miss Sheila Cameron	1965 - 1972
T (Tom) Langley	1945 - 1958	Miss Stephanie Hope	1965 - 1966
John Green	1945 - 1954	Miss Victoria Suder-Pole	1965 - 1965
Lennard ('Jack') Woodason	1945 - 1964	Mrs Judith Atkinson	1967 - 1979
Mary Cole	1946 - 1980	William JH (Bill) Parker	1967 - 1967
Jean Saunders	1946 - 1946	Miss Shelia Smith	1967 - 1972
Jimmy Elliott	1947 - 1973	Miss Sarah Hutt	1967 - 1972
Walter Newton	1947 - 1958	Miss Jane Saunders	1967 - 1967
F Butler	1947 - 1949	Miss Veronica Thatcher	1967 - 1972
Ernest Pearce	1948 - 1968	W (Bill) Burkey	1968 - 1979
Jeannette Bearen	1948 - 1949	Mrs Chris Clark	1968 - 1981
Miss ES Barnard	1949 - 1951	Miss A (Ann?) Barfoot	1968 - 1968
Barbara Crockford (Newton)	1949 - 1958	Miss Judith Burkey (Cull)	1968 - 1972
Patricia Newport	1949 - 1951	Miss Wendy Burkey	1969 - 1972
John Perkins	1949 - 1950	W (Wynford) Clarke	1969 - 1979
R L Grover	1950 - 1953	Mr Wood	1969 - 1972
Miss Ann E Taylor	1951 - 1953	Mr Howitt	1969 - 1969
Miss Ann E Moles	1952 - 1953	Mrs White	1969 - 1969
Keith R Goddard	1952 - 1966	Mrs Jo Burkey	1970 - 1978
RG Brown	1952 - 1953	David Deakins	1970 - 1976
Miss L Langley	1952 - 1954	Mrs H Deakins	1970 - 1976
Miss GN (Gill) Glennie	1952 - 1954	Nicholas Cole	1970 - 1970
Miss CE Phillips	1952 - 1955	Mrs Nellie Pearce	1971 - 1987
Ernic H (Harvey)* Mitchell	1953 1958	John Ellsworth	1971 - 1974
Mr B Lawrence	1954 - 1954	Mrs H Elsworth	1971 - 1974
Miss Gillian Piggott	1954 - 1956	Miss M Smith	1971 - 1972
John Watts	1956 - 1960	Francis J Moore	1972 - 1980
Michael J Lewis	1956 - 1958	Mrs Audrey Moore	1972 - 1980
Mrs G Cozens	1957 - 1961	Miss Galagher	1972 - 1973
Miss Jane Huckings	1957 - 1962	Mrs Lamb	1973 - 1973
Miss Furth	1957 - 1957	Mrs Lavinia Tildesley	1973 - 1975
Miss Henderson	1957 - 1957	BJ Creed	1973 - 1975
Miss Jane Kennett	1957 - 1957	Denis Pearce	1973 - 1976
Mr Palterman	1959 - 1962	Stephen Skates	1973 - 1978
Miss Brant	1960 - 1960	Miss W Hastings	1973 - 1973
Miss Ingram	1960 - 1960	David Ellsworth	1974 - 1974
Miss Muriel Longhurst	1961 - 1975	Janet Clark	1975 - 1979
Mr Grist	1961 - 1961	Alison Moore (Barber)	1977 - 1985

Lindsey Moore	1977 - 1979	E John Wells	1986 - 1987
John A Harrison	1978 - 2008	Julie B Branson (Goodchild)	1987 - 2008
David M Dewar	1978 - 1989	Joanna Dyer	1987 - 1991
Evan* Kozakiewicz	1978 - 1985	Rachel Longley	1987 - 1989
Betty M Tomlinson	1978 - 1992	Sarah Mack	1987 - 1987
Simon J Tomlinson	1978 - 1989	Linda M Williams	1987 - 2008
Robert J (Bob) Chapman	1978 - 1982	John A Harding	1987 - 1999
Jane Chapman	1978 - 1982	Richard Smith	1987 - 1987
Theresa A (Terry) Scott	1978 - 1992	Jill Jones	1990 - 1990
Ruth Hosken	1978 - 1978	Christine Roper	1990 - 1998
W Stewart Gibson	1978 - 1999	Andy Slay	1990 - 1992
Pearl J Gibson	1978 - 1999	Fiona J Harrison	1990 - 1992
Pamela A (Pam) Vassie	1979 - 1981	W Nigel G Herriott	1991 - 2000
John GP Scott	1979 - 1992	Jenny M Herriott	1991 - 2000
Martin Hosken	1979 - 1979	Mike S James	1991 - 1996
Sarah Chapman	1979 - 1982	Clare Allison	1992 - 1992
Angela Chapman	1979 - 1982	Catie Smith	1992 - 1995
Francesca Shearcroft	1980 - 1985	Mark Webb	1992 - 1992
Jon P Tutcher	1981 - 2008	Gary Webb	1992 - 1992
Clare Lovett	1981 - 1985	Stephen J (Steve) Noyes	1993 - 1999
Helen Domm (Mahoney)	1981 - 1986	Jaqui Longley	1993 - 1993
Louise J Clements (Cole)	1981 - 1986	Clare Amner	1993 - 1993
Hilary A Moss (McPherson)	1981 - 1987	Alex Henson	1993 - 1993
Susan Bedborough	1981 - 1981	Paul Arnold	1993 - 1995
Alison McLaren	1981 - 1981	Helen Roper	1994 - 1997
Martin Layley	1981 - 1981	Teresa Proudlock	1996 - 2001
Sheila M Williams	1981 - 1989	C Arthur Moss	1996 - 2008
Brianey Ilot	1982 - 1986	Charles WG Herriott	1997 - 2000
WM David Collis	1982 - 1982	Jonathan P Goodchild	1997 - 2008
Richard J Woodward	1982 - 2008	Jane A Mellor	1997 - 2008
Eve M Reader	1983 - 2008	Nigel AL Mellor	1997 - 2008
Alex Nelson	1983 - 1989	Katie J Tutcher	1998 - 2008
Phillipa Moon	1983 - 1984	Pauline Branson	1998 - 1999
Helen Porter	1983 - 1983	Elizabeth J (Liz) Barter	1998 - 2006
Rebecca Briault (Arcari)	1984 - 1985	Evan* Kozakiewicz	2001 - 2008
Barbara G Smith	1984 - 2008	Andrew L (Andy) Smith	2001 - 2007
Helen Layley	1984 - 1986	Charlotte Kozakiewicz	2002 - 2008
Alan Capper	1984 - 1985	Mary Spence	2005 - 2008
Jonathan Johnson	1984 - 1984	Simon C Farrar	2005 - 2008
John Reader	1984 - 2008	Mhairi C Miller	2006 - 2008
Aathony G (Tony) Pullan	1984 - 1988	Emily J Mellor	2006 - 2008
Stephen R Smith (1)	1984 - 2008	Lucy Bricheno	2007 - 2007
Martin Mahoney	1985 - 1986	Michael Johnson	2007 - 2008
Steven J Field	1985 - 1986	Ceila J Tinsley	2008 - 2008
Stephen R Smith 2	1985 - 1987		

Annex C: Rules

We know that the Society of Honorary Ringers adopted a set of rules when it was formed in 1873, but no record of them remains. The rules were modified in 1907 to increase the number of 'stated ringers' from 8 to 10. The earliest rules whose record survives were adopted in 1935, at the time of Gilbert Thurlow's arrival, and the start of the earliest surviving minute book. The post-war band revised and extended them in 1946, and again in 1967. There were amendments in 1979 and 1980. In 1990, they were completely revised to produced a more formal constitution[1], with minor amendments in 2001 and 2008.

Rules adopted 1935

1 There shall not be more than 16 ringers.
2 There shall be an annual meeting to be held as early in the year as possible at which the necessary officers shall be elected.
3 There shall always be a sufficient number of Ringers present on Sunday for service who shall be expected to attend church at least once a Sunday and the same reverence shall be observed in the Belfry as in any other part of the Church
4 The Ringing on Sunday shall commence at 10 a.m. and 6 p.m. or at such other times as shall with the consent of the Rector be decided upon.
The weekly practice shall be held on Monday at 7-30 pm.
5 No person shall be admitted to the Belfry without permission.

Rules adopted 1946

1 The Society shall be called "The All Saints Society of Church Bell Ringers"".
2 That "Members of the Tower" may be elected by existing members up to the number of 16. They must be change ringers and when elected shall share in all pay and privileges.
3 Teams of Ringers shall be arranged for service ringing, and placed in the belfry by Monday. Any member unable to attend shall find a substitute.
4 The Belfry being part of God's House, the same reverence shall be observed in the Belfry as in any other part of the Church.
5 The Ringing on Sunday shall commence at 10 A.M. and 6 P.M. or at such other times, as shall, with the consent of the Rector, be decided upon, and shall always be preceded by a prayer.
6 The weekly practice shall be held on Monday at 7-30 P.M.
7 There shall be an Annual meeting to be held as early in the year as possible.
8 No person shall be admitted to the Belfry without permission.
9 The fee for ringing for weddings shall be £3-0-0.

Rules adopted 1967

1 The Society shall be called "The All Saints Society of Change Ringers[2]".
2 That applicants for membership may be elected by existing members
3 That they must be change ringers, and when elected shall share in all pay and privileges.

---

[1] The model constitution in *The Tower Handbook* [20] was based on this.
[2] The name changed, but not the intent – the 1946 rules insisted that members be change ringers.

4 All members are requested to attend at Sunday service ringing; notice of absence to be given as soon as possible.

5 Sunday service ringing shall commence at 10 AM and 6 PM. and at such other times, as shall, with the consent of the Rector, be decided upon, and ringers attending are requested to be punctual.

6 Ringers for weddings, special services etc, will be nominated by the Foreman or his deputy, and their names placed on the notice board in the Belfry. Any members unable to attend shall find a suitable substitute.

7 The weekly practice to be held on Mondays at 7-30 PM prompt, with the exception of Bank Holidays.

8 That an Annual meeting be held as early in the year as possible.

9 The Belfry being part of God's House, the same reverence shall be observed as in any other part of the Church.

10 No person shall be admitted to the Belfry without the Foreman's consent.

Amendment 1979

The upper limit on members should be at the discretion of the Foreman.[3]

Amendment 1980

Officers should be elected annually and a term of office should not normally exceed 3 years[4].

Rules adopted 1990

1 **Name:** The Society shall be known as "All Saints Society of Bell Ringers"

2 **Objectives:** The aims of the Society shall be:
a) to glorify God by the ringing of bells,
b) to ensure regular ringing of the bells at All Saints Church Wokingham for all major services
c) to advance the quality of ringing at All Saints Church.

3 **Affiliation:** The Society shall be affiliated to the Oxford Diocesan Guild of Church Bell Ringers (hereafter called "the Guild") and shall support the objectives of the Guild.

4 **Officers:** The officers of the Society shall be (a) Foreman (b) Deputy Foreman (c) Secretary/Treasurer (d) Steeplekeeper

5 **General meetings:** An Annual General Meeting (AGM) shall be held each year in January, chaired by the Rector of All Saints Church or his nominee.
All Officers shall retire at each AGM; they shall be eligible for re-election but any one term of office shall not normally exceed three years.
An Extraordinary General Meeting (EGM) may be called upon 14 days notice
(a) by the Officers or (b) by written request of a simple majority of members.
Casual vacancies among the Officers shall be filled by convening an EGM.

6 **Membership:** New members of the Society shall be elected by a simple majority vote at an AGM or EGM.   Between such meetings, the Officers shall be

---

[3] This rescinded the 1935 rule limiting members to 16, but since no such rule was included in either the 1946 or 1967 rules, why was it necessary to do so?

[4] This was to encourage periodic change of officers, and avoid an individual getting 'locked in' to a post. Including 'normally' allowed a waiver when there wasn't a sensible alternative.

empowered to grant membership to ringers who are eligible, subject to ratification at the next AGM.

The following shall be eligible for membership:

a) Ordinary members of the Guild who pay their subscription to the Guild through the Society.

b) Life and Honorary members of the Guild who register their membership through the Society.

c) Any regular Sunday service ringer at All Saints Church who is not a member of the Guild.

A member who claims eligibility under (a) above shall not be entitle to vote or attend general meetings until his or her Guild Subscription for the current year has been paid to the Secretary/Treasurer.

Membership shall terminate:

y) Upon a member giving written notice to that effect to the Secretary/Treasurer,

z) Upon a member ceasing to be eligible for membership as in (a), (b) or (c) above.

7 **Finance:** The Society shall hold and maintain its own funds; these shall be owned jointly by the members and shall not be part of Church funds.

The Officers shall be empowered to open and maintain a bank or building society account, any one Officer's signature being sufficient authority for withdrawal.

The Officers shall be empowered at their discretion to subsidise (up to 100%) the annual Guild subscription of particular ringers; this shall in no way affect the beneficiaries' eligibility for membership of the Society.

The financial year shall end on 31st December each year; a statement of account shall be presented to the ensuing AGM.

8 **Duties and conduct:** Membership of the Society shall imply an obligation that the member will make every reasonable effort to attend Sunday service ringing, at practices, and when called upon to do so, at weddings and special functions.

All members shall conduct themselves appropriately while in the ringing chamber.

Amendment 2001

The posts of Secretary and Treasurer may be held by separate people.

Amendment 2008

A new post of Ringing Master was created, to run the ringing, and to take primary responsibility for developing the band's capability. The post may be held separately or in addition to one of the existing posts.

Annex D: Sources and references

[1] Oxford Diocesan Guild of Church Bellringers annual reports (1882 - 2008)

[2] Sonning Deanery Branch of ODG, minutes and records (1881 - 2008)

[3] Wokingham Parish Notices (later Parish Magazine) (1865 - 2008)

[4] All Saints Wokingham tower AGM minutes (1935 - 1978), (1979 - 1996), (1997 - 2008)

[5] All Saints Wokingham Peal Book

[6] Conversations with Mary Cole

[7] Conversation with John Rance

[8] Conversation with Keith Goddard

[9] Correspondence with Barbara Newton

[10] *All Saints Wokingham † The Life of a Parish Church*, John Clemetson, 1990

[11] *The Inns and Public Houses of Wokingham*; Dennis Ayers & Judith Hunter, Berkshire Books, 1994,

[12] *Change Ringing – The History of an English Art* Volume 1, Ed. J Sanderson, 1987.

[13] *Change Ringing – The History of an English Art* Volume 2, Ed. J Sanderson, 1992.

[14] *Change Ringing – The History of an English Art* Volume, 3, Ed. J Sanderson, 1993.

[15] *The Bells News and Ringers' Record* 1881 - 1915

[16] *The Ringing World* 1911 – present

[17] *Early Prize Ringing Around Reading*; Cyril Wratten (in *The Ringing World* October 1978)

[18] *The Bellringer (Plain Guides to Lay Work No. 8)*; Rev. CDP Davies, 1927.

[19] *The Church of All Saints Wokingham*, Rev AGG Thurlow, 1937.

[20] *The Tower Handbook*, John Harrison (Ed), CCCBR 1998.

[21] *The Church of All Saints Wokingham – Its History and Archtecture,* Anon, 1961

[22] Card index of quarter peals in Oxford Diocesan Guild towers published in *The Ringing World* (held in the Guild library)

[23] AJ Buswell's card index by tower of quarter peals published since 1966

[24] Notes by Bertram Long (held in Berkshire Record Office, WO/D1))

[25] Correspondence with Muriel Longhurst

[26] All Saints tower website – http://AllSaintsWokinghamBells.org.uk/

Index